ISSUES
IN
CANADIAN
HISTORY

The 1911 General Election: A Study in Canadian Politics

Edited by
PAUL STEVENS

THE COPP CLARK PUBLISHING COMPANY
TORONTO

ISBN 0 7730 3113 8

[1676]

The 1911
General Election:
A Study in
Canadian Politics

ISSUES IN CANADIAN HISTORY

Consultant
J. T. SAYWELL

General Editor
J. L. GRANATSTEIN

Available

The French Canadians, 1759-1766
The United Empire Loyalists
The King-Byng Affair, 1926
Racism or Responsible Government
The Family Compact
Joseph Howe
The Manitoba School Question
The Bennett New Deal
Canadian Foreign Policy Since 1945
The Acadian Deportation
Louis Riel
Imperialism and Nationalism
Quebec in the Duplessis Era
Henri Bourassa
The Frontier Thesis and The Canadas

In Preparation

The Shaping of Canadian Federalism
The Dirty Thirties
The Alaska Boundary Dispute
Upper Canada and the Rise of Discontent
The Impact of the Conquest
The Maritimes and Canadian Regionalism
B.C. and Canadian Regionalism
Groulx
The Prairies and Canadian Regionalism
St. Laurent

Contents

PART VI: The Results and Post Mortems   181

Introduction

The general election of 1911 was in some ways the most important election in Canadian political history. It was crucial because it brought into focus many of the issues which had confronted Canadians for a number of years. It crystallized opinion on the long standing debate between nationalism and continentalism that the election of 1891 had not resolved and that had found renewed expression during the meetings of the Joint High Commission in 1898, the Alaskan boundary dispute and in the establishment of the International Joint Commission. The basic issue, declared Robert Borden, was "whether a spirit of Canadianism or of Continentalism is to prevail on the northern half of this continent". Ultimately, the debate over reciprocity introduced once again the problems of race and creed into national politics. It underlined the growing cleavage between the protectionist East and the free trade West. And it revealed much about the manoeuverings of politicians and the nuts and bolts of party management.

The origins of Laurier's decision to adopt reciprocity with the United States are far from clear. Laurier always considered himself a free trader and was convinced that a large measure of free trade between Canada and the United States would be advantageous to both countries. In the summer of 1910, he made a tour of Western Canada and heard farmers clammering for tariff reductions wherever he stopped. He may have believed that the prospect of a free American market for farm products would provide a formidable offset outside of Montreal to the *nationaliste* movement in the Province of Quebec. Or he may just have concluded that his government needed a new and dramatic policy after almost fifteen years in office.

Yet Laurier seems to have committed himself and his party to reciprocity as much by accident as by design. Of mounting con-

1

cern to the Liberal leader throughout his political career were Canada's diplomatic relations with the United States. The setting up of the International Joint Commission in 1909 to settle questions relating to the boundaries of the two countries, and the agreement in 1910 to refer the problem of the North Atlantic Fisheries to the Hague Court, were the marks of a new spirit of accommodation between Ottawa and Washington which had gradually replaced the animosity engendered by the Alaskan boundary dispute. When the Americans proposed that the two countries consider possible mutual reductions in their tariffs at the beginning of 1910, Laurier was reluctant to jeopardize this accord by rebuffing the overture. Only after the discussions had begun in November did the Canadian negotiators realize the breadth of the American proposals, and two months later they accepted an agreement which was much more comprehensive than they had originally expected.

Whatever the explanation, the reciprocity proposals were presented to Parliament on January 26, 1911. They provided for free trade between Canada and the United States in a long list of natural products and a few selected manufactured goods and for reciprocal tariff reductions on several other articles. They were approved by a special session of the American Congress in July 1911, but they ran into considerable difficulty in Canada. Although members of both political parties initially approved the agreement, including a number of western Conservatives and the Conservative Toronto *News* and Ottawa *Journal*, opposition began to appear in the ranks of both the Liberals and Conservatives.

Much of the opposition came from the business, financial and manufacturing community in Toronto and Montreal. In the vanguard of the suddenly mounting wave of resistance to reciprocity was a group of eighteen Toronto Liberals led by Zebulon Lash, a leading Toronto lawyer, and Sir Edmund Walker, President of the Canadian Bank of Commerce. On February 20 they issued a manifesto opposing the agreement and calling upon the country to block its approval. Reciprocity, they claimed, would destroy the Canadian economy which had developed on an east-west axis and would lead eventually to Canada's absorption into the United States. As the days went by the public protest took on formidable proportions. Opponents of the agreement set up the Anti-Reciprocity League in Montreal and the Canadian National League in Toronto, the latter under Lash's direction, to organize meetings, circulate petitions and churn out pamphlets. By the beginning of March their efforts had been so effective that the Governor-General, Lord Grey, reported that "the feeling in Montreal and Toronto against the Agreement could hardly be stronger if the United States troops had already invaded our territory."

Conservative M.P.'s took renewed heart from the success of the campaign and began to mount an attack of their own. They received a considerable boost from Clifford Sifton and a small group of disgruntled Liberals who let it be known that they were unable to support the Government's proposals. The former Minister of the Interior, who had broken with Laurier in 1905 over the Autonomy Bills, had publicly opposed reciprocity while the negotiations were in progress. And at the beginning of February he and five other members of the Liberal caucus asked Laurier to postpone consideration of the agreement until it had been ratified by the American Congress. Laurier refused, and on February 28 Sifton denounced the proposals in the House of Commons. Although there was little new in his address to the House, it provided the opposition with a wealth of statistics and considered arguments with which to assail reciprocity. Of more immediate importance, it led to an agreement with Robert Borden. On March 1, Sifton, Lash, John Willison, the editor of the Toronto *News*, and Lloyd Harris, the Liberal M.P. for Brantford, met privately with Borden and presented him with seven conditions upon which they would cooperate with the Tories to oppose reciprocity and bring down the government. And when the Conservative leader agreed to "use every possible endeavour to give them effect," they pledged to proceed at once to organize for the coming battle.

Debate in the House continued for twenty-five days. Conservative speakers concentrated their initial volleys on the economic aspects of the agreement, arguing that it would be of uncertain duration, would present a direct threat to Canadian transportation interests and a variety of Canadian producers including farmers, cattlemen, and fruitgrowers who would be forced to compete with foreign imports. But as the debate picked up tempo, and the political implications became more apparent, the opposition shifted its ground. Speaker after speaker predicted that reciprocity would lead to separation from Great Britain and annexation by the United States. It would destroy the British preference, eliminate interprovincial trade, and put an end to the country's fiscal freedom. In their flood of oratory, Conservative backbenchers made particular use of the indiscretions of some American politicians, including a letter written by President Taft which noted that "the amount of Canadian products we would take would produce a current of business between Western Canada and the United States that would make Canada only an adjunct of the United States . . . I see this argument made against Reciprocity in Canada, and I think it is a good one."

The Liberals replied that reciprocity would produce larger markets for Canada's natural products and result in greater prosperity across the country. This, they contended, would stimulate the development of the nation's natural resources, provide a larger market in western Canada for Canadian manufactures, and supply Canadian railways with more freight. Some argued that the consumer would benefit through lower prices, though as the Conservatives were quick to point out, this was hardly consistent with the Liberal proposition that reciprocity would mean higher prices for Canadian farm products. Liberal orators met Conservative predictions about annexation with unconcealed scorn, and they insisted that increased prosperity would make the country more independent politically. But from the outset of the debate, they were constantly on the defensive. And as party spokesmen failed to launch a vigorous counter-offensive against the anti-reciprocity propaganda machine, particularly in Ontario, their arguments appeared less than convincing.

Conservative strategy apparently was designed to hold up the agreement in the House while the anti-reciprocity forces outside Parliament gathered funds and marshalled their forces. Frederick Monk, Borden's Quebec lieutenant, made the first move at the beginning of the debate when he moved that the question be submitted to the people before proceeding. The motion was defeated and both sides settled down to a battle of nerves. In the middle of March the Conservatives and rebellious Liberals threatened to withhold supply until Laurier agreed to make certain changes, but the Prime minister refused and supply was granted only at the last moment. At the end of April Borden laid his cards on the table. "There is unanimous resolve," he declared in a statement to the press after a meeting of caucus, "to offer firm and determined resistance to the proposals to the bitter end. The Conservative party will make no truce on this question which involves the national existence of the country and gravely affects its relations to the Empire."

The crunch came with the approaching Coronation and Imperial Conference in London. Replying to a question on April 28 from the leader of the opposition, Laurier announced that he had booked passage for May 12 but would remain in Canada if necessary. To allow for his departure, Borden then proposed three alternatives: Parliament might continue to sit while the Prime Minister attended the conference; the session might be ended, allowing reciprocity to stand over to the following session; or the session might be adjourned until Laurier returned from London. For his own part, the Liberal leader preferred another alternative —dissolution of Parliament and an immediate election. But the majority of the cabinet were strongly opposed, and the government decided to adjourn the House for two months until July 18. At the same time, Laurier left instructions that the voting lists be prepared in the event that the Conservatives continued to obstruct and a fall election became necessary.

It was not a wasted effort. While Laurier made headlines in London, Borden mended his political fences in the western provinces. And if the Conservative leader failed to convert many of the Grain Growers, the response to his speeches in eastern Canada provided overwhelming evidence of the strength of the nationalist and imperialist appeal. When the members returned to their desks, the Conservative barrage continued with even greater intensity. Morning sessions were to no avail, and on July 29, the government dissolved the House and called for an election on September 21.

But while the stage had shifted from Parliament Hill to the political hustings, the lines were the same. Only in Quebec did reciprocity play a secondary role. In "la belle province" the tone was set by Henri Bourassa and his nationalist supporters in the editorial columns of Le Devoir and at numerous assemblies during August and September. Bourassa had maintained for many years that reciprocity with the United States would be desirable, largely because it would prevent any Imperial Zollverein. And when the details of the agreement were first announced, he admitted that it would benefit the farmer without injuring Canadian industries. It was only when an election appeared imminent that he saw it as a weapon to oppose Laurier and began to argue that it should not be ratified on the grounds that Canada could obtain better terms.

But with Bourassa the question of reciprocity paled into insignificance before the primary issue of Canadian autonomy. What concerned Bourassa and the Conservatives in Quebec was Laurier's decision to establish a small navy, owned, manned and directed by Canada, but which could be placed at the disposal of the British Admiralty in times of emergency. Not only would Canada be dragged into every Imperial war, Bourassa contended, but conscription would follow and thousands of lives and millions of dollars would be sacrificed in conflicts in which Canada had nothing at stake. Of greater importance were the constitutional consequences: participation in Imperial wars would necessarily lead to compensation to Canada in the form of an Imperial preference for Canadian wheat and eventually to Imperial Federation. "It is time," Bourassa editorialized, "for the people of the province of Quebec to prove to Mr. Laurier that if they admired him when he served the interests of the country well, today he has prevaricated, today he has duped us."

Politically, the result of the controversy was a realignment of the parties in Quebec. The Conservatives under Frederick Monk coalesced with the *nationalistes* and accepted Bourassa as their leading spokesman. In theory at least, the *Autonomistes*, as they labelled themselves, were to be independent of both national parties, "men of good principles who would not be swayed by opportunism or partisanship to support the anti-national policy of Imperialism". The results of the alliance had been fully shown in November 1910. During a stormy by-election campaign in Drummond-Arthabasca, Monkite Conservatives helped to elect a *nationaliste* candidate in a seat which the Liberals had held since 1887. In the general election their hopes were pinned on gaining sufficient seats in the new Parliament to hold the balance of power, then using their leverage to ensure the defeat of Imperialist designs.

The election of 1911 presents a number of questions for the student of Canadian history.

Historians have long been fascinated with the problems of election analysis. It is therefore surprising that historians in Canada have developed few of the tools required for more than a cursory study. In their analyses of the election of 1911 they have concentrated on the issues—repiprocity, the naval controversy and the loyalty cry. They have generally overlooked other factors which may have been significant in the outcome of the campaign. In their haste to attribute the result to reciprocity, they have usually dismissed the role which regional and provincial leaders play in the Canadian political system. They have failed to consider party organization as a factor in the campaign. Even basic questions such as why people vote and the relationship between campaign issues and electoral behaviour have yet to be considered.

The traditional approaches have not provided an adequate explanation of the results of the reciprocity campaign. In 1911 reciprocity should have been popular in many parts of the country. On the hustings both the Liberals and Conservatives merely repeated the arguments they had developed in the House. As they had done during the debate, the Conservatives were successful in distorting the issue from the economics of reciprocity to the national and imperial question. This may have been the result of a majority of Canadians genuinely believing that reciprocity would be destructive of a Canadian nationality. Or it may merely have been a reflection of the fact that the Conservatives had the personnel and organization necessary to put their position across at a time when the Liberals did not.

Part I

The Debate in the House

The Minister of Finance, William S. Fielding, ended months of conjecture on January 26, 1911 when he announced the terms of a reciprocity tariff agreement with the United States in the House of Commons. From the gallery above, the correspondent for the *Montreal Herald* wrote that the members were instantly aware that history was being made. "The limited list had swelled and swelled and swelled and as it grew to the proportions of a nation's commerce, and members leaned forward to catch every word, triumph was written on the faces of the Liberals and dismay painted on the visages of the Opposition. There was not much cheering. Interest was too keen to tolerate interruption. But there were occasions when enthusiasm mastered curiosity Free fish, free wheat, oats, barley, and buckwheat, free potatoes, free dairy products and free hay conceded by the United States brought forth a tumult of appreciation which for a moment halted the Finance Minister in his triumphant recital. And when he closed the Liberals cheered and cheered again."

The magnitude of the agreement stunned the opposition. Although Borden quickly appealed to the government to do nothing that would imperil Canada's position in the Empire, it was not for some days that Conservative leaders begain to realize the national and imperial implications. George Foster, one of the party's chief financial experts, set the tone for the debate on February 9 in a speech which Clifford Sifton later declared to be unanswerable. The agreement, he contended, would profoundly affect Canada's destiny: it would cut interprovincial trade, end the British preference, put an end to Canadian fiscal freedom and make the country dependent upon the United States.

The most detailed indictment, however, came from within the government's

6

own ranks. Clifford Sifton surprised few observers when he broke with his party to attack the agreement. Although his speech provided few arguments that were new to the debate, it was a comprehensive case against reciprocity, providing the opposition with valuable material for election literature and a working model for anti-reciprocity speeches.

The task of replying to Sifton fell to Sydney Fisher, the Minister of Agriculture. Fisher represented the Quebec constituency of Brome, a rural constituency in the Eastern Townships where reciprocity in hay and other farm products appeared to be an attractive proposition. In a private letter to John Dafoe, the editor of the *Manitoba Free Press*, he countered Sifton's arguments. It is interesting to speculate what the result might have been had the debate been conducted along these lines.

Laurier's speech nine days later was typical of many he delivered throughout the reciprocity campaign. It was not one of his better speeches, but it reflected one of the central aspects of his political philosophy. Like all philosophical Liberals, Laurier believed that men were rational and that moments of emotional hysteria were no more than temporary aberrations. Ultimately, he was convinced that reason and common sense would prevail over emotion and self-interest. He believed that increased trade meant increased prosperity; he could not conceive that better commercial relations with the United States could affect political relations with Great Britain. As usual, he assumed that moderate men would agree once they understood the facts of the agreement.

W. S. Fielding, House of Commons, *Debates,* 1910-1911, January 26, pp. 2440-2441, 2447-2460, 2466-2475, 2476.

The Introduction of Reciprocity

. . . the action of this government in consenting to reopen negotiations with the government of the United States with a view to bringing about if possible a satisfactory reciprocal trade arrangement, has been very severely criticized in many quarters. From that fact we may properly infer that there must be some people in this Dominion of Canada who hold the opinion that the commercial policy of the 92,000,000 people who live to the south of us is of no concern to the inhabitants of this Dominion. No other conviction could justify the action of those who have objected to the opening of negotiations. One may easily understand, Sir, that there would be room for difference of opinion as to the merits of any arrangements into which it might be proposed to enter, but that there should be opposition to the reopening of negotiations in response to the friendly approach of the United States government seems to us, in the light of history, to be very strange indeed. Sir, for us, for this government, for this parliament, for this

Dominion, to set itself against a discussion of the question of the trade relations between our country and the neighbouring republic would be to emphatically reverse the historic policy of the Dominion from the first day of confederation down to the present time, and not only the policy of the Dominion but the pre-confederation policy of every province out of which the Dominion was subsequently formed. Whether we desire it or not, Sir, the conditions of our two countries, lying side by side, must always make us of much interest one to the other.

The 92,000,000 people to the south are willing to acknowledge that they are interested in the commercial policy of Canada, and we, representing 8,000,000 people are not ashamed to confess that we have the deepest concern in the policy which those people may adopt in relation to their commerce with the world at large. It is because we have the feeling that there is a mutual interest, that we have entered upon the negotiations as to which my privilege now to address you.

. . . we have conducted negotiations first at Ottawa and afterwards at Washington, covering the whole question of trade relations. We have now been able to come to an understanding, and if we are able to bring about some of the good results which this country has been seeking for many years, I earnestly hope that the action will be one in which all parties in this House and in this country will be able to join and say, that that is for the good of Canada and for the good of the United States as well. Let me proceed to tell you, first in a summary way and afterwards in detail, exactly what the arrangement is.

In the first place, I am glad to be able to tell the House that at a very early stage in our negotiations, several months ago indeed, we informed the representatives of the United States government that while we desired to make a friendly reciprocal arrangement, while we were most anxious to broaden our trade conditions and to establish and continue friendly relations with them, we believed that could be now brought about as well by mutual legislation, as by the more definite form of a treaty; and therefore we informed them that while we were prepared to proceed with the negotiations and to make the arrangement as broad and generous as we could, it must be understood that we preferred the form of concurrent legislation, and that it was not our purpose to bind the Dominion of Canada or the United States in the way of a treaty. . . .

The next point is that we have arranged that there shall be a large free list. We have agreed upon a schedule containing a large number of articles which are to be reciprocally free. These are chiefly what are called natural products, though there are some things in them which would hardly be classified in that way. Some of these things are already free in Canada, but have been subject to duty in the United States. We have been able to arrange that the United States shall take off the duty, and therefore, instead of having what some of our hon, friends have sometimes called a lop-sided free trade, there will be real free trade in this matter, and the thing that is free in Canada shall also be free in the United States.

In another schedule we have provided a rather numerous list of items on which there shall be a common rate of duty in both countries. A very common criticism on the part of gentlemen who have not viewed this matter as favourably as we would have wished, has been: If the United States want to make a tariff arrangement with you, let them come down to your rates of duty. It seemed to be taken for granted that that was what the United States would not do. But that is exactly what we asked them to do, and what they have agreed to do, respecting a large number of articles. They have not only come down to our rates, but in some cases they have come below them, and in those cases, in order to reach that common rate, we have had to make reductions. But as our tariff is a moderate one, while theirs, in the main, is a high tariff, the result has been that in order to arrive at a common rate, we have had to make only moderate reductions, while they, in many cases, have had to make quite large reductions. There are a few exceptions to this general rule. We found a few cases with which we desired to deal, but with respect to which we were not able to agree upon a common rate. In some instances it was not so much the rate itself as the classification and the phraseology. Dealing with these cases as exceptions, we have provided one schedule of articles on which the United States impose the rates of duties therein mentioned on the products of Caanda, and another schedule of articles on which Canada imposes the rates of duties therein mentioned on the products of the United States. The idea of reciprocity is in the arrangement, but it does not require both countries to adopt the same rate or the same classification. These two schedules, however, will be found to contain not many items. . . .

. . . now I propose to present to the

House the form in which the arrangement is made.

Washington, January 21, 1911.
Dear Mr. Secretary,—

1. The negotiations initiated by the President several months ago through your communication to His Excellency the British Ambassador respecting a reciprocal tariff arrangement between the United States and Canada, and since carried on directly between representatives of the governments of the two countries, have now, we are happy to say, reached a stage which gives reasonable assurance of a conclusion satisfactory to both countries.

2. We desire to set forth what we understand to be the contemplated arrangement, and to ask you to confirm it.

3. It is agreed that the desired tariff changes shall not take the formal shape of a treaty, but that the Governments of the two countries will use their utmost efforts to bring about such changes by concurrent legislation at Washington and Ottawa.

4. The Governments of the two countries having made this agreement from the conviction that, if confirmed by the necessary legislative authorities, it will benefit the people on both sides of the border line, we may reasonably hope and expect that the arrangement, if so confirmed, will remain in operation for a considerable period. Only this expectation on the part of both Governments would justify the time and labour that have been employed in the maturing of the proposed measures. Nevertheless, it is distinctly understood that we do not attempt to bind for the future the action of the United States Congress or the Parliament of Canada, but that each of these authorities shall be absolutely free to make any change of tariff policy or of any other matter covered by the present arrangement that may be deemed expedient. We look for the continuance of the arrangement, not because either party is bound to it, but because of our conviction that the more liberal trade policy thus to be established will be viewed by the people of the United States and Canada as one which will strengthen the friendly relations now happily prevailing and promote the commercial interests of both countries.

5. As respects a considerable list of articles produced in both countries, we have been able to agree that they shall be reciprocally free. A list of the articles to be admitted free of duty into the United States when imported from Canada, and into Canada when imported from the United States, is set forth in Schedule A.

6. As respects another group of articles, we have been able to agree upon common rates of duty to be applied to such articles when imported into the United States from Canada or into Canada from the United States. A list of these articles, with the rates of duty, is set forth in Schedule B.

7. In a few instances it has been found that the adoption of a common rate will be inconvenient and therefore exceptions have to be made.

8. Schedule C specifies articles upon which the United States will levy the rates therein set forth when such articles are imported from Canada.

9. Schedule D specifies articles upon which Canada will levy the rates therein set forth when such articles are imported from the United States

10. With respect to the discussions that have taken place concerning the duties upon the several grades of pulp, printing paper, &c.— mechanically ground wood pulp, chemical wood pulp, bleached and unbleached, news printing paper and other printing paper, and board made from wood pulp, of the value not exceeding four cents per pound at the place of shipment—we note that you desire to provide that such articles from Canada shall be made free of duty in the United States only upon certain conditions respecting the shipment of pulp wood from Canada. It is necessary that we should point out that this is a matter in which we are not in a position to make any agreement. The restrictions at present existing in

Canada are of a Provincial character. They have been adopted by several of the Provinces with regard to what are believed to be Provincial interests. We have neither the right nor the desire to interfere with the Provincial authorities in the free exercise of their constitutional powers in the administration of their public lands. The provisions you are proposing to make respecting the conditions upon which these classes of pulp and paper may be imported into the United States free of duty must necessarily be for the present inoperative. Whether the Provincial Governments will desire to in any way modify their regulations with a view to securing the free admission of pulp and paper from their Provinces into the market of the United States must be a question for the Provincial authorities to decide. In the meantime, the present duties on pulp and paper imported from the United States into Canada will remain. Whenever pulp and paper of the classes already mentioned are admitted into the United States free of duty from all parts of Canada, then similar articles, when imported from the United States shall be admitted into Canada free of duty.

11. The tariff changes proposed might not alone be sufficient to fully bring about the more favourable conditions which both parties desire. It is conceivable that Customs regulations which are deemed essential in some cases might operate unfavourably upon the trade between the United States and Canada, and that such regulations, if made without due regard to the special conditions of the two countries, might to some extent defeat the good purpose of the present arrangement. It is agreed that the utmost care shall be taken by both Governments to see that only such Customs regulations are adopted as are reasonably necessary for the protection of the Treasury against fraud; that no regulation shall be made or maintained which unreasonably hampers the more liberal exchange of commodities now proposed; that representations on either side as to the unfavourable opera-

tion of any regulation will receive from the other all due consideration, with the earnest purpose of removing any just cause of complaint; and that, if any further legislation is found necessary to enable either Government to carry out the purposes of this provision, such legislation will be sought from Congress or Parliament as the case may be.

12. The Government of Canada agree that, until otherwise determined by them, the licenses hitherto issued to United States fishing vessels under the provisions of section 3 of chapter 47 of the Revised Statutes of Canada, granting to such vessels certain privoleges on the Atlantic coast of Canada, shall continue to be issued and that the fee to be paid to the Government of Canada for such license by the owner or commander of any such United States vessel shall hereafter be one dollar per annum.

13. It is understood that upon a day and hour to be agreed upon between the two Governments, the President of the United States will communicate to Congress the conclusions now reached and recommend the adoption of such legislation as may be necessary on the part of the United States to give effect to the proposed arrangement.

14. It is understood that simultaneously with the sending of such communication to the United States Congress by the President, the Canadian Government will communicate to the Parliament of Canada the conclusions now reached, and will thereupon take the necessary steps to procure such legislation as is required to give effect to the proposed arrangement.

15. Such legislation on the part of the United States may contain a provision that it shall not come into operation until the United States Government are assured that corresponding legislation has been or will be passed by the Parliament of Canada; and in like manner the legislation on the part of Canada may contain a provision that it shall not come into operation until the Government of Canada are assured that correspond-

ing legislation has been passed or will be passed by the Congress of the United States.

Yours faithfully,

(Sgd.) W. S. FIELDING.

WM. PATERSON

The Honourable P. C. Knox,
    Secretary of State,
        Washington, D.C.

. . . Let me now read the reply of the Secretary of State, the Hon. P. C. Knox:—

Department of State, Washington,
        January 21, 1911.

The Honourable W. S. Fielding, and
The Honourable William Paterson,
        Washington.

Gentlemen,—I have the honour to acknowledge the receipt of your communication of this date in relation to the negotiations initiated by the President several months ago for a reciprocal trade arrangement between the United States and Canada, in which you set forth and ask me to confirm your understanding of the results of our recent conferences in continuation of these negotiations.

I take great pleasure in replying that your statement of the proposed arrangement is entirely in accord with my understanding of it.

It is a matter of some regret on our part that we have been unable to adjust our differences on the subject of wood pulp, pulp wood and print paper. We recognize the difficulties to which you refer growing out of the nature of the relations between the Dominion and Provincial Governments, and for the present we must be content with the conditional arrangement which has been proposed in Schedule A attached to your letter.

I fully appreciate the importance, to which you call attention, of not permitting a too rigid customs administration to interfere with the successful operation of our agreement, if it is approved by the Congress of the United States and the Parliament of Canada, and I desire to confirm your statement of our understanding on this point. I am satisfied that the spirit evinced on both sides gives assurance that every effort will be made to secure the full measure of benefit which is contemplated in entering into this arrangement.

The assurance that you give that the Dominion Government proposes to require only a nominal fee from the fishing vessels of the United States for the privileges in Canadian waters for which heretofore a charge of $1.50 per ton for each vessel has been required is most gratifying.

I heartily concur in your statement of the purposes inspiring the negotiations and in the views expressed by you as to the mutual benefits to be derived by both countries in the event our work is confirmed, and I take this opportunity to assure you, on behalf of the President, of his appreciation of the cordial spirit in which you have met us in these negotiations.

I have the honour to be, gentlemen.

Your obedient servant,

(Signed) P. C. KNOX.

This agreement deals with the rates of duty on Canadian products going into the United States, with the rates of duty on American products coming into Canada, only that and nothing more. If my hon. friends will permit me, I will now read the schedules:

Articles the growth, product or manufacture of the United States to be admitted into Canada free of duty when imported from the United States, and reciprocally articles the growth, product or manufacture of Canada to be admitted into the United States free of duty when imported from Canada:

Live animals, viz.:—Cattle, horses and mules, swine, sheep, lambs, and all other live animals.

Poultry, dead or alive.

Wheat, rye, oats, barley, and buckwheat; dried pease and beans, edible.

Corn, sweet corn, or maize (except into Canada for distillation).

We can impose a duty on corn for distillation. In the United States they do not. We maintain our duty for the purpose of distillation, but the corn is free otherwise.

Hay, straw, and cow pease.

Fresh vegetables, viz.:—Potatoes, sweet potatoes, yams, turnips, onions, cabbages, and all other vegetables in their natural state.

Fresh fruits, viz.:—Apples, pears, peaches, grapes, berries and all other edible fruits in their natural state.

Dried fruits. viz.:—Apples, peaches, pears and apricots, dried desiccated or evaporated.

Dairy products, viz.:—Butter, cheese, and fresh milk and cream. Provided that cans actually used in the transportation of milk or cream may be passed back and forth between the two countries free of duty, under such regulations as the respective Governments may prescribe.

Eggs of barnyard fowl, in the shell.

Honey.

Cotton-seed oil.

Seeds. viz.:—Flaxseed or linseed, cotton-seed and other oil seeds; grass seed, including timothy and clover seed; garden, field, and other seed not herein otherwise provided for, when in packages weighing over one pound each (not including flower seeds).

Fish of all kinds, fresh, frozen, packed in ice, salted or preserved in any form, except sardines and other fish preserved in oil; and shell fish of all kinds, including oysters, lobsters and clams in any state, fresh or packed, and coverings of the foregoing.

Seal, herring, whale, and other fish oil, including cod oil.

Salt.

Mineral waters, natural, not in bottles or jugs.

Timber, hewn, sided or squared otherwise than by sawing, and round timber used for spars or in building wharfs.

Sawed boards, planks, deals and other lumber, not further manufactured than sawed.

Paving posts, railroad ties, and telephone, trolley, electric light and telegraph poles of cedar or other woods.

Wooden staves of all kinds, not further manufactured than listed or jointed, and stave bolts.

Pickets and palings.

Plaster rock or gypsum, crude, not ground.

Mica, manufactured or rough trimmed only, and mica ground or bolted.

Feldspar, crude, powdered or ground.

Asbestos not further manufactured than ground.

Fluorspar, crude, not ground.

Glycerine, crude, not purified.

Talc, ground, bolted or precipitated, naturally or artifically, not for toilet use.

Sulphate of soda, or salt cake; and soda ash.

Extracts of hemlock bark.

Carbon electrodes.

Brass in bars and rods, in coil or otherwise, not less than six feet in length, or brass in strips, sheets or plates, not polished, planished or coated.

Cream separators of every description, and parts thereof imported for repair of the foregoing.

Rolled iron or steel sheets, or plates, number fourteen gauge or thinner, galvanized or coated with zinc, tin or other metal, or not.

Crucible cast steel wire, valued at not less than six cents per pound.

Galvanized iron or steel wire, curved or not, numbers nine, twelve, and thirteen wire gauge.

Typecasting and typesetting machines and parts thereof, adapted for use in printing offices.

Barbed fencing wire of iron or steel, galvanized or not.

Coke.

Round rolled wire rods in the coil, of iron or steel, not over three-eighths of an inch in diameter, and not smaller than number six wire gauge.

Pulp wood mechanically ground; pulp of wood, chemical, bleached or unbleached; news print paper, and other paper, and paper board, manufactured from mechanical wood pulp or from chemical wood pulp, or of which such pulp is the component material of chief value, coloured in the pulp, or not coloured, and valued at not more than four cents per pound, not including printed or decorated wall paper.

Provided that such paper and board, valued at four cents per pound or less, and wood pulp, being the products of Canada when imported therefrom directly into the United States shall be admitted free of duty, on the condition precedent that no export duty, export license fee, or other export charge of any kind whatsoever (whether in the form of additional charge or license fee or otherwise) or any prohibition or restriction in any way of the exportation (whether by law, order, regulation, contractual relation, or otherwise, directly or indirectly) shall have been imposed upon such paper, board or wood pulp, or the wood used in the manufacture of such paper, board or wood pulp, or the wood pulp used in the manufacture of such paper or board:

Provided also that such wood pulp, paper or board, being the products of the United States, shall only be admitted free of duty into Canada from the United States when such wood pulp, paper or board, being the products of Canada, are admitted from all parts of Canada free of duty into the United States.

Note.—It is understood that fresh fruits to be admitted free of duty into the United States from Canada do not include lemons, oranges, limes, grape fruit, shaddocks, pomelos, or pineapples.

These things are largely free in Canada. In the United States they do not want to make them free, so they are not included in the fruits that are made free.

It is also understood that fish oil, whale oil, seal oil and fish of all kinds, being the product of fisheries carried on by the fishermen of the United States shall be admitted into Canada as the product of the United States, and similarly that fish oil, whale oil, seal oil and fish of all kinds, being the product of fisheries carried on by the fishermen of Canada, shall be admitted into the United States as the product of Canada.

That refers to fish taken beyond the three-mile limit, which would not be strictly a Canadian or a United States product; but if it is taken by Canadian fishermen it assumes the character of a Canadian product, and if it is taken by United States fishermen it assumes the character of a United States product, and is treated accordingly.

SCHEDULE B

Articles the growth, product or manufacture of the United States to be admitted into Canada at the undermentioned rates of duty when imported from the United States; and reciprocally the same articles the growth, product or manufacture of Canada to be admitted in the United States at identical rates of duty when imported from Canada:—

Articles.	Rates of Duties
Fresh meats, viz.:—beef, veal, mutton, lamb, pork, and all other fresh or refrigerated meats excepting game	One and one-quarter cents per pound.
Bacon and hams, not in tins or jars	One and one-quarter cents per pound.
Meats of all kinds, dried, smoked, salted, in brine, or prepared or preserved in any manner, not otherwise herein provided for	One and one-quarter cents per pound.
Canned meats and canned poultry	Twenty per cent ad valorem.
Extract of meat, fluid or not	Twenty per cent ad valorem.
Lard, and compounds thereof, cottonlene and cotton stearine, and animal stearine	One and one-quarter cents per pound.
Tallow	Forty cents per 100 lbs.
Egg yolk, egg albumen and blood albumen	Seven and one-half per cent ad valorem.
Fish (except shell fish) by whatever name known, packed in oil, in tin boxes or cans, including the weight of the package:—	
(a) when weighing over twenty ounces and not over thirty-six ounces each	Five cents per package.
(b) when weighing over twelve ounces and not over twenty ounces each	Four cents per package.
(c) when weighing twelve ounces each or less	Two cents per package.
(d) when weighing thirty-six ounces each or more, or when packed in oil, in bottles, jars or kegs	Thirty per cent ad valorem.
Tomatoes and other vegetables, including corn in cans or other air-tight packages, and including the weight of the package	One and one-quarter cents per pound.
Wheat flour and semolina; and rye flour	Fifty cents per barrel of 196 pounds.
Oatmeal and rolled oats, including the weight of paper covering	Fifty cents per 100 pounds.
Corn meal	Twelve and one-half cents per 100 pounds.
Barley malt	Forty-five cents per 100 pounds.
Barley, pot, pearled and patent	One-half cent per pound.
Buckwheat flour or meal	One-half cent per pound.
Split pease, dried	Seven and one-half cents per bushel of 60 lbs.
Prepared cereal foods, not otherwise provided for herein	Seventeen and a half per cent ad valorem.
Bran, middlings and other offals of grain used for animal food	Twelve and one-half cents per 100 pounds.
Macaroni and vermicelli	One cent per pound.

Articles.	Rates of Duties
Biscuits, wafers and cakes, when sweetened with sugar, honey molasses or other material	Twenty-five per cent ad valorem.
Biscuits, wafers, cakes and other baked articles composed in whole or in part of eggs or any kind of flour or meal when combined with chocolate, nuts, fruits or confectionery; also candied peel, candied pop-corn, candied nuts, candied fruits, sugar candy and confectionery of all kinds	Thirty-two and one-half per cent ad valorem.
Maple sugar and maple syrup	One cent per pound.
Pickles, including pickled nuts, sauces of all kinds, and fish paste or sauce	Thirty-two and one-half per cent ad valorem.
Cherry juice and prune juice, or prune wine, and other fruit juices, and fruit syrup, non-alcoholic ..	Seventeen and a half per cent ad valorem.
Mineral waters and imitations of natural mineral waters, in bottles or jugs	Seventeen and a half per cent ad valorem.
Essential oils	Seven and a half per cent ad valorem.
Grape vines, gooseberry, raspberry and currant bushes	Seventeen and a half per cent ad valorem.
Farm wagons, and finished parts thereof	Twenty-two and a half per cent ad valorem.
Ploughs, tooth and disc harrows, harvesters, reapers, agricultural drills and planters, mowers, horse-rakes, cultivators; threshing machines, including windstackers, baggers, weighers, and self-feeders therefore; and finished parts thereof imported for repair of the foregoing	Fifteen per cent ad valorem.
Portable engines with boilers, in combination, horse-powers and traction engines, for farm purposes; hay loaders, potato diggers, folder or feed cutters, grain crushers, fanning mills, hay tedders, farm or field rollers, manure spreaders and windmills; and finished parts thereof imported for repair of the foregoing, except shafting	Twenty per cent ad valorem.
Grindstones of sandstone, not mounted, finished or not	Five cents per 100 pounds.
Freestone, granite, sandstone, limestone, and all other monumental or building stone, except marble, brechia, and onyx, unmanufactured, or not dressed, hewn or polished	Twelve and a half per cent ad valorem.
Roofing slates	Fifty-five cents per 100 square feet.
Vitrified paving blocks, not ornamented or decorated in any manner, and paving blocks of stone	Seventeen and a half per cent ad valorem.
Oxide of iron, as a colour	Twenty-two and a half per cent ad valorem.
Asbestos further manufactured than ground; manufactures of asbestos, or articles of which asbestos is the component material of chief value, including woven fabrics wholly or in chief value of asbestos	Twenty-two and a half per cent ad valorem.
Printing ink	Seventeen and a half per cent ad valorem.
Cutlery, plated or not, viz.:—pocket knives, pen knives, scissors and shears, knives and forks for household purposes, and table steels	Twenty-seven and a half per cent ad valorem.
Bells and gongs; brass corners and rules for printers	Twenty-seven and a half per cent ad valorem.
Basins, urinals and other plumbing fixtures for bath rooms and lavatories; bath tubs, sinks and laundry tubs, of earthenware, stone, cement or clay, or of other material	Thirty-two and a half per cent ad valorem.

Articles.	Rates of Duties
Brass band instruments	Twenty-two and a half per cent ad valorem.
Clocks, watches, time recorders, clock and watch keys, clock cases, and clock movements	Twenty-seven and a half per cent ad valorem.
Printers' wooden cases and cabinets for holding type	Twenty-seven and a half per cent ad valorem.
Wood flour	Twenty-two and a half per cent ad valorem.
Canoes and small boats of wood, not power boats ..	Twenty-two and a half per cent ad valorem.
Feathers, crude, not dressed, coloured or otherwise manufactured	Twelve and a half per cent ad valorem.
Antiseptic surgical dressings such as absorbent cotton, cotton wool, lint, lamb's wool, tow, jute, gauzes and oakum, prepared for use as surgical dressings plain or medicated; surgical trusses, pessaries and suspensory bandages of all kinds	Seventeen and a half per cent ad valorem.
Plate glass, not bevelled, in sheets or panes exceeding seven square feet each, and not exceeding twenty-five square feet each	Twenty-five per cent ad valorem.
Motor vehicles other than for railways and tramways, and automobiles, and parts thereof, not including rubber tires	Thirty per cent ad valorem.
Iron or steel digesters for the manufacture of wood pulp	Twenty-seven and a half per cent ad valorem.
Musical instrument cases, fancy cases or boxes, portfolios, satchels, reticules, card cases, purses, pocket books, fly books for artificial flies, all the foregoing composed wholly or in chief value of leather	Thirty per cent ad valorem.

SCHEDULE C.—Articles the growth, product or manufacture of Canada to be admitted into the United States at the undermentioned special rates of duty when imported from Canada:—

Articles.	Rates of Duties
Aluminum in crude form	Five cents per pound.
Aluminum in plates, sheets, bars and rods	Eight cents per pound.
Laths	Ten cents per 1000 pieces.
Shingles	Thirty cents per thousand.
Sawed boards, planks, deals and other lumber, planed or finished on one side	Fifty cents per M. feet B.M.
Planed or finished on one side and tongued and grooved, or planed or finished on two sides	Seventy-five cents per M. feet B.M.
Planed or finished on three sides, or planed and finished on two sides and tongued and grooved	One dollar and twelve and a half cents M. feet B.M.
Planed and finished on four sides	One dollar and fifty cents per M. feet B.M.
In estimating board measure under this schedule no reduction shall be made on board measure on account of planning, tonguing and grooving.	
Iron ore, including manganiferous iron ore, and the dross or residuum from burnt pyrites	Ten cents per ton of 2,240 pounds.
Coal slack or culm of all kinds, such as will pass through a half-inch screen	Fifteen cents per ton of 2,240 lbs.

SCHEDULE D.—Articles the growth, product or manufacture of the United States to be admitted into Canada at the undermentioned special rates of duty when imported from the United States:—

Articles.	Rates of Duties
Cement, Portland, and hydraulic or water lime, in barrels, bags, or casks, the weight of the package to be included in the weight for duty	Eleven cents per 100 pounds.
Trees, viz.:—Apple, cherry, peach, pear, plum, and quince, of all kinds, and small peach trees known as June buds	Two and a half cents each.
Condensed milk, the weight of the package to be included in the weight for duty	Two cents per pound.
Biscuits without added sweetening	Twenty per cent ad valorem.
Fruits in air-tight cans or other air-tight packages, the weight of the cans or other packages to be included in the weight for duty	Two cents per pound.
Peanuts, shelled	One cent per pound.
Peanuts, unshelled	A half cent per pound.
Coal, bituminous, round and run of mine, including bituminous coal such as will not pass through a three-quarter-inch screen	Forty-five cents per ton.

This completes the schedules which, I am sorry to say, have occupied the attention of the House longer than I thought they would. . . .

We present the arrangement to you to day, Sir, not as a triumph of one country over the other, but as the result of an effort to do justice to both; we commend this arrangement, Sir, to the judgment of this parliament as the President of the United States will commend it to the judgment of the Congress. The one fear I have is that there may be people who will say that we have made so good a bargain that the Congress should not approve of it. In times past friendly arrangements have been made with the United States government which have failed to receive the approval of the Congress, but we think the time is more favourable now. We think we have found the psychological moment for dealing with this question; we think we are within reach of some of the commercial advantages for which our people have struggled now for half a century. We commit this matter to the care of the Canadian parliament with the firm conviction that it is going to be a good thing for Canada, a good thing for the United States, and that we will continue to have it and maintain it not because there is any binding obligation to do so, but because the intelligence of the people of the two countries will decide that it is a good thing for the promotion of friendly relations and for the development of commerce of the two countries.

George Foster, House of Commons, *Debates*, 1910-1911, (February 9, 1911), pp. 3327, 3336-3342; (February 14, 1911), pp. 3530-3563.

The Battle Joined

[Feb. 9]

. . . I may be wrong, but I have given a great deal of thought to trade matters in the course of my political life, and my conviction is that we have never had in Canada any question quite so important as this present one—any issue upon which hung more far-reaching consequences. The only one that, in my mind, approached it, was the struggle in 1891, when commercial union with the United States and discrimination against Great Britain was the slogan of hon. gentlemen opposite, and the cry around which centred one of the greatest political battles ever fought in Canada. I think it is a situation which involves in a large degree the fiscal freedom and political independence of Canada . . .

Now, what does this measure do? In the first place it alters the fiscal conditions of interchange, not for a few unimportant articles, but a long list of most important products. It alters the fiscal conditions of interchange for all our dairy products, all our animals, all our grains, a large proportion of our lumber, all our natural food products, all our fish products except sardines, all our fresh vegetable products, our mineral products, our wood pulp and paper, by transferring them in one block from the dutiable to the free list. Do we know just what that means and can we sense just exactly how far that reaches? But it goes further than that: Our meat products, our grain products, our prepared vegetables and food products, a large slice of manufactures, are transferred to a lower reciprocal list, and another fairly large number of important products are transferred to a non-reciprocal but specified list in which the duties are lower. In gross, it takes $95,000,000 of products and at a stroke of the pen transfers them from dutiable to free or from a higher dutiable to a lower dutiable list. Every man knows that if you change the fiscal conditions of interchange of $95,000,000 worth of products in this country you effect in some degree every other of our products or nearly so. As I have shown $47,800,000 of our imports, and $47,300,000 of our exports are affected. Now, Mr. Chairman, I do not want to labour these different points beyond what is necessary to get them under advisement and thought. Every man in this House must realize the importance of a measure which at one stroke of the pen lifts $95,000,000 of interchangeable products out from old established conditions and makes a different fiscal system for interchanging them. Such a measure must be of a far reaching and wide importance. How far it goes requires business men of the best calibre to figure out adequately. But, this arrangement does something even more important: It shifts the base and conditions of production. It is true that production is of greater importance than interchange or trade, because trade is founded upon production and without products you cannot have trade. You must have at least two different productions in order to have a trade; one man raises one thing, another man raises another thing and there you have the basis of interchange and that interchange you measure by your trade figures of the value of each. Therefore, though trade is important, the conditions and the base of production is more important still to be considered. And, this agreement if it goes into operation, shifts the base of production and not to the advantage of Canada in my opinion. For example, British Columbia is particularly adapted to the raising of fruits, and British Columbians have invested their capital and risked their future in the business and they have done well and aim to do better. They have accomplished their success so far through being fairly protected from the southern fruit growers who compete in their market. There you have the production of fruit that employs labour and capital and is of great importance to that province. East of the Rockies they produce grain and cattle; British Columbia has to get grain and the prairies have to get fruit, and there you have the basis of interchange between these two parts of our Dominion, and the products are both raised in Canada. Now, what does this measure do? It changes the base of production; it says to the prairie buyers: Men in the United States will raise fruits and will supply them to you and you need not deal any more with British Columbia: it says to the prairie provinces: You may still raise grain and cattle, but you will send them down to the United States. You have the same grain and cattle raised, you have the same fruit raised, but one of your products has been shifted from its base

in Canada and transferred to the United States. That, Sir, is the defect of this instrument which is before us to-night. These gentlemen opposite say: We are in favour of reciprocity? Are you? What would be the best reciprocity?—Reciprocity between the different sections in Canada itself that raise different productions and have different capabilities. Why, if you favour reciprocity should you kill, or deteriorate, or diminish the reciprocity between British Columbia and the prairies? That is but a sample, but there are other instances. Take fish which is a great natural industry and a great business industry as well. Within the last 20 years a fish trade of large dimensions has been built up between the lower provinces and the rest of Canada running as far as the Rockies.

There is a production in Canada. The eastern Canadians want cattle, want grain, or want flour, which is raised in the western provinces. There are the elements of a reciprocity which builds up this country—both productions made in Canada and an interchange between the different sections of Canada. Now, what are you going to do? You are going to say to the fish industry in the eastern provinces: Go, seek your markets somewhere else. The fishermen of the lakes and the fishermen of the Atlantic shore, because they have shorter routes and cheaper routes, maybe, to the heart of the great west, will get and give the fish that are required in the west. It will no longer be reciprocity between two sections of our own country. It will be reciprocity between the United States in one production and the west in another production. Now, Sir, that runs through the whole of this reciprocity arrangement. You talk about your foreign trade, and you bellow about it as though it were the greatest thing in Canada. I was going to say that it was almost the least thing in Canada. What is the greatest thing in Canada? The interprovincial trade, which is founded upon the many productions in the east, and the wheat, grain and cattle productions in the west—the two complementing each other. What has made Canada so strong, and so great in her progress is this, that you have filled her veins with the rich blood of interprovincial trade, stimulating productions in various parts, and then interchanging these productions one part with the other part. This instrument has for its object, can have no other, the shifting of the base of production, and giving as far as possible at least one-half to the United States of America, and taking it from Canada, with this proviso, which is important, that the kind of production you leave to Canada is the production so dearly loved by the Minister of Customs. To Canada, he says, dig out your ore; the United States will manufacture it up through a thousand processes until you get it at great value, and then send it back to us to buy. Frontenac, dig your talc, and employ a few hundreds of men; send over the product of your pick-men and your shovellers to the United States, and let them do the perfecting processes upon it, and get the employment, get the accrued wealth, and get the national development. That is what it means. The part you call for Canada to keep is that which employs the least labour; what you give to the United States as the result of that employment of the least labour in raw material—is what employs the greatest labour and runs up into the great figures of value which labour adds to the raw material in perfecting the product. The real reciprocity for Canada is the reciprocity between these different provinces. I put it to you, Sir, that if it were now 1867 and

the provinces were asked to federate, with the alternative of free reciprocal trade with the United States of America, would we have any federation of these provinces? It would have been absolutely impossible, and if this measure is to have the effect that its promoters and sponsors in the United States hope for it, it will turn us backward, and lead us towards the pre-confederation days when our maritime provinces traded with New England, and our large central provinces with the states on the border—there was no prairie then—and when British Columbia traded with the border states on the Pacific. My count against this measure, stronger and deeper than any, is that it threatens the best and highest production in this country, that it threatens thereby the stream of interprovincial trade which is absolutely the life and essence of this country as a whole. It also vitally affects and changes the direction of the channels of trade and the great transport routes. Now, that does not need to be argued at all. Everybody admits that. The only thing that is said with reference to it is this: Granted that what we have gone to such expense for, what we have been for forty years building up what we have now in the great trunk lines of communication east and west—granted that they will be affected—and if your reciprocity amounts to anything, they will be largely affected —there will be enough grown to keep them going and to keep the southern lines going too. Is that the sum and substance of our national aspirations to-day? Twenty years ago you could have said of one straggling line of railway in there, it can carry more than is produced, but in a little while production will overtake it, and surpass it, and the southern lines will have what they want, and that line will have all it can do. That was not the ambition of Canada. The ambition of Canada was to keep her transportation routes even and adequate for the increased production of the country. . . .

This agreement restricts freedom of legislation. I have a quarrel with the government because, without giving ear to the market gardeners or fruit men or any other interests, they have made a pact and rushed it through, and while they are rushing it through, these men come and complain that it cannot fail to do them damage. But the Minister of Customes, with loud voice, says to these people: You do not know anything about it; it will be the best gift God has ever given you. These people have to submit, because this government has contracted to push the thing through, they must get it through, and they are pledged to the United States administration to keep it there, after it is through. Two years pass and the market gardeners and other men come again to the government and say: our industry is absolutely gone; we can not subsist another year; you told us it would be all right, but it has not turned out all right; on the contrary, we shall be ruined unless you come to our relief. hat does the government say to that? All they can say is: We cannot help it. Why? Because if we do, that will break up the whole compact, and that we cannot do. What then is this parliament asked to do? It is asked to absolutely give away its independent power of redressing grievances. . . .

I have one other point to make and it is this—that this measure vitally affects the labour interests of this country. I have made my argument in reality on that, all I have to do is to state the proposition. If the effect of this measure is to shift producing centres from this country to the United States, to give us half and the

United States half, it means that half of the labour possibilities for the future are taken from this country, and shifted to the other side or kept upon the other side. If it is true, as I have stated, and I believe it is, that we are keeping the more raw processes for our country and leaving the more finished processes for the other country, and that the raw processes employ the least labour and at the smallest wage and the finishing processes the greatest amount of labour at the highest wage, we are cutting again into the great future of the labour men of this country. I do not need to carry that out a single step further.

[Feb. 14]

. . . The most important factor in the development and progress of any country is its productions in kind and variety. The twin factors which aid in producing are capital and labour, and I propose, for a few moments, to consider what will be the effect of the proposal before us in respect of the productions of Canada and their co-operative factors, capital and labour. As I have already said, we are disposed to pay too much attention to the figures of trade, which, after all, are but indexes of something which is basic and far more important. In all the foreign trade of Canada there are two productions, as far as geographical distribution is concerned—one of them in Canada and one outside Canada—and the one production is exchanged for the other. But the interprovincial trade is infinitely more important than foreign trade, as indexed by the foreign trade figures, because in the former all the products are made in Canada and the elements necessary to production are furnished and operated in Canada itself. The aim and

THE DEBATE IN THE HOUSE

object of this country for the last 40 years has been, as far as possible, to stimulate the number of productions in Canada itself, which usually form the article of exchange between the different parts of the country and to diminish as far as possible—and it is only possible relatively to diminish them—the productions of outside countries required in exchange for the productions of Canada. That is to transfer, as far as possible, all the elements of labour and capital and profit which go towards making up foreign productions, to transfer these to some section, province, or part of Canada where they shall be sent out and shipped for other productions in Canada made in some other province, section or part of Canada. To-day, when I read the American papers and scan the American speeches, and look at the American arguments, I do not find that they are saying very much as to the employment of American capital in the establishing of American industries in Canada. In the past and present condition of things we have noticed that as a factor, and a very important one, in the development of this country. It is stated, and I think without doubt, that at least $226,000,000 have been transferred in equipment and plant from factories in the United States towards the establishment of branch factories in the Dominion. Senator Beveridge, deploring that fact, substantiates it, but wonders whether it would not be much better for the United States, instead of transferring branch factories to the Dominion, to bring about a condition of tariffs, in which it would not be necessary for these American industries to transfer branches beyond the line. And Governor Foss, another very strong advocate of this reciprocity arrangement, deplores the same fact, and says that if it goes on hun-

dreds of millions more will be so transferred, and he thinks the time has come for the United States of America to accept Canada's offer, make the way easy and clear between the two countries and thereby keep the production, the capital, the labour and profits, the homebuilding and wealthmaking in the United States, instead of transferring it to Canada.

Why are they solicitous for this trade treaty with Canada? It looks out upon every page of their argument; it slips off the tongue of every advocate of the proposal. It is that the United States of America covets the rich natural resources of the Dominion of Canada—covets these resources not with a view to coming where the resources are, bringing labour and capital, and working them up where they exist; not that, but covets them to draw them away to their own manufacturing industries, to the centres of their own country, to make them up with their own labour to their own profit, directly and with all the subsidiary gain which accrues to manufacturing in the United States. 'How will they get these raw resources'? you say. Well, Sir, outside of what they already own in this country—and they own, probably, more than any one who has not looked into quite understands— this arrangement will not have been in operation for five years before the big trusts and moneyed interests of the United States will own everything that is loose in this Dominion in the way of great natural resources. What they do not wish to buy from the man in Canada who raises it or digs it from the mine, they will raise and dig on their own properties under their own direction in this country. They will have these natural resources, they will command them. And, as I have said, I want the people of Canada to keep this in mind—that the object in all this is not to work up the raw materials in Canada but to work them up in the United States of America. They will allow the cheaper and less skilled and less concentrated operations of labour to be performed in Canada, but the better paid, the more skilled, the more aggregated, are to be carried on in the United States. They will let Canadians take out the ore, catch the fish, fell the trees, raise the cattle and other stock, do the mechanical and exhausting farming work and—all the rougher processes of industry; but all the progressive processes of perfecting the raw material with all that pertains to those processes, and the distribution of them with all the profits that pertain thereto, these they covet for themselves. And the tendency of this arrangement is to put it within their power to carry out this purpose.

What I want to ask is this: Of what particular benefit will that be to the Dominion of Canada? You say: It is not possible for them to take away all the raw material. I do not press the argument that far; but I do say that the tendency is and will be to draw, as far as possible, the rawer resources of Canada to their centres and work them up there. And that they will do more and more, and in larger proportion as the years go by. I say that the broad effect of this agreement if it is to be as successful as these advocates argue, will be to leave the rawer rougher processes of the work, the digging, the mining, the felling, the collecting, all the processes of common labour at lesser wages, to the people of Canada, and as few as possible of the perfecting, more highly-paid and better-conditioned processes to the United States of America.

If that be true, what is the first effect? The first effect is to exhaust, in proportion to what they draw from us, the natural resources of the Dominion of Canada and to husband what they have left of their own resources as far as they possibly can for future generations; to take away from Canadians the higher and better processes of development in their own country, and to transfer these to the United States. . . .

How is capital to be affected by this? And how is labour to be affected by this? For forty years we have had a fairly stable policy in this country. The national idea came to birth in 1867 and it has ruled in this country from 1867 to this day. The national spirit carried with it the National Policy. And the national spirit and the National Policy appealed to the capital of the old country and of other countries, on the ground that this was to be a national development under a settled policy. And capital, which is eminently sensitive, which looks long before it invests itself, has gradually invested itself in the great public works and important national enterprises of Canada, until today $1,800,000,000 of British capital lies in our great routes of transport and the public undertakings of this country. Under what conditions was that placed there? Take the capital invested in your east and west lines of communication, was it ever dreamed in Britain, Sir, that the time would come when a change of policy would be inaugurated by the men who petitioned for the money, who plead for the investment of capital and got it at long last, was it ever dreamed that when this capital was securely fixed and invested, the long lateral lines of railway should be tapped every few miles by communication to draw off the trade intended for them to southern routes and do away with the long haul of the east-and-west lines?

So this proposition of the Finance Minister absolutely changes the conditions of all capital that has been invested in that way, invested from Great Britain in our great national concerns. In those times we wanted money, and our credit, though good, was based more upon hope than fulfilment; it was what we expected to happen in this country upon which we made our appeal for finances, to bring what we expected to birth and to fruitage. But, Sir, as the years went on, and expectations began to be fulfilled, that stream of money widened and deepened, and to-day it is coming into this country from Great Britain at the rate of $150,000,000 a year, and increasing from year to year. The men who have their money fixed in it have to stand the new conditions, they cannot get their investments out. Canadians have not been simply trying to get investments in the past, but they have, as we know, been endeavouring to make the flow deeper and more plentiful into this country for the ever ripening and recurring development which it is necessary for us to make in a new country like ours. How will this instrument affect capital that has not come, that is ready to come, but which, under doubt and uncertainty, will hesitate to come and invest itself in this country? I do not follow that out any further, it is not necessary.

Let me state another thing: That just as the flag follows trade, just so labour follows capital, and capital is going to be sensitive and careful of investing itself in this country on account of the unstable conditions which are imported by this arrangement, and will go to the side where there is the largest population, where there is the greatest market, where there is the greatest fixity and stability of financial conditions. For you find no intimation amongst the powers that be, or the powers that are to be, in the United States, that while they are quite willing, for purposes which I shall hereafter disclose, to open the barriers and to make free trade between Canada and the United States, they are at all disposed to throw any barriers down against the rest of the world. They do not intend to do it. Then, Sir, the investor, under this precious document which the Minister of Finance has laid upon the table for our approval, the investor says: Here is in instrument which works in a certain direction, how long is it to be valid? The Finance Minister says he does not know. It can be made invalid any day that this legislature or that legislature chooses to make it so. What money will invest itself then in enterprises which run in the lines of trade which are established between the United States and ourselves? If they have money to invest, what will they say? We think we had better go to the other side of the line and invest it. Then, if this thing bursts up we will be, with our investment, with our establishment, with our labour, with our product, where the ninety-three millions are, and where we will be protected against the rest of the world. . . .

I wish to ask a few more questions on the trade side of the question. In the first place, I want to ask what is the effect of this upon our trade with other countries. The first effect that we have is a singular one—no I am not quite right in saying that, under this government it is not singular, but it is one of which we have had repeated instances. There is again in this case, as there has been in other cases, the gift of free trade privileges, or lower duty privileges, to foreign countries who give us no compensation of any kind.

By what right in this stage of commercial competition and warfare so to speak does the government of Canada give to countries already upon a good basis of trade with Canada further concessions upon entering into our markets when Canada gets no single thing in return for the same. At least it is questionable as to whether we should carry out that operation too far and repeat it too often. What is done in this case? I find that most favoured nations receive a benefit of $165,254 of trade made free to them on the basis of their dealings with Canada last year, and $580,317 of trade in which the duty has been lowered to them under this treaty, taking the goods they sent to Canada in 1910. That is to say, a total trade of $745,671 has been effected favourably to certain countries of the world and for this no single thing in the way of compensation has been given to us in return. So much for that. There is also, however, this to be noted, that in some of the articles which we have made free to the United States of America, these favoured countries come in not only theoretically but practically with the ability to send large exportations into the Dominion, free, or at a modified rate of duty. Animals, grains, vegetables, fruits, butter, cheese, fish, salt and other articles can come in from Argentine, Austro-Hungary, France and Algeria, Norway, Russia, Switzerland and some other countries. With that superior smile which more frequently graces the face of my right hon. friend the Prime Minister when he labours for lack of information than otherwise, the Prime Minister rather smiles now at I suppose the silliness of my argument; nevertheless each man has to make his argument according to his light, and each man has a perfect right to judge of it as he wishes.

Sir WILFRID LAURIER. And to smile also.

Mr. FOSTER. My right hon, friend can smile and take a smile for all I care; I won't quarrel with that. But what is more important—and now perhaps my right hon. friend will rather want to take a smile than to smile—what does happen is this, and it is rather an important point it seems to me. I want to remind my right hon. friend of a statement made in cold blood by the Primine Minister of Canada; a statement which he is supposed to have known the meaning of, and which no honourable statesman would fail to carry out. Sitting in that chair the other day, he said to the 1,500 that were interviewing him: Gentlemen, I am sorry you come too late; if you had come a few weeks before, why, we could have interchanged opinions and you could have had your questions taken up. Afterwards, hearing some of these gentlemen talk, one said to the other: Oh, well you see, this is the misery of the thing, we did not come early enough; didn't you hear what the Prime Minister said; if we had come earlier we would have got all we wanted maybe. Yes—said the other, didn't we have the Prime Minister's pledge as a public man and a gentleman that he didn't propose to make any adjustment and revision of the tariff until he had appointed a tariff commission? I thought the answer was a good one. I make the same answer to my right hon. friend here to-day. Why did he make that promise and why did he fail to fulfil it? Why did he pledge himself in the west and pledge himself here in this House of Commons in the early part of the session unless he honestly intended to abide by the pledge? In reply to my hon. friend the leader of the opposition, he said:

I stated that we would have a commission of investigation before we undertook a revision of the tariff. Does any member on the other side of the House take issue with the promise I make. Would any of them advocate rushing into a revision of the tariff without previous investigation. Hon. members may laugh at that but they will dare not to say that they would favour such a course.

Mr. HUGHES. Who said that?

Mr. FOSTER. This was said by the right hon. gentleman who sits opposite to us now, and who as Prime Minister, made that statement in the west and made it here. And, he will get up after me, and he will try to crawl out of that by saying that this is not technically a revision of the tariff. Now, will he? It will be the smallest hole that any large sized man ever tried to get through. When you transfer the immense number of products which have been transferred from the dutiable to the free list, and when you affect the dutiable list in others, what is it but de facto a revision of the tariff, and a good big revision, and a revision upon which most important consequences hang. I say that never in the history of Canada, has a more fateful and more important revision of the tariff taken place than has been brought about by this agreement with the United States, and the legislation which is to call it into force. I charge the right hon. gentleman with bad faith with the people of the west, with bad faith with this parliament of Canada, with bad faith with this whole people of Canada, when he lulled every interest to sleep by saying to the wide Dominion: Don't fear, gentlemen, there will be no revision of the tariff until a tariff commission has been put to work and you shall have an opportunity to make your representations

before that tariff commission. My right hon. friend made this other statement:

There is in the Fielding tariff a cardinal principle. It is the principle of British preference, and that preference will not be interfered with by anything we do with the United States.

I ask the right hon. gentlemen if he has implemented that promise? I charge him to his face that he has broken it. Right under my hand here, are the proofs that he has broken it. He made that statement not once, or twice, but over and over again, and, Sir, I noticed that the Finance Minister took the unusual course of sending a reasoned argument by cable to the High Commissioner at London to be used by the Prime Minister of the empire, filled with many half statements that would have been clearer had they been made whole statements, and with many presentations which would have been nearer the truth if they had been whole instead of partial presentations. But, Sir, on the basis of it, Mr. Asquith rose in the House of Commons and in the debate which took place there he said:

The American-Canadian agreement had been carefully watched by the British Ambassador at Washington on behalf of British interests, and he had been assured that so far as British importations into Canada were concerned, British preference would be scrupulously maintained.

. . . I challenge the statement that imperial preference has been scrupulously maintained. I have here only a partial table which will show what I mean. Counting up the items, I find that there are 102 in which there has been a lowering of tariff without going so far as perfect freedom from impost. Of those, 28 involve importations from Great Britain which have not had the preference impaired; 74 involve importations from Great Britain in every one of which the preference has been impaired and lowered. In the list of goods made free there are 69 items. On 39 of those British preference has not been touched; on 30 of them it has been absolutely wiped out, for the goods have been placed on the free list. There is involved altogether $6,387,336 worth of British goods imported under the preference in 1910, on every dollar's worth of which the imperial preference has been either absolutely wiped out or has been materially diminished. Now, it is no excuse to say: But that six millions, compared with our whole foreign trade, is but a trifle, and therefore we have scrupulously maintained the preference. That would be quibbling unworthy of even any member of the present government. . . .

Where is the argument for the men who advocate the imperial preference arrangement with Great Britain? On this side of the water, they will say it would have been a boon to us then, but we have got free entrance into a market of 93,000,000, we have got all we want, do not talk to us about British preference. On the other hand, they have struck a fatal blow on this side, in this way. They have included all the articles on which the British people would be willing to give a preference in the free list to the United States, and every one of them could be sluiced through Canada into the empire under a preferential arrangement with Canada. And you could not help yourself. Preference then will not be with Canada alone in these articles, but with Canada plus the United States. These considerations justify me in saying that a fatal

blow had been struck at British preference, and I want no better corroborative argument than this, namely, the joy that broke out in the British House of Commons among the anti-tariff reformers when this news came to them, which, it was declared, dished tariff reform in Great Britain forever and aye. This is how imperial preference has been treated. . . .

. . . Reciprocity, I think, has this as a prime condition—that it shall be between two countries, each producing a surplus, but a surplus in a different line of articles, and each wanting articles of which the other's surplus is made up. More than that, for ideal reciprocity, this should not be a mere occasional surplus, but should be the result of fixed conditions of climate, soil, and so on, that will make the surplus permanent. Two countries that show ideal conditions of reciprocity in trade would be the West India islands and Canada. The West Indies produce a surplus of tropical fruits, of which we produce none. But they produce absolutely no dairy products, none of the food products of the temperate zone, of which we produce a great surplus. These are examples of two countries between which a reciprocity trade arrangement could be made with great profit. In the same way, reciprocity between us and Great Britain is possible in lines or articles which will readily suggest themselves to the minds of hon. members. But in the case of the arrangement we are now discussing, you are trying to establish reciprocity between two countries, each of which has a surplus, and a surplus of exactly the same products. With the exception of cheese and fish, the United States of America has a surplus of every article which goes from Canada, under this arrangement, into the United States. And not a slim surplus, but in every respect a substantial surplus, and in some respects a very large surplus. . . .

. . . And President Taft, in his message to the United States Congress, says that what the United States must set itself to do is to increase its exports on the line of manufactured goods. That is its future. It cannot expect to make large exportations of food and other products. What we want, he says, is raw material close at hand, what we want is cheap foodstuffs, so far as we can get them from the northern country in order that we may be better provided and furnished for this increased product and increased export of the industries of this country, in which our future lies in respect of the world trade. That is the policy shining out in every statement, shining out in every line and article of this proposed agreement. The United States knows what it is after, with a tariff wall against the world, desiring to preserve its own unused natural resources so far as it can, dipping into the virgin resources of Canada so far as it may be able, fortifying itself by the conservation of its own and by the destruction of ours, making itself the great manufacturing country of the world, and increasing its wealth and its power in that way.

So I say that the elements of real reciprocity are not found in the conditions of the two countries. The reciprocity that you will have between this country and the United States will be largely a sectional, fitful, occasional reciprocity. If the hay crop is poor in the United States, and we have a good crop, that will be our opportunity to a certain extent; although if the hay crop is very poor in the United States, and the existence of their cattle depended upon hay being got, no matter what the duty was in reason, they would have to pay for the hay and

pay the duty. But the Finance Minister laid little stress on this part of the arrangement, that whilst the United States gave us a market we gave the United States a market as well. If we can turn our products into their country in certain sections where drouth or frost has made a shortage at certain seasons, when, from any circumstance, there is a failure of any particular crop in whole or in part, the very same thing can be done by the United States when these adverse circumstances visit the Canadian crops, and the Canadian farmers. There is a market given to us, but there is also a market given by us. As I said before, the reciprocity between the two will be largely a fitful, sectional reciprocity. . . .

Now the great argument of the Finance Minister, and the argument that is used throughout the country, is this: We have given you another market for your wheat. As I said before, there are two markets for wheat now. The Canadian northwest farmer need not sell his wheat to the miller if the miller does not give him the fair ruling price; he can export it to London and Liverpool and get the price that the world gets, which fixes the price that the miller gives, outside of certain incidental circumstances of location and the like of that. Thus he has two markets now. But the Finance Minister forgot to go any farther, forgot to trace out just what he was doing when he presented the gift of free entry of Canadian wheat into the United States market. He forgot to point out that the miller of the Canadian west, and the miller of the west United States, has in the end, after the local supply is satisfied, to find the same market in London and Liverpool. He forgot to point out that he made it possible for the United States miller to get Canada's No. 1 hard wheat, to mill it in the

United States mills and satisfy the people in the United States who ask for high grade flours and pay fancy prices for them and then take the less strong flours and export them to the European market, which is largely, as I am informed, for those grades not the strongest and not the best. So that what happens is this: The Canadian miller will be at a disadvantage in competition in the export market in flour with the United States miller, who draws on his best, who has the offal to supplement his gains, and to diminish his charges, and has at least shorter and possibly cheaper routes of exit to the old country markets. The milling industry is an important industry in this country. It is important because of the by-products and the absolute necessity for those by-products if we are going to have improved and intensive farming in that great northwestern country. Did you notice that President Taft and Mr. Hill in their arguments, lay great stress on this? They say that the people of the United States should now turn their attention more and more to improved and intensive farming. Is not that as good advice for Canadians as it is for the people of the United States? and if that impetus is given to the export of raw wheat because you have got a more facile market, and may be at times a better market, although it is certain at other times to be a less good market, you make a set and tendency in that great northwestern country to shear off the wheat and sell it with less trouble of farming and by doing that, neglect the improved and intensive and mixed farming which alone can restore your impoverished soil, bring it to its natural state as productive and as valuable as it was at first. The more milling you have in the west, and the more offal for feeding the better you will attain this end. . . .

So much with reference to reciprocity. The next point I wish to make is, that this instrument restricts and may ultimately destroy our fiscal freedom. Has this people of Canada lost its sense of what is due to it as a responsibly governed people. I do not believe it. But it is hard not to believe it just at this particular time. I put the matter in this way before, and I put it again, because it is vitally important: Here are two men, members of the government that have absolutely had no mandate from the people of any kind or sort; no mandate because they declared to the people that they have done with reciprocity and were cultivating now the British market. These two men with no extraordinary business ability or experience go down to Washington, make a pact with the administration there, sign it with their hand and seal, come back here and present it to the free parliament of Canada, to the free people of Canada. And when the people get their breath they say: What does this thing mean; why, this goes the wide length of the Dominion; it enters into productions of every sort and kind, it makes an absolute change in our fiscal relations, it may go further and affect the productions of our country immensely, it may go further still and affect our national ideals and our imperial relations. And, yet Sir, these two men with their limited knowledge, consulting with nobody but 14 other men of equally limited knowledge—and I give them credit for all they are worth; I was there myself once and I know how limited really the knowledge of a minister of the Crown is with reference to these things—these two men bring back an instrument and without asking leave of the people, without giving to parliament a free hand they impose that as a pact, and backed up by the whole party force and power they put it into operation no matter whose back is broken, no matter what interest is invaded, no matter what great national consequences hang upon it, and what interests may be injured thereby. I say, Sir, that if such a thing had happened 30 years ago in any province of the Dominion of Canada there would have been a revolt in that province. It amazes me to think that men could dare to assume such rights; it amazes me still more to think that they dare to assume such responsibility. Why, when this pact was made I can imagine the Minister of Finance and the Minister of Customs, two good men, two simple-minded men, two men of fair but limited knowledge, with two clerks with them, facing the trained men of business at Washington, going down there with fear and trembling, wondering if they could get a little bit of a slice so as to justify their going, creeping into Washington, and when they meet, the United States representatives suddenly hand out to them a proposition which in their wildest imaginings they did not suspect would be offered to them. Overwhelmed, overpowered, they pick it up and telegraph back to Ottawa: Goodness gracious, Sir Wilfrid, see what they have given us, shall we take it. And Sir Wilfrid looks at it, and he says it is the whole thing, and he telegraphs back: Take it, take it, take it. And the pact is signed. Sir, the gift is brought back but the mortgage has to be met. And if this is passed the future of this country economically and nationally will pay that mortgage to the last cent and curse the men who made that mortgage possible. . . .

So, as I have said, from this time out, if this holds, Canada's interests cannot be met and satisfied by the Canadian parliament in the Canadian forum. Our hands are tied. Ninety-three millions of people plus eight millions have to give their assent. The predominant partner has to be seen and has to give his consent, and to every grievance brought by the individual interest the government must answer;—we know we are wrong, we see you are going to be destroyed but it is the whole pact or none, we cannot let you off or the whole business goes by. Now, let me put this to my right hon. friend: You started out on the right track in 1910 just before the big stick was lifted; you told us in parliament that you were brave and that you would continue to be brave; you said you would do what was best for Canada and let the United States do as it liked, and you carried through the French Treaty in that fit of bravery and courage. But the February of 1910 came when a surtax of 25 per cent was possible within a month of going on, when the big stick was raised, and then Sir, you wilted; you forgot your brave words and your brave sayings even in parliament, and you came here with the excuse: Well, it was unjust, we knew it was, we should not have asked to do it, it was not neighbourly treatment, we had treated them splendidly and they have treated us in niggardly fashion; they had no right to do it, but see here we cannot face a disturbance and dislocation of the $300,000,000 worth of trade between the United States and Canada, and, therefore, we give in. And if this pact should increase your trade between Canada and the United States to $600,000,000 as you say it will, then let a demand come from the other side equally as unjust as that, and you will again say: It is unjust, it should not have been, we should not be asked to make a sacrifice like that but here is $600,000,000 of trade involved and we cannot disturb and dislocate it. Don't you see the fetters you have put about you; don't you see the bonds in which you have wrapped yourselves up, the more this is successful in stimulating trade between the two countries the more we are in the power of the predominant partner. Let a man with $8,000 go into business with a man with $100,000, and who manages that business? It makes no difference that the man with small capital is wiser than the man with large capital, the man with small capital sees his interests are not being well cared for and sees he is subjected to injustice, and he goes to the predominant partner and says: I want this thing changed, and the other says: You do, do you, well I don't want it changed; what are you going to do about it? So the United States can say to Canada.

I am the predominant partner; I have a hundred millions in this, and you have only eight millions; do you want to sell out, or are you prepared to grin and bear it, and take the injustice? One or the other; and it is not an alternative for a young nation to have placed before it. It does not square with that spirit which has been cultivated for the last forty years, and you know it does not. Then why don't you simply say so, and say as patriots and good citizens have said before, in every crisis of their country's history: Sacrifices, if necessary, we will make that our country may be saved and our flag may be preserved. I say, therefore, that we have given up our fiscal freedom to a large extent, and we have endangered it absolutely. This country is young; it develops rapidly. Who is wise enough to say to-day that five years from this we ought not to have a totally different alignment of our tariff? But under this you bind yourselves; you are not free to make it. Suppose that, five years from this, this country came to

the conclusion that with regard to one of these products Canada's duty to herself, and her people was to prohibit the export of it, or to put restrictions upon it that it should be manufactured in this country with our own capital, with our own labour, and for our own first uses. You come up against the fact that the predominant partner says: You cannot do that without disturbing the whole arrangement; are you going to imperil $400,-000,000 worth of trade? The argument is not irresistible, but it is almost irrestible practically. Theoretically you are free; practically you are bound; your strength and your power and your sovereign right of first service to your own citizens in your own country has been bartered away, and bartered away, in my opinion for a petty mess of pottage. . . .

I venture, now, with some timidity and in all humility to approach this question from a national standpoint. I make no apology for doing it. The economic side of this question is important, but no good citizen will satisfy himself by keeping his mind fixed simply on the economic side, if he believes that there is in the thing itself a peril to the nation and his country. Unless you admit that, you deny that countries can exist, you deny that there is anything like patriotism, you deny the right of the people to keep up their own national home for themselves and make sacrifices for that object. If a foreign army threatened us on the border every Canadian would rise and take up arms to defend his country, but have we no duty, no service to perform in defending our country in times of peace? Battalions of armed men are not the greatest menace to the country. Oft times the peaceful warfare of trade and pact is more fatal than open arms. You cannot get away from the proposition that there comes a time in the

have to look at the national as well as
the economic side. If it be for the better
preservation and maintenance of your
national ideas and your national life, well
and good. But what is the American view?
My hon. friend the Finance Minister
appealed to history. I am also going to
appeal to history. What has been the
American view since the American republic came into existence with reference to
this British North American country? At
the first they tried to persuade this country by every art to rebel against the
mother country and join in the revolution
and become a part of the United States.
They failed in that. They next sent their
armed detachments to conquer us into
submission and annex us forcibly. In that
also they failed. Afterwards they took a
long, tedious and annoying course of trade
restrictions, prohibitions and harrassment
of our fishery grounds, the negation of our
fishery rights, the assumption of privileges
which they did not possess under the
treaty, and for long years they worried
and harassed us on these lines. For what
purpose? For the avowed purpose of
tiring us out and inducing us to throw in
our destinies with them. Is there any
doubt about that? But they found a people,
sturdy, independent and strong, who did
not urge unreasonable pretensions, but at
the same time did not give away its well-
known rights, and I make this assertion,
that to-day the United States have a respect for us, a hundred times greater, than
they would have had if, like poltroons, we
had given way to their influence and
menaces. Consequently there is absolutely
the best of friendly feeling between us and
our neighbours. It is of no use for hon.
gentlemen opposite conjuring up the existence of some dangerous feeling between
us and the United States, which it requires

sacrifices on our part to assuage. There is
nothing of the kind. The American people
respect and admire us, and they do so for
one thing. They respect and admire us
because we have clung to our rights, our
nationality and our own standards. Well,
after this long course, Senator Sherman,
speaking in 1888 in the United States
Senate, pointed out to his countrymen a
change of method. He said:

Now, Mr. President, taking a broader
view of the question, I submit if the time
has not come when the people of the United
States and Canada should take a broader
view of their relations to each other than
has heretofore seemed practicable.
Since the conquest of Canada by
Great Britain in 1763, she has been a continuous warning that we cannot be at peace
with each other except by political as well
as commercial union. Canada should have
followed the fortunes of the colonies in the
American revolution. The way to union
with Canada is not by hostile legislation,
not by acts of retaliation, but by friendly
overtures. This union is one of events that
must inevitably come in the future. The true
policy of this government then is to tender
freedom in trade and intercourse, and to
make this tender in such a friendly way that
it shall be an overture to the people of
Canada to become a part of this nation.

That was the advice given by a far-
seeing man, and a senator of the United
States. Years go by, and in 1903 the
Chamberlain idea was to the fore, and we
find a representative New York paper,
the 'Post,' in combating the Chamberlain
idea, saying this:

Instead of any such mad course as retaliation, the path really open to us is one
that will quietly, peaceably and forcibly defeat the whole project of discrimination
against our goods. Canadian reciprocity is,

in our judgment, the only road of safety and profit now open to us.

Mr. Blaine was at that time trying to make a treaty with Newfoundland.

The Boston 'Herald' says:

The underlying motive of Blaine's Newfoundland treaty was to draw the British colonies into the net of annexation.

And the Springfield 'Republican,' a very representative American paper said:

There need not be any hesitation in saying that the Newfoundland treaty should be regarded as a stepping-stone to a similar one with all Canada, and that the great end in view which should appeal to any American statesman with imagination and foresight is the ultimate peaceful combination of Canada's destiny with our own.

That is explicit. But the objective is still there, just as strongly as it was in 1775, or in 1812, or in all the years since then. But here was a change of methods suggested. And now we come to President Taft's message to Congress. He carries out the very same idea:

They are coming to the parting of the ways.

Who? Canada. What ways? One the broad highway that we began to construct in 1867 running transversely across this continent with its east-and-west lines and ending, for our market, in the grand old mother country, the emporium of the markets of the world. And what is the other way? It is the way brushed out and trailed by Messrs. Paterson and Fielding, leading off this old and well-beaten highway down amongst unknown obscurities and hazards, but ending in the United States

of America. These are the two ways; and we are at the parting of the ways, says President Taft, and something must be done.

They must soon decide whether they are to regard themselves as isolated permanently from our markets by a perpetual wall or whether we are to be commercial friends.

Is that a threat? If we are to think of a perpetual wall, who put up the wall? —42 per cent high on their side while our neighbourly wall was only 26 per cent; a wall that gave us a paltry $33,000,000 of free entry into the United States, while we gave $104,000,000 of free entry into Canada for the goods of that country. Is it a threat that, while we are looking nation-wards, forces us to a path looking United States-ward? Does it mean?— Come down this path at the peril of isolation and commercial war between your country and ours.

Should we not now, therefore, before their policy is too crystallized and too fixed for change, meet them in a spirit of real concession, facilitate commerce between the two countries and thus increase the natural resources available to our people.

President Taft is, I believe, a very far-seeing man. He knew the history of these men—knew it well. He knew that in the Finance Minister (Mr. Fielding) he was dealing with a man who, not so many years ago, declared that the maritime provinces could not live and endure as part of this Canadian confederation; who headed a campaign in his own province to take Nova Scotia, and, if possible, New Brunswick and Prince Edward Island along with Nova Scotia out of this union. President Taft knew the Finance Minister's history and felt that there was reasonable ground for working upon a man with such a record. He knew that the Finance Minister, in 1891, pledged his party to, and fought tooth and nail for, commercial union with the United States as against closer trade relations with Great Britain; and he thought he had good hopes when working upon a man with such a history. And the Finance Minister had with him the Minister of Customs (Mr. Paterson) behind whom was the towering figure of the old knight of Ontario, Sir Richard Cartwright, who had declared in the halls of Boston that Boston, New York and Portland ought to be the metropoli of the maritime provinces that nature had so made it and the decrees of nature ought to be carried out; who declared that there was no market in the world which would compensate us for failure to acquire free access to the United States of America, and who, when asked the question: Would you go into a scheme like that and discriminate against the mother country? Answered promptly: Yes I would discriminate. And Mr. Taft had some very fair idea that he could work upon a government which had members such as these. Then he had the right hon. leader of the government (Sir Wilfrid Laurier). President Taft knows the right hon. gentleman's history from A to Z. It has been tortuous work following it, but President Taft is a very active minded man, and he has good men to help him. I have not the least doubt that there is not a political path that the right hon. gentleman has trod, in which he has turned and twisted, but President Taft has followed his course, either himself or through some of his advisers. And he knew well that the Right Hon. Sir Wilfrid Laurier stood in the market-place of Boston and declared that trade should not

follow sentiment, that the time would come when Canada's interest would differ from the interest of the mother country, and when that time came he would look to Canada's interest; that the right hon. gentleman had declared that the interest of Canada lay with the United States rather than with Great Britain. President Taft knew all that. So, knowing the history of these men, knowing that they were guided by no principle save political opportunism President Taft thought that this thing should be clamped now before the 'policy became too crystallized' as it might very well be if these gentlemen happened to go out of office and another government came in. Can there be anything more clear than President Taft's opinion? He did not say: You have to come into this country, and this is the first step. But he said what was equivalent to it, absolutely equivalent to it; and it is in the lines I quoted.

But I not only take President Taft then, I take President Taft since. He is now stumping the United States in favour of reciprocity, and as he goes he grows a little more and a little more decided. At Columbus, Ohio, he declared:

> The greatest reason for adopting this agreement is the fact that it is going to unite two countries with kindred people and lying together across a wide continent, in a commercial and social union to the great advantage of both.

What says Mr. Hill, the railway magnate?

> I want to say to you that we cannot afford to let this opportunity pass. It is said that 'opportunity calls once at every man's door,' but that if you leave the door open it will come again. Let me say to you that the conditions in the British Empire are such that if we let it pass it will never come

again. If we neglect the opportunity that is now manifesting itself, if that is refused, it is almost a certainty that imperial federation will follow, and if it does, where is your independence, where is your market?

What says Senator Beveridge? What says Governor Foss? What say the newspapers from one end of the country to the other? What is the allusion, what is the call to the United States for viewing this question, not simply from the low business standpoint, but from far-sighted reasons of statesmanship and National Policy? What does it mean? It means that the old objective is there, it means that the methods have changed, they propose to have the Trojan horse with its big gifts introduced into the fortress. Sir, 'I fear the Greeks when they are bearing gifts.'

I could go on quoting from one and another; these are but samples of what I could quote, and therefore, are indicative of the general trend in the United States. All their methods of the past we have withstood and met, and we are on terms of absolute good friendship with the United States. I want to repeat what I said before, that to-day they have more respect for us in Canada, and more admiration for our enterprise and our work, than at any other period in the history of these two countries; and we on this side have just as high an appreciation of them as they on their side have of us. There is absolutely to-day no cause of dissatisfaction or ill will between us and the United States. But it does not follow that, because you are friendly with your neighbour and are doing each other good turns, you should give him half or three-quarters of your house and install him in it. Neither does it follow that because we want to be on good terms with the United

States we are to hand over the rich possessions we have hewn out and made for ourselves, and go into a dangerous partnership with them. Nor does it agree with our policy, our instincts and our ideals. It was the conquest of Canada aimed at in 1775; it was the conquest of Canada aimed at in the years around 1812, and since; it was the conquest of Canada and its incorporation with the United States aimed at by the methods I have spoken of in respect to our trade and fisheries; and the dominant spirit in the United States that is pushing reciprocity through to a successfully enactment today is not economic, it is political. It is still the conquest of Canada. But it is conquest of Canada by peaceful means and large gifts, to bring about the time when, from the frozen north to the Mexican gulf, there shall be but one power predominant, and that the United States of America, and when British and European influence shall be banished forever from this North American continent. . . .

. . . This land is ours, we have made it, we and our fathers—please God we will keep it for our children and our children's children, to the remotest generation. We have not wrought so in order to bestow a great gift upon a rich nation, we have wrought to build ourselves a national home with a fireside and altars for ourselves and for those who come after us in this great far-flung country that God has given to us for our own.

This proposal cuts square across that national ideal, challenges it at every point, will endanger it undoubtedly, may destroy it entirely. Should we not think before we enter into it? Ninety-three millions to the south of us mean it in the way of absorption and hegemony and mean it in no other way, hence these gifts. This proposal cuts our country into sections and at every section bleeds the life blood from it. The well-filled arteries of interprovincial trade will be drained until the whole system grows anemic and flabby. Do not treat it lightly. The sustained pressure of ninety-three millions to eight millions, the far-reaching effect of business affiliation, the close proximity and constant efflux and influx, the seductions of commercialism, the constant intercourse of business, social and official life, will inevitably weaken the ties of empire and wean the thoughts of our newer generations, if not of ourselves, to wards the predominant power, and create new attachments, until like Samson we would arise and would shake ourselves and find that our strength is gone.

I utter the most solemn words I have ever uttered in my life, and I believe them to the very bottom of my heart, that there is danger, and deep danger ahead. This path entered upon leads us away from home to a strange country. I pray, Sir, that the full meaning of this first step may sink into the hearts of members of parliament and into the hearts of the people of this country until there shall burst forth a protest of such strength that the steps contemplated will be recalled to the old paths, leading east and west, in and out amongst our own people, converging on the great metropolis of the mother land, and which we may follow without uncertainty and without menace to our national existence.

Clifford Sifton, House of Commons, *Debates*, 1910-1911, February 28, pp. 4385-4409.

Reciprocity Under Attack

. . . I agree with what has been said by members of the House who have preceded me respecting the very great importance of the question we are now discussing. I have found it the most important question which has come before this House since I have had the honour of being a member of it, and when I say frankly to the committee that the result of my investigation has been to lead me to the conclusion that I cannot follow the leader of the party with which I have been identified practically all my lifetime it will be very evident that to me at least it is an extremely important question. . . .

. . . I dissent altogether from the proposition that everybody in Canada has been in favour of reciprocity with the United States for the last forty years. I do not know of any warrant at all for the statement that both the parties, or that one of the parties, for the last forty years has been in favour of reciprocity. There can be no doubt that the Liberal party was in favour or reciprocity twenty years ago; there can be no doubt that in the

platform of 1893 there was what might be called a look at reciprocity; and there can be no doubt that later on, I think it was in 1898, that under the Joint High Commission, the right hon. leader of the government attempted to get some measure of reciprocity from the United States. But there is equally no doubt that when the Joint High Commission ceased to act, the right hon. gentleman expressly made his position clear, and that in the general election of 1900, in the election of 1904, and in the election of 1908, there was no mention whatever of reciprocity by either of the parties. As a member of the government in the first two of those elections I should be credited at least with having a general idea of the policy of the government of which I was a member, and I do not think there would be any individual in Canada more surprised than I if I had been told in either of those elections that it was a part of the policy of the government to seek reciprocity. If there was anything that was clearer than another in connection with the policy of the two political parties in those three successive general elections, it was that neither of them made any claim to advocate the policy of reciprocal trade relations with the United States.

I agree with what has been said that the government has no mandate to make these proposals. I do not mention that point because of a desire to fill up the cup or to aggravate the argument against my hon. friends, and I furthermore say that I think oppositions very often say what can hardly be supported on grounds of reason or law in opposition to what is done by governments on the ground that they have no mandate. But I do not think the principles which often apply apply in this case. We have not, it is true, a system of government by delegation.

Our governments are not elected to do specific things; that is not the nature of our constitution. We are elected under a very wide system of parliamentary responsibility, and a great discretion is vested in the House of Commons, and in the government which is the executive committee of the House of Commons in connection with the transaction and new business, business which was not discussed when they were before the electors. They may do a great many things that were not discussed when they were before the electors, but they may not constitutionally or properly do everything, and I venture to say that when the fiscal policy of a country has been thoroughly canvassed and settled, discussed, debated and approved in the year 1900, discussed, debated and approved in the year 1904, discussed, debated and approved in the year 1908, that there is no constitutional warrant for the members of the government reversing that policy radically without any consultation and practically without the knowledge of the people. There is a discretion vested in the government, there is a discretion vested in the House of Commons, but Mr. Chairman, it must be remembered that the discretion that is exerciseable by those who occupy important positions under our form of government is not an arbitrary personal discretion, it is a constitutional discretion which must be exercised in accordance with the principles of the constitution, and the constitutional rights of the people we represent, and I want to say and to say it not as I said simply for the purpose of making another point against my hon. friend, but I want to say that I do not believe, speaking from my own experience and from the experience of many men whom I have met in various walks of life and largely members of the Liberal party,

I do not believe that in the recent history of Canada anything has happened which has given to the thinking people of Canada so painful and so sudden a shock as the sudden realization that four or five gentlemen who, by reason of their ability, their years of service and their high position in their party, are in control of the affairs of the dominant political party, can suddenly, of their own motion, without discussion, without debate, without the knowledge of the country, commit the country to a radical change of fiscal policy. That is not, I am bound to say, the doctrine of constitutional government as I was taught it in the Liberal party, and I do not think that there could be possibly a more dangerous innovation.

Sir, what we are asked to do in these resolutions is to reverse the fiscal policy of the Dominion of Canada. . . .

. . . And what will be the effect of this proposed revolution in our fiscal policy? I do not intend to overstate it or to say anything which can possibly be regarded as overstating it. But I am surely within the mark, when I say that there will be a very great dislocation and disturbance of business, that there will be individuals who will suffer very great loss, and that even if these individuals succeed in rectifying their position, still, the disturbance for considerable portions of the community will be of a very serious character. As to the general progress of Canada, the production of Canada is so enormous, the immigration is so great, the impetus we have received so strong, the development of our resources so rapid, that no possible mistake of fiscal policy can prevent this country making enormous progress in the future. Nevertheless, the effects will be serious. Let me enumerate what I think will be a few of those effects.

Some industries will be destroyed—

there can be no doubt about that. What reason can be given for drawing your pen through an item of the tariff and thereby shutting up an industry which is not accused of combining as against consumers, of charging illicit prices, or of any other evils?—what reason there can be for selecting that industry and wiping it out of existence, I do not see. I am bound to say that it does not appeal to my common sense. I think that the meat packing industry of this country will be destroyed. I have given that subject a good deal of consideration. I thought when I saw and read carefully the memorial of the packers, that the meat packing industry would be injured, and I am prepared to say now that if this treaty goes into effect, and continues in effect for any length of time, the big packing industry of the Dominion of Canada will be wiped out. There is no more chance of the meat packing industry standing against the beef trust of the United States than there would be of my standing up against this building if it fell upon me. That is precisely the position in which the meat packers will be put. . . .

Will this proposition assist in transferring American capital to the construction of factories in Canada, which has been going on in Canada for several years past at a very rapid rate? Surely we cannot conclude that it will. These factories have been established because it was thought that the fiscal policy of Canada was settled, that we had settled down to a definite fiscal policy, and people came along and built factories here and built factories there, thinking they were perfectly safe. I have no doubt that those who are engaged in putting up factories will continue and complete their work; they cannot afford to do anything else. But is it reasonable to suppose that many

business men with money to invest in factories will readily decide to do so unless they get some definite assurance that what has happened in this particular case is not going to happen again? I do not see how they can get the assurance; I do not see how it will be possible for parliament to prove that what has been done in this case will not be done in every case in which ministers, with the best motives, may see fit to do it. . . .

What are the compensations? It is said that the farmers will have better prices and better markets. It is very difficult for a private individual to make an exhaustive examination of prices. He can only be expected to go into a limited number of subjects, and his information must necessarily be limited. I have made as careful an examination as I could of the prices of the various staples which the farmers of Canada sell in the open markets, and I have before me the result of that examination. It is not necessary that I should enter into any considerable number of details, but will give you a few of the conclusions which appear to be absolutely established by the facts. First, I will take hogs, one of the most important products of the province of Ontario. The average price in the provinces of Ontario and Quebec is better than it is in the United States. As far as cattle are concerned the prices are variable, and as far as eggs are concerned the prices of the better grades are higher, and of the other grades, lower. It is said that the market for lambs will be good if we get reciprocity with the United States. From the 1st of December up to the present time lambs have been cheaper in Chicago than in Ontario. The best creamery butter sells at a higher price in the United States, but all the lower grades are cheaper, and it seems to be quite clear from an investigation of the market conditions by those who are familiar with the subject, that we shall lose our local market for butter and eggs—in the case of eggs to the United States and in the case of butter to countries like New Zealand, Denmark and possibly Australia. While we may get some advantage by selling a small portion of the higher grade of the product to the United States, we shall lose upon a great portion of the lower grade, which, as everybody knows, is the greater proportion of the product. In poultry the higher grades will be higher and the lower grades will be lower. Hay is one product that is substantially higher in the United States than in Canada. Barley is higher and oats lower. Looking over the whole case, it is not possible to figure out any general advantage to the farmer in getting these markets even if we take prices as they are without having any reference to the general effect upon the market which may take place in other ways. As to the quality, everybody knows that there is a perfectly good market for all that our farms produce. There is no glut in the market of Canada if the produce is reasonably prepared, and if it is not reasonably prepared for the market then the United States market will be of no assistance to the man who allows himself to be in that position.

Then, there are some general features of the case which require to be considered. This, Mr. Chairman, is a conclusion which you cannot possibly escape: Under this arrangement, which means free trade in farm products, the markets for farm produce will be absolutely dominated by the United States and favoured nation countries. There can be no possible question about that. The meat packing industry will be destroyed. . . .

The meat trust in Australia and New Zealand is so sinister in its operations that the government of the commonwealth has to take the field against it, and we are here taking down the barriers and inviting it to come in and dominate the market of Canada. That trust will oppress our farmers, it is not a beneficent institution, it is not a philanthropic institution, and when it dominates the market, we will say of Ontario, and any hon. gentleman on this side of the House or on the other side of the House finds that the farmers of his constituency are not getting fair play in the matter of prices, may I ask what that gentleman will do, may I ask what his remedy will be, may I ask how he is going to apply that remedy if he has any? I do not know what the remedy will be. The head office of your trust will be in Chicago or New York, it will be outside of our jurisdiction and there is only one thing we can do, just one thing—we can put the duty back where it is now and start all over again to build up the local industries which we are threatening to destroy.

The whole tendency of this arrangement is to induce the farmer to adapt his raw product to the United States market. The whole tendency is to do away with the by-products which are so essential for intensive farming, the whole tendancy is to break down the system of interrelated industries which makes the present prosperity of the province of Ontario and the other provinces. Under that system, Mr. Chairman, brought about by the policy which my hon. friends upon the Treasury Benches have pursued for the last 13 years, the great province of Ontario raised $250,000,000 worth of farm produce last year and nobody heard that there was no market for any of that produce.

Take the provinec of Quebec. . . .

. . . The province of Quebec is not

very well farmed at the present time—there is good farming in some parts of it, there is good farming in a good portion of it, and moderate farming in other portions of it. The agricultural problem of the province of Quebec is to induce the farmer to keep his hay at home and to follow a system of intensive farming. . . .

. . . What happens—comes along this treaty and puts a bonus on poor farming by inducing the farmers of the province of Quebec to ship their raw products to New England, and deplete the fertility of their soil.

Take the prairie provinces— I am perfectly aware of the fact that there are a great many people in the western provinces who think that this treaty will be a great thing for them. I have before seen premature conclusions arrived at in the course of 23 years in public life during which I have had an experience that not many members of the House have had because I have had the honour of representing to-day in this House the same people who elected me first as a young man to the legislature of Manitoba, and in the legislature or in this parliament I have been their representative ever since. During that time I have seen a good many questions of this kind come up as to what was going to benefit the farmer and as to what would be in his interests, and I am not so sure, when this question comes to be discussed, that the farmer of the Northwest will be impervious to reason and common sense and good judgment when he gets the case put before him. It was first said: Well, but the farmer of the Northwest is going to get more for his wheat; the price of wheat south of the line in Dakota is higher than it is in Manitoba. That is true. It is a little higher; it always or nearly always rules a little higher, and they said: If the farmer can

get into that market he will get more for his wheat. Now comes along Mr. Hill, the president of the Great Northern railway who is a great advocate of reciprocity and a very fine man and in a way a friend of my own, and he says: The duty does not make any difference; it is true the Dakota farmer gets a little more for his wheat but it is not on account of the duty, it is on account of the local circumstances. Now, Mr. Chairman, Mr. Hill is either right or he is wrong; there are just two ways to look at it. If he is right and the duty does not make any difference, then the Manitoba farmer will not get any more for his wheat when the duty is taken off. That's clear. If he is wrong and the duty does make a difference what is going to happen? Why, what is going to happen is this: That so soon as the immense exportable surplus of the Canadian Northwest is let into the Dakota market then the Dakota man's wheat goes down to the export level, and the Dakota man gets less, but the Manitoba man does not get any more. There is no doubt about that: it has happened already. . . .

Then there is the question of cattle and that is one question in respect of which there is no doubt that the western farmer will get a benefit under his agreement, for the present at least. There is no doubt that the market for the second grade of cattle in the prairie provinces, is a poor market at the present time—why? Because it is a new country. It is only a short time since the country was sufficiently settled to have a sufficient production to organize this business. In fact, we have hardly got to that point yet. The result is, that there is at the present time a very poor market for cattle in the western provinces. But that is no reason for throwing the country away, or for considering that we can never have a market.

That is a reason for taking up the subject and dealing with it in an intelligent way. The farmers' delegation, which came here recently, said to the government:

We wish also to draw attention to the danger we are in while we leave the opportunity open for the United States meat interest to capture and control the export trade from our country.

What are they going to do now? They will capture and control all the cattle of the Northwest—the very last hoof will be controlled from Chicago. What I say is, that we should establish a chilled meat industry. It has been done in Australia and New Zealand. Dr. Rutherford has reported in favour of it. There would be no great difficulty in the government doing this, and it would be worth while taking the trouble when you have a country like the Northwest of Canada. We could afford to hire ten men at $10,000 a month rather than lose this business. The members of this House know that I am an enthusiastic friend of the Northwest. The best years of my life were given to the settlement of that country, and I cannot tell you how I feel about that great country being made a backyard to the city of Chicago. I have differed with my friends in my own constituency, and I do not know, but that there are many men who have supported me for years, who differ with me on this subject; but I take the liberty of thinking that I know as much or more about it than they. I have studied these questions all my life with the object of learning the way in which the affairs of that country should be organized so as to be of some benefit to themselves and the rest of the country, and I say that we should organize that country in a business way. If we do, we shall

have duplicates of the stock yards of Kansas City, Omaha and Chicago in our Northwest.

What is the general effect of this treaty? The general effect is, that we put the Dominion of Canada on a absolutely free trade basis, so far as farm products are concerned. The farmers of Canada are on a free trade basis for what they sell and on a protective basis for what they buy—protection for the purchaser, free trade for the seller. Do you think they are likely to stand that for any length of time? I do not. I tell you, that if you have had delegations from the Northwest, you will have them again if this treaty goes through. After it has been in force for a few years, I venture to say that there will not be any question of the duty on agricultural implements or on any other manufactured goods, for we shall be compelled to take all those duties off, and have practically commercial union with the United States. As men of common sense, let us apply to this question the same business rules that we apply to any other business matter. We open our market to the world. Read the list of favoured nations along with the United States, and if there is in that list of countries of production anybody who can raise any one of the commodities in this list, cheaper than it is in the Canadian market, a commodity unsaleable and unmarketable, it can be shipped and dumped into the Dominion of Canada. I cannot conceive of what our friends in the government were thinking of. I leave this question of markets and prices, and record my conviction, that if ever a government made a monumental mistake, if ever a government got in wrong on a subject from first to last, my hon. friends have got in wrong on this subject. The House may think that I am very much in earnest about it. Sir, I would not break away from the political party with which I have acted for 23 years, practically all my life, if I were not in earnest about it.

What is the commonest phrase in the mouths of the people of Canada? We hear it in the speeches of public men, we read it in the editorials of newspapers; we even see it in the compositions of our school boys—what is it? Binding the scattered provinces of Canada together. I would like to know if this treaty is intended to bind the scattered provinces of Canada together. It binds, but it binds the other way; it binds British Columbia to Oregon and to Washington and to California; it binds the provinces of the Northwest to the states immediately to the south of them; it binds Ontario and Quebec to the states south of us; and it binds the maritime provinces to the states of New England. And we are expected to believe that a policy of that kind is a broad national policy, one to promote a broad and strong nationality. What have been the main features of our transportation policy? We have spent scores of millions of dollars for what purpose? What has been in our mouths at all times, Liberals and Conservatives alike, on every platform? Send our goods through Canadian channels, from one province to another, and from the astern provinces across the sea. What did Sir John A. Macdonald mean when he nailed his colours to the mast and said that the Canadian Pacific railway must be built around the north shore of Lake Superior, and appealed to the people of Canada on that policy and got their support? My right hon. friend the leader of the present government later came before this House and said: We shall build another line of railway from ocean to ocean, every foot of it on Canadian soil, and he appealed to the people

of this country for their support, and they supported him in doing it. They said: Yes, we believe in that policy. Why should we turn from that policy now?

If it does not make any difference which way the traffic goes, why spend $50,000 or $60,000, or $133,000 per mile to build a railway from Quebec through to Moncton and duplicate the Intercolonial, which we had before? Why do that, if it does not make any difference whether or not the traffic goes over Canadian soil? For my part, I can see no reason. What is the reason for the right hon. gentleman's change of view? I could take the 'Hansard' and read to you the strong words of the right hon. gentleman when he said, in this House, that of all things in connection with the policy of Canada as related to the United States, the one thing we must do is to be independent of the Americans. That is a policy, Sir, which I believe in. He never said a word in the whole course of my close association with him with which I agreed more fully than I did with that statement, but the difference is that I believed it then and I believe it now, and so long as I have the honour to have anything to say about the public affairs of Canada in the most humble capacity I shall continue to support what I believe to be the loyal policy that the people of Canada desire to have followed. We know why it is that the other policy is being supported. We know why the milling trust of St. Paul and Minneapolis are in favour of this proposal: it is because they want to get the hard wheat of the Canadian northwest without paying duty and drive our millers out of the export market. That is just as easy as adding two and two together. The northwest miller of the United States gets $2 or $3 a ton more for his offal than the miller in Canada, and that makes the difference; the Canadian miller has no chance in the world in the competition which is brought about in this way. The northwest miller of the United States would get the wheat free now if he could. The meat trust would get meat free if they could. We have often been told that they might take the duty off if they wanted to, but they cannot take the duty off, because they have a population of farmers who do not propose to permit these gentlemen to manipulate the duties to suit themselves. But we understand why the milling people would want this arrangement in regard to transportation, why the meat trust would want it and why the United States Steel Corporation want to get into our markets. We can understand why the Chamber of Commerce in New York, always in favour of reciprocity, should favour this arrangement, because in this last year they have been conducting an inquiry to ascertain why Montreal has been growing so rapidly and becoming a rival of their in connection with the export trade. We know why it is that the New England States, looking jealously upon the commercial development of our St. Lawrence route, should support this treaty to get the great trade which is building up Montreal and the St. Lawrence route down by their own channels. But can anybody in the world tell me why a Canadian, devoted to the interests of Canada should support the arrangement which we have here?

What will be our future relations with the United States? I read the argument presented by the hon. member for North Toronto (Mr. Foster) upon that aspect of the case. I see no possible answer to it. It seems to be perfectly clear to me that every day in which we adapt ourselves to the markets of the United States, that every day in which we cater to those mar-kets, that every day in which we adapt all our arrangements to catering to those markets strengthens the grip of the United States upon Canada. And while everybody, of course, repudiates as absurd the idea of any conscious interference either with our political independence, or with our commercial independence, I do not believe that if this treaty goes into effect there will ever again, so long as it goes on, unless a rupture takes place, be a revision of our tariff in which United States interests, United States lobbyists, and United States pressure will not be brought to bear on this parliament. What is the only possible effect? The only possible effect is domination of the smaller by the larger, and if you say you do not think there is any danger of any domination I say that I think the domination has come now, that we have it in the discussion of this treaty. How did it get here, what brought it about? For 30 years the United States had nothing to say to us, and then, when we have finally, definitely won our commercial independence and put ourselves into such a position that we were perfectly independent, what happened? They shook a club over our heads, they threatened a surtax. It was threatened a year ago. Then our friends of the government were asked to make concessions in order that this surtax might be avoided. The government made some concessions. I think they were very trifling in character: I do not think they were of much importance, but I do think it would have been as well if the government had stood its ground at the start. Nevertheless, we all know that in international matters it is necessary to leave a great deal to the government. You cannot know everything that passes, and you must leave a great deal to the discretion of the government in international matters. But I am prepared to say now that I think we all made a mistake. I think the time to have stood our ground was the first time the club was flourished. What has been the history of our relations with the United States? For the last 30 or 40 years we have been ignored and buffeted by them, and during all that time we have taken our way secure, firm, serene under the strong arm of the British Empire. Now we come to the point when we are of some use; we are just beginning to be of some use. Up to nearly the present time we have been more or less of a nuisance to the empire; now we are beginning to get to the point when we add something to the prestige of the British Empire, to the point when, if necessary, we can send some men, or some ships, or some money; we can be of some use to the empire that has given us our liberties and all the traditions of our citizenship. When we get to that point what happens? The United States beckons from Washington and we are asked, the first time anybody beckons, to turn from the path that leads to the capital of the empire, and to turn towards the path that leads to Washington. I say, so far as I am concerned: Not for me.

Public Archives of Canada, *J. W. Dafoe Papers*, Sydney Fisher to John Dafoe, March 10, 1911.

A Brief for the Defence

Ottawa, March 10, 1911

My dear Dafoe,

... Now let me say a word in regard to the political situation, and here again I am going to talk very freely to you. We were all disappointed in Sifton's speech. He said nothing that was new. He put his points forcibly and well, as he always does. Coming from a man in the very front ranks of public life in Canada, on the occasion of such a man's announcement of leaving his party, it attracted very great attention and carried weight. Some days before Sir Wilfrid asked me to prepare to follow him. I confess I was nervous when I went into the House that afternoon. After Sifton had spoken half an hour, I was quite satisfied I could reply to his arguments, and many, from whom I did not expect such, said I succeeded. You can judge of that for yourself, as I am sure you have read the speeches.

The situation seems to resolve itself into this: This arrangement grants to our farmers what they and the whole country have for years been saying would be a great thing, viz., reciprocity in natural products. We have been debarred from getting this because the Americans insisted upon a large measure of reciprocity in manufactured articles. We have succeeded now in securing it without that string attached. Indeed the only complaint of the farmers is that we did not go far enough in that respect.

Of course, the manufacturers are making an outcry, but, sifted to the bottom, it resolves itself into the fear that as we have free trade in natural products we will be tempted to go farther and get free trade in manufactured articles. I do not think I need argue that with you or the West. In the East, however, we do not wish to lose Liberal manufacturers whose sympathies are with us and who are reasonable in tariff matters. There is no doubt these have been startled and some of them alarmed, and the shrieking outcry of the Tories and the INTERESTS have contributed. Our record is entirely against any such conduct. We have in all our tariff legislation since '97, by radical reductions all round so framed and picted as to still let the industrial concerns live and, indeed, cause them to prosper. Since that time in many cases that have been lost sight of we have reduced the duty a little here and there so as to ease the consumer, and nearly always at the same time lowerd the duty on the raw products of the corresponding manufacturing industries so that the latter were still able to flourish more than ever.

In 1907 we further revised the tariff, generally adopting a Liberal policy, and consulted the people through the investigations: and again the tariff was to a certain extent eased up on the consumer, and yet no industry hurt. In this very arrangement we have displayed the same caution in regard to *all* industry in the country. Mr. Fielding and Mr. Paterson could have secured an arrangement with the Americans in two days, had they been willing to accept a large measure of reciprocity in manufactured goods. They fought it out and secured the arrangement now before us.

Why should we go back on our record? Why should we be suspected of having any intention of doing so? We have not perhaps done as much as extremists have asked for. I think, however, we have satisfied the mass of reasonable farmers. If by reason of the resistance of the manufacturers this arrangement is imperilled, I venture to say there will be aroused amongst the farmers a resentment that will sweep out of existence any Government in Canada which does not go much farther in the way of reductions of duties and probably British preference. Being myself strongly in favour of free trade, I would naturally not be adverse to this; but free trader as I am, perhaps the most extreme in the Government, I have accepted the principle that, in this country while working always to a lesser incidence of tariff taxation, we must not create any industrial or commercial crisis. We must do our work moderately and so cautiously that there will be no commercial disturbance. Perhaps it will be said that in this arrangement we have not followed this principle. I believe we have. I believe the greatest protection due to the feeling of greater confidence amongst the farmers as to the disposal of their products, will enormously stimulate production in Canada, and that our commercial classes or transportation interests or banks will be better off than they were before, while with no appreciable reduction in the duty on manufactured articles our industries will have the same protection they have had before and the evidently better home market in which to sell.

In other words, although our farmers will have two strings to their bow in selling, the other commercial interests in Canada will be the same.

There are three interests which will be interfered with: First, the millers, who with the grain exchanges in Winnipeg have had control of the prices paid for grain, and who will now have to suffer the competition of the American buyer; Second, the packing houses, who, in the persons of Pat Burns, Gordon, and Ironsides in the West, and in the person of Fearman, the Davies people etc. in the East, have had the control of the purchase of our animals for the business: these will now have to suffer competition with the American buyer in their preserves; and third, the group of handlers of dairy products, chiefly in Montreal, who have had absolute control of the prices paid in Canada for butter and cheese from the Canadian factories: these, especially along the lines in Quebec and along the St. Lawrence River, will have to submit to the keen competition of the American buyers who want our butter, cream and milk for the American cities to the south of us. These people naturally resent this invasion of their preserves, but I do not think the farmers who have been resentful of these people's control of their markets will object to having the competition for their products.

Sifton must know that the American meat trust, in the person of the Swift's, is already in Winnipeg and Calgary, and, therefore, his contention that under the new arrangement the meat trust will come into Canada is ridiculous. The trust is, however, operated under our laws of inspection by my Department, and under the combines and trust laws of Mackenzie King's Department. We will efficiently and strongly enforce these laws just as we do now; and our laws compare with the American laws very much in the same way as our Western administration compares with theirs. The ruffian in the mines in the United States can flourish and shoot off his revolver. In Canada, he must leave it at home and behave himself. The same is true of the trusts. I need not, however, go more at length into the arguments. You probably know them already. . . .

Yours sincerely

Wilfrid Laurier, House of Commons, *Debates*, 1910-1911, March 7, pp. 4751-4771.

The Summation of the Defence

Let us, I say, approach the question from the point of view of common sense —and I am glad that my remarks on that point evoke some response from the other side; we will see how far they will go. If, Sir, I were to state to my hon. friends on the other side that amongst civilized mankind, all those who work, work with the object of disposing of the product of their labour, I should be told, this is a truism that is running in the street. If I were to add that the man who works has the legitimate ambition of getting the greatest possible remuneration for his labour, I should be told, this is a mere truism. If I were to say that the man who works, will be better remunerated the more clients he has, seeking the products of his labour, I should be told, this is a truism. And yet, this is the very thing, this very truism, which is embodied in the proposition now before you. All that we ask under these resolutions is to obtain for the man who works in the fields, the best possible remuneration for his labour.

And does that proposition require any defence? Is it not simply on the line of common sense? Is it not the first of all principles? How, then, is it that it is not accepted at once? I will give the reasons. . . .

I stated a moment ago that the agreement we made, is simply to get better prices for the product of the Canadian farmers. This is a proposition so obvious that I am surprised it should have received the treatment it has received on the part of our friends opposite. But the objections made to this agreement are not to be found within the four corners of the same; they are all based upon extraneous grounds. The opposition, the Conservative party, are against this agreement because, as they tell us, it will produce consequences which will be deplorable for this country,—I have listened with some care to nearly all the speeches that have been deliverd in this House on this question, and those which I had not the opportunity to hear, I have read with equal care; and I think I am fair in stating that the objections made to this arrangement are fourfold. The first objection is that the effect will be to deflect the carrying trade from Canadian channels to American channels. The second is that it will destroy our natural resources. The third is that it will imperil our industries. And the fourth—and certainly not the least—is that it will dissolve our autonomy and land us ultimately in the American Republic. I think I have there fairly stated what are the objections of hon. gentlemen on the other side; and the House will perhaps permit me to discuss them. Let us take the first—the objection that this arrangement is going to deflect trade from Canadian channels into American channels. This question is to be discussed from two points of view: from the point of view of goods going from Canada into the United States for the purpose of being carried over to Great Britain, and goods going from Canada to the United States for consumption therein. Now, regarding the first, those goods sent from Canada to the United States, to be carried to Great Britain, in what way does this arrangement undo the system now in existence? It does not affect it one iota. At the present time, goods go from Canada to be shipped from Boston, New York or any American port without paying duty. In the same way, American goods come to Canada to be shipped out by Montreal, Halifax, or St. John without paying duty. A cargo of wheat can leave Winnipeg for New York, and there be discharged and put on board ship without duty being demanded. A cargo of grain can leave Minneapolis to be taken to Montreal and shipped thence without paying duty. This is by virtue of the bondage privilege which has been given by each government to the other, for the purposes of transportation. It has been in existence for something like sixty years, and I have never heard a complaint that it was unfair to one party or to the other. There was a time when I felt nervous on reflecting that the bonding privilege was simply an act of good will on the part of the United States towards us. That was the time when we had no communication of our own to the sea. But now that we have a continuous communication on Canadian soil from sea to sea, we feel that the United States can remove the bonding privilege at any time they please, and if they do so, they will suffer more than we shall. But Sir, our condition in that respect is absolutely safe, whether this treaty passes or not.

Now, Sir, it does not follow that for my part I am opposed to the policy of retaining in our channels Canadian trade; on the contrary, I am very solicitous in that respect, and I think I can show by the records of this government that we have favoured the building of lines through Canadian territory from east to west with the intent of keeping trade in our own channels. But I may say this to the hon. member for North Toronto (Mr. Foster), to the leader of the opposition (Mr. Borden), and to the member for Brandon (Mr. Sifton) especially, that if they expect to keep trade within Canadian channels by legislative enactment, by trade impediments, they make the greatest of all mistakes, a mistake which was tried once and had to be abandoned. Sir, when the Canadian Pacific railway was created in 1881 it was with the avowed policy of creating a channel of communication between east and west, the policy was to keep, so far as legislation could do it. Canadian trade in Canadian channels. Now my hon. friend from North Toronto commented upon the aspect of our policy rather severely, and with great force of language as to the results upon the credit of Canada, as to those who had invested their money in these enterprises, when they learn that by this legislation the lines east and west could be diverted from channels running east and west to channels running north and south. This is the language which the hon. member for North Toronto made use of on that occasion, and I quote it in view of what I shall say a few minutes later:

Take the capital invested in your east and west lines of communication: Was it ever dreamed in Britain, Sir, that the time would come when a change of policy would be inaugurated by the men who petitioned for the money, who pled for the investment of capital and got it at long last? Was it ever dreamed that when this capital was

severely fixed and invested, the long lateral
lines of railway should be tapped every few
miles by communication to draw off the
trade intended for them to southern routes
and do away with the long haul of the east
and west lines?

My hon. friend should have had in
his mind when he spoke that way the
circumstance that in the contract with
the Canadian Pacific Railway Company
precautions had been taken to keep the
trade flowing east and west. In that contract with the Canadian Pacific Railway
Company the following clause was in-
serted as clause 15:

For twenty years from the date hereof
no line of railway shall be authorized by the
Dominion parliament to be constructed
south of the Canadian Pacific railway from
any point at or near the Canadian Pacific
railway, except such line as shall run south-
west or to the westward of southward, not
to within fifteen miles of latitude 49.

Mark the words. The men who invested their money in that enterprise had
this inducement, that the Canadian
government would not for twenty years
permit any railway to be built south of
the line of the Canadian Pacific railway,
and that for fifteen miles south of the
boundary line there should be absolutely
no railway at all. Therefore, under those
circumstances, trade could not be diverted
from Canadian to American channels,
there could be no possible communication. That was the extreme precaution
which was taken by the government of
that day, that was a restriction upon the
energy, upon the enterprise of the people
of the west which was to last for twenty
years. Under that restriction the capital-
ists of the world were invited to put their
money into the enterprise, and they did

it, upon the faith of the Canadian government. How long did this restriction last?
Did it last twenty years? Sir, it lasted just
six years, and at last, after six years, the
Canadian government had to recall that
legislation. And how did it occur? This is
one of the most dramatic pages of the
history of our country, and no one knows
it better than my hon. friend from Brandon. I do not know if he was then in the
legislature, but I know he was a young
politician, and he could not have been
indifferent to what was taking place.
There was a restriction put upon the
energy, upon the enterprise of the people
of the west, and of the province of Manitoba in particular. The people of Manitoba wanted power to trade north and
south, they wanted to trade with their
neighbours, the American people, they
wanted to have railway communication
with them. But there was a statute, there
was an Act of parliament, there was the
authority of the Canadian government
which prevented them from trading with
their neighbours to the south, and the
Canadian government attempted for six
years to keep that legislation in force. The
legislature of Manitoba passed Acts char-
tering railways, allowing them to cross
that zone of territory which the government was attempting to reserve from
civilization and from the benefits thereof.
The legislature of Manitoba wanted railways to communicate north and south,
they chartered railways to that effect, and
these charters were disallowed one after
another, disallowed in 1881, disallowed
in 1882, disallowed in 1883, disallowed
in 1884, disallowed in 1885, disallowed in
1886, disallowed in 1887. Year after
year the legislature of Manitoba petitioned parliament, to do away with this
restriction, and year after year that prayer
was denied. At last in 1887, after this

restriction put upon their energy, the government of Manitoba, with the assent of the whole people of Manitoba, passed another Act authorizing a railway to run from Winnipeg to the boundary line where it could reach the American system of railways, and this Act was disallowed. The province passed beyond that disallowance and proceeded to build the railway, though there was no legislation empowering them to do so. It was practically an act of rebellion. My hon. friends from Manitoba, my hon. friend from Brandon, remembers that on a certain day in the month of October, 1887, when the Canadian Pacific Railway Company challenged the right of the province to cross their line towards the south, 200 citizens from the city of Winnipeg, members of the government, members of the legislature, financial men, professional men, merchants, bankers, went in a body to the point of crossing determined to repel force by force, to allow the crossing of the Canadian Pacific railway by the provincial line. Then, Sir, the Canadian government came down, and at the following session the privilege was repealed, a privilege that had to be bought back by the Canadian government from the Canadian Pacific railway. Now I ask the hon. member for North Toronto, what became then of those investors who had put their money into the Canadian Pacific railway upon the faith of the Canadian government. Were they ruined by it? What became of this turgid rhetoric of my hon. friend which I read a moment ago:

Take the capital invested in your east and west lines of communication: Was it ever dreamed in England, Sir, that the time would come when a change of policy would be inaugurated by the men who petitioned for the money, who pled for the investment of capital and got it at long last?

No, they did not dream of it, but it was done all the same, and the result was that their stock, which was worth at that time 30, has now reached 213. I repeat, if you attempt to prevent the people from trading in natural channels, no amount of legislation will accomplish that object, but let nature alone, and then the trade will be carried on on Canadian lines. Why? Because we have the interior and the shorter and the better lines. Take the condition of things to-day; Winnipeg can trade with Europe by way of the United States, it can trade with Europe by way of Canada. The line of railway from Winnipeg to Montreal is 1,414 miles, and from Montreal to Liverpool 2,760 miles, a total of 4,174 miles. From Winnipeg to New York by way of Minneapolis, Chicago and the American lines, the distance is 1,790 miles, and from New York to Liverpool 3,026 miles, a total distance of 4,826 miles. The American line is 4,826 miles, the Canadian line 4,174 miles, a difference in favour of the Canadian line of 652 miles. Do you require any legislation, I want to know, to compel trade to choose the Canadian channel? Is it not obvious that for very self-interest trade will always take the Canadian line, because it is the shorter one? Well, Sir, that is not all. We have had experience as to what has happened, and our experience has been that our trade over the Canadian channels has increased by leaps and bounds as against the trade by the American channels. In 1900 the total amount of Canadian wheat exported from Montreal was 4,000,000 bushels; in 1910 it had increased from four million bushels to 14,140,000 bushels. Of American wheat the total number of bushels exported from Montreal in 1900 was 5,000,000 bushels, and in 1911 that had increased to 10,000,000 bushels. So therefore, there is no doubt on this point, the Canadian line must have the preference, because the Canadian line is the best and the shortest. But, Sir, the question now has to be examined from the point of view of goods which are exported from Canada to the United States with a view to consumption in that country. My hon. friend the leader of the opposition (Mr. Borden, Halifax), when he spoke upon this subject, stated that our policy ought to be to favour interprovincial trade. To this, Sir, everybody agrees; we all favour interprovincial trade in preference to trade with other nations, and I am prepared to admit with my hon. friend that the home market is the best for all kinds of products. But I have to observe to my hon. friend that this whole amount of our natural products, and my hon. friend will not contend that the Canadian people can consume the whole production of our natural products. My hon. friend from Brandon (Mr. Sifton) the other day stated that the home market would require about 80 per cent of our products. It is difficult to secure reliable statistics upon this point, so as to arrive at a satisfactory conclusion how much of meat, of eggs and of fruit is consumed by a population. This depends much on the means and wealth of the population, but it is possible to obtain not only satisfactory, but conclusive evidence and statistics as to the amount of wheat which is consumed by a population, and it is far less than 80 per cent of our production. Thirty years ago, or thereabouts, the opinion was held that the consumption of wheat was about five bushels per head, and to-day I am satisfied that it is much larger. I discussed the matter some few

weeks ago with a prominent miller, and his opinion is that at the present time the consumption of wheat is between 6 bushels and 7 bushels per head. If that be the case, the Canadian consumption of wheat, assuming a population of 8,000,000, would be about 50,000,000 bushels. If that be the proportion of the consumption to the production of Canada, then Canada consumes only 50 per cent of her production of wheat. Where is the balance to go? My hon. friend will tell me we have the English market. So we have, the English market is quite ample enough to take the surplus production of wheat in this country for many years to come, although we are sure the production will increase tenfold by and by.

But, Sir, there are other products than wheat, which the British market cannot absorb, or cannot absorb with the same convenience as the American market can. The hon. member for Brandon (Mr. Sifton) spoke of hay in Quebec, and rather hinted, although he did not say so, that the sending abroad of hay is bad business for the farmer. I can tell my hon. friend from Brandon (Mr. Sifton) that no hay will be exported from the hillsides of the eastern townships of the province of Quebec, but as the Minister of Agriculture reminded my hon. friend from Brandon, we have in the province of Quebec natural meadows, which require no tillage, and upon which the best of timothy has been grown, not for 50 years, but for 100 years. Along the two shores of Lake St. Peter there are natural meadows a few inches only above the level of the water, which are yearly flooded, and which, to the knowledge of every one in the province, have been for a hundred years or more growing hay and nothing else. The counties of Berthier, Montmagny and St. Maurice on the north shore, and the counties of Nicolet, Yam- aska and Richelieu on the south, are so situated that they have a population of, perhaps, 1,000, who are growers of hay and for whom this treaty, if it becomes law, will be the most positive boon. To- day they cannot sell any hay in the United States because there is a duty of $4 a ton. Let the duty be removed and immedi- ately there will be an immense trade in that section of the community, as there was some 30 years ago. The same thing applies in the case of eggs, poultry and mining products. For this reason it is to our advantage that we should have not only the British market, but the Ameri- can market also. The hon. member for Brandon (Mr. Sifton) made the argument that if you were to adopt this arrangement our present facilities for transportation to Great Britain would become useless. I differ from him altogether. The trade will go on just the same, but we will raise more of those commodities than we raised before.

Then there is the cattle trade. Years ago we had a cattle trade with Great Britain. We have some yet, but it is not as large as it ought to be, because every- body knows that it has been constantly retarded by the embargo put on it some 20 years ago or so, and, therefore, if we are not able to sell all the cattle we can raise in Great Britain there is a ready market in the United States.

Now, I come to a very important point. It has been stated in this discus- sion, and repeated in the press; indeed, the statement has been alluded to in Great Britain, that by this arrangement we were putting an end to every possibility of mutual preferential trade with Great Britain. My hon. friend from Brandon made that argument, and I have heard it from the other side of the House. I take

positive issue with that statement, and I say more: that statement does not bear criticism; it has only to be analysed for its falseness to be shown. Sir, we on this side of the House have never taken part, we have refused to take part, in the con- troversy which has been long going on in England on the question of mutual pre- ferential trade. We would not take any part in the contest between the tariff reformers and the free traders. We thought it would not be dignified, we thought it would not be any part of our business, we thought it would be an act of impudence for us to take part in this controversy, whether on the one side of the question or the other, and we pre- ferred to remain silent upon that point, having laid our policy before the English people. And what was our policy? Our policy was set forth by the Canadian ministers in Great Britain at the confer- ence of 1902, and it was in these words:

The Canadian ministers stated that if they could be assured that the imperial gov- ernment would accept the principle of pref- erential trade generally, and particularly grant to the food products of Canada in the United Kingdom exemption from duties now levied or hereafter imposed, they (the Canadian ministers) would be prepared to go further into the subject and endeavour to give to the British manufacturer some increased advantage over his foreign com- petitors in the markets of Canada.

This was our policy laid down at the Imperial Conference of 1902. This is our policy in this year 1911 at the confer- ence which is soon to take place. We have been told by the other side of the House that the action we have taken with regard to this agreement has made it impossible to implement the policy thus laid down. How can that be argued seriously? The

Canadian ministers at the conference in 1902 stated that they were prepared to give to Great Britain a preference on manufactured goods in our market if Great Britain would give us preference on our natural products in her market. Great Britain does not export many natural products; on the contrary she is a large importer of natural products. We are exporters not of manufactured products, but of natural products, and we are large importers of manufactured products, and we have given to the Americans a free entrance to our markets only for their natural products as they have given us a free entrance to their market for our natural products and how can that affect the British Islands? Surely in no way at all can it affect our trade with Britain. The United States can enter our market with their natural products, but it is certain that England will never send a bushel of any kind of grain to Canada. However, England can give us a preference in her market for our natural products if she chooses to change her policy, and then we are prepared to give her upon her manufactured products a corresponding advantage. Sir, the policy of Canada is just the same as it was three months ago when this arrangement was made; nay, it is the same today as it has been for the last 12 years and it will be the policy of the Canadian government at the next Imperial Conference which will open in May next. What then of all the shrieks and lamentations and imprecations we have heard from all sides upon this point? Surely the question has not been properly thought out for if it were it would have answered itself. Perhaps it is just as well now, since I am reviewing all the objections to this agreement, that I should take up another point which has been made against it and

which has drawn many a tear from the eyes of some gentlemen sitting on the other side. I refer to the consequences of the agreement on what are known as the Most Favoured Nations. There are in existence certain old treaties between England and other countries in which it is provided that if England or any of her colonies should give a preference to any country in the world the same treatment shall be given to those nations with which England has these old treaties. These treaties were in the past of so little consequence that we never troubled about them. When in 1896 we found in our way the treaty with Germany and the treaty with Belgium we asked for the renunciation of these treaties. Similar treaties with other countries were not in our way, and, therefore, we did not trouble about them. However, all of a sudden these treaties have assumed enormous magnitude in the eyes of some, and a few days ago we heard a gentleman on the other side of the House say that we were practically opening our doors to the whole world. Well, the whole world is a big phrase, but let us examine in detail what it is composed of in this sense. The whole world in detail, so far as these treaties are concerned comprises, Venezuela, Switzerland, Sweden, Spain, Russia, Japan, Denmark, Colombia, Bolivia (and who ever heard of any trade with Bolivia) Austria-Hungary, and the Argentine Republic. Let us see what our trade is with these nations. All told last year we exported to Venezuela $14,000 worth and we actually imported from Venezuela $53,000 worth, a trade which would probably supply the next corner grocery. And, in this $53,000 worth of trade of Venezuela there is not included any of the natural products we mention in our agreement with the United

States. Then from Switzerland we imported $2,633,000 worth and we exported to Switzerland $10,000 worth, and our imports from Switzerland were chiefly silks and cottons and manufactures of silks and cottons. Sweden our exports last year were $111,000, and our imports $207,000, and there was not a dollar's worth of anything included in the agreement. We exported to Spain last year $51,000 worth and imported from Spain $1,040,000 worth, and our imports included fruits, but they were oranges and tropical fruits of that character such as are not provided for in the agreement at all. With Russia our exports were $59,000 last year and our imports $138,000 and I cannot find among them a single article which would come within the scope of the agreement. To Norway and Sweden our exports were $487,000 and our imports $168,000, and amongst these there are some fish, and Norway would have the benefit of free fish under this agreement and that is the first item we find which is at all affected. Then, we have some trade with Japan, but does any one imagine that Japan will send us wheat or butter or cereals? With Denmark we had some trade, but not very extensive, our exports being $425,000 and our imports $86,000, and while Denmark is a butter exporting country not a pound of butter came to Canada from Denmark. Then, with the State of Columbia our exports were $42,000 and our imports $28,000, but they included nothing mentioned in the arrangement. Bolivia—we have not any trade with it; we do not import anything from it or export anything to it. Austria-Hungary—our imports at $1,410,000 and our exports $60,000; the imports are chiefly laces and things of that kind. Then I come to the last—the Argentine Republic; our total exports are $2,869,000, and our total imports $2,181,000; but I find that we have not imported from the Argentine a single article that is included in this agreement. The Argentine, however, is a wheat-growing country, and it exports wheat; but if ever the Argentine Republic sends wheat to Canada, there is no reason why Canada should not send wheat to the Argentine, so that objection is wholly exploded and may be dismissed without further reference.

Another objection which has been taken to this agreement is that it will destroy our natural resources. My hon. friend from North Toronto was particularly indignant on this point. He grew eloquent and asked us what we meant by establishing a Conservation Commission for the preservation of our natural resources and then proceeding with ruthless hands to destroy their work. I have to say to my hon. friend that the Commission for the preservation of our natural resources was intended to deal not at all with questions of political economy, but with questions of physical science. My hon. friend told us that we should preserve our natural resources for our children and for our children's children; but I ask my hon. friend, what is the object of these natural resources? Soil, water, forests, minerals, have been given to man by the Creator for the use of man, and all civilized nations have acted accordingly. Why did our ancestors leave their respective lands and come to this country and take it from the Indians if it was not for the purpose of taking hold of the natural resources of the country and using them for their benefit? The Indians were men after the heart of my hon. friend from North Toronto—they were great preservers of natural resources. They kept them not for themselves, but for their children and the children of their children. They never used them to any great extent. The territory they inhabited contained many minerals; but when our ancestors came here, they found the Indians using implements made of bone and stone. They never cultivated the soil; they lived on fish and game. They were in the midst of immense forests, but they never felled a tree to build a house. They lived beside the most noble streams in the world, but they did not use them to turn a wheel; they never even used water to wash. They were people after the heart of my hon. friend from North Toronto. Our ancestors who came here, came to enjoy the natural resources of the land. Unfortunately, they not only used, but also abused them. It is the reproach of the white settler that if he has used these natural resources, he has been imprudent, and has destroyed them much more wantonly than he has consumed them for his own benefit. It is charged to-day against the Canadian farmer that he is not cultivating the soil, but mining it, and taking all the fertility out of it. It is charged against the Canadian lumberman that he is not only cropping the lumber, as he should, but in his operations, is destroying much more than he uses. I think it is admitted that in this valley of the Ottawa, where timber has been cut for the last one hundred years, the lumbermen have destroyed more timber than they have ever carried away. Sir, the object of the Conservation Commission is simply to instruct the farmers the lumbermen, and others, how to use the natural resources of the country. But if that be the case, the Commission, which is ably presided over by my hon. friend from Brandon, will do an immense service in showing all our people how to use these resources with prudence, so that they will be preserved

for our children and our children's children.

But, Sir, what has this to do with this agreement? My hon. friend says that our resources will be taken by the Americans. Well, the Americans will take them if they pay for them; but whether they take them or not, whether this agreement goes into force or not, the natural resources of the country will be made use of, and I hope in a more prudent manner than they are at the present time. My hon. friend from North Toronto need have no more apprehension on that point.

I pass to a more important objection, really the only objection of any consequence that I know of. That objection is that this agreement will imperil our industries. How will it imperil our industries? This agreement is concerned chiefly with natural products. There are no manufactured products dealt with in it, except agricultural implements. In negotiating this agreement we have adhered strictly to the terms of the resolution which was adopted at the Liberal Convention of 1893, in which the Liberal party declared for a treaty of reciprocity in natural products and a carefully-considered list of manufactured products. Why did we put this restriction in our resolution? Why did we state in so many words that the reciprocity which we would negotiate, if it ever became our lot to do so, would be general for natural products, and would be confined to a carefully prepared list of manufactured products? Because, Sir, there is a vast difference between reciprocity in natural products and reciprocity in manufactured goods. This is the reason we have acted with this prudence. I was not present at the Conference which took place between my two friends beside me and Mr. Knox; but it is not a great effort of imagination to suppose that the Americans were far more concerned about obtaining reciprocity in manufactured products than in natural products; but our negotiators would not consent to any reciprocity in manufactured products, but insisted on limiting the agreement simply to such manufactured products as agricultural implements.

Well, we limited our negotiations to that, and in doing this, I know that we have not gone as far as certain sections of the community wanted us to go. A certain section wanted free implements altogether, but we did not think it prudent or advisable to go that far. And why? The reason is that the men on the treasury benches, who are responsible, recognize in tariff matters the wide difference between manufactured and natural products. It is easy enough to put up a customs duty or enact a protective duty, but it is always a difficult task to decrease or remove such a duty. The reason is well known. It is obvious that if you raise the customs duty or impose a protective duty you create at once a fictitious economical atmosphere; and if the industries established under that tariff and under that temperature and condition, have to face suddenly a removal of the duty, you might annihilate in the course of one night millions of capital and reduce to non-employment thousands of operatives. That is why we have acted as we have done. We have gone very cautiously, with great care into this agreement. When we came into office in 1896, we had the same problem before us, and we took the utmost possible precaution—whilst giving, as we were bound to do, to the consuming public an abatement of the tariff—we took every precaution in so doing not to injure any

existing industry, and I think we have been successful.

Although it was part of our policy to obtain reciprocity with the United States, we have acted carefully in so doing and have not injured any industry. The only industry affected is that of agricultural implements, on some of which the duty has been reduced from 17½ per cent to 15 and on others from 20 per cent to 15 per cent. It would have been pleasing for myself at all events to have gone beyond that, but we considered that if we did, we would perhaps not do justice to the large number who have invested money in these establishments.

This government does not exist for the farmers alone or the manufacturers alone or for any one class, but for the manufacturers and farmers and for all the classes which compose our nation.

I do not admit that there should be any antagonism between class and class. I do not admit that there should be any antagonism between the manufacturer and the farmer. The manufacturer is the best friend of the farmer, and the farmer is the best friend of the manufacturer. Let them walk hand in hand, let each profit by the trade of the other; but so far as we are concerned, for 14 years we have administered the government of this country on these lines, trying to do away with collisions between class and class, trying to keep all abreast of one another keeping always in mind the motto: Freedom for all and privileges for none. That has been our policy and that policy we shall continue. There are men who believe that we are going to recklessly ruin industry and capital. Capital is timid under all circumstances and the man who is at the head of affairs and the ministers who assist him, would not be worthy of the public confidence if they were not always careful to see that capital will be safe, whenever it is invested in any industry in this country.

I now come to the last of the objections raised against us. If it is difficult to find within the four corners of this agreement the latent, the insipient destruction of our industries, it is still more difficult to find there the fatal germ which is to dissolve our autonomy finally landing it into the American Republic. Autonomy! They speak of autonomy. Why, it was only last year we heard the same men rebuke us because we paid too much attention to autonomy.

But, whether they approve of autonomy, or whether they combat it, they show clearly, in one instance as in the other, that they never understood or appreciated the true meaning of the word. This new-born zeal for autonomy, when reduced to actual exposition, is generally expressed somewhat in this way: There may be, perhaps, no danger to our autonomy in this agreement itself; but this is only a first step that will be followed by others. This, they tell us, is a trade agreement confined to natural products; another time the agreement will be extended to manufactured products; this will be followed by commercial union and lastly by political union. Such logic, Sir, will carry you any distance, in any direction, to any conclusion which hope, fear or any other passion may suggest. With such logic the world has long been familiar. Was there ever, in any land, at any time, a reform proposed which was not immediately denounced as revolution by all the forces of reaction? With this logic we have been particularly familiar in this country ever since the first days of responsible government. Open the records of our own old discussions, and you will find that when the

reformers of that day were asking for responsible government, all the Tories denounced the idea as being the first step towards annexation. It is not, therefore, to be wondered at that, if, upon this occasion, the whole Conservative party have been moved by the old instincts of Toryism. But the manner in which this reform which we now bring forward is opposed, will be seen by anybody who examines the question, to be an insult to the intelligence and character of the Canadian people. What are the arguments we hear against this agreement to justify the position which is taken that this is a first step towards the dissolution of our autonomy? We are told that this agreement may, perhaps, lead to certain satisfactory results for some time, but that later it may be removed, and if removed, may be followed by a high protectionist tariff, and under such circumstances the Canadian people would not have the stamina to resist the dislocation of trade but would be forced to seek refuge in the American union. This is the argument which we have heard from the leader of the opposition (Mr. Borden, Halifax); this is the argument of my hon. friend from North Toronto (Mr. Foster). Nay, this is even the argument we have heard from my hon. friend from Brandon (Mr. Sifton), who, on this occasion of all occasions, has deserted the principles of Liberalism to join the principles of Conservatism. Let me refer to the resolutions of the Board of Trade of Toronto, —I take these because they contain in condensed form all the arguments with which we have been deluged in this House. The third resolution says:

3. That any present benefit to any section of Canada or to any interest therein which might accrue from said agreement

would be more than offset by the loss and injury to other sections and interests.

There is an admission that in this agreement there will be a benefit at least to some sections of the community. It may be qualified, but it is there all the same. And the fourth and fifth resolutions read:

4. That the proposed agreement would weaken the ties which bind Canada to the empire.

5. That to avoid the disruption of trade which after some years under said agreement would result were said agreement terminated and a protective tariff against Canada established by the United States, Canada would be forced to closer trade relations with them, which would still further weaken those ties and make it more difficult to avert political union with the United States.

Mark those words—'Canada would be forced to closer trade relations.' Well, Sir, if Canada would be forced, what would force it? Nations there have been which, in the face of a great emergency, a great national calamity, would rise to the occasion, and even the women throw their jewels and ornaments into the common fund for the protection of the country. But we are told here by Canadian Tories that if a crisis, an economic crisis, were to arise in which their pockets would be liable to suffer, they would hesitate between their pockets and their loyalty.

Sir, the Tories of fifty years ago were made of sterner stuff. In 1854, the treaty which was negotiated by Lord Elgin, with Francis Hincks as his Prime Minister, resulted in immediate prosperity. Ten years afterwards the treaty was repealed, and a high protective tariff substituted for it. At that time, did Canadians falter? Did they hesitate? Were

they forced into closer relations with the United States? Did they seek a refuge in political union? No, in the face of that action they conceived and organized the Canadian confederation.

The treaty of 1854 was negotiated by Lord Elgin, when, as I have said, he had as his First Minister Francis Hincks. It was ratified in 1854 by the first Liberal-Conservative administration that we had. That administration was presided over by that staunch, stalwart Tory, Sir Allan Macnab, and one of its members was the young man, John A. Macdonald. Did Sir Allan Macnab, or did John A. Macdonald falter. Did they say to Lord Elgin that they would not advise the ratification of the treaty for fear that, if it were afterwards abolished, the Canadian people would be forced into closer relations with the United States? On the contrary, their advice to Lord Elgin was to ratify the treaty. It never occurred to them that, even if the treaty could be repealed, as it was repealed ten years later, there would be a single Canadian who would be led by the dislocation of trade to seek to change his country's allegiance. But imagine what would have been the colloquy between Lord Elgin and his advisers, if, instead of being advised by such men as Sir Allan Macnab and John A. Macdonald, he had been advised by the present leaders of the opposition, my hon. friend Mr. Borden and my hon. friend George Eulas Foster. 'Sir,' they would have said, 'do not ratify this treaty.' Lord Elgin would ask them, 'Why; will not the treaty be a cause of satisfaction to the people?' 'It would,' they would answer; 'but that is the very thing we dread. It may bring us prosperity. But, after prosperity comes, the treaty may be repealed and replaced by a high tariff: and we are not sure that our knees would be firm enough and our spines strong enough to resist the aggression of the Americans.'

Away with this timorous advice of faint-hearted men, we stand by the example of the stout-hearted men of fifty years ago. Reviewing the situation as it is placed before us, far from sharing the forebodings, the lugubrious forebodings, uttered concerning what is to follow the application, not of a new principle but of an old policy, it seems to me there are evidences not a few, that we are now entering upon a new era in our relations with our neighbours, that we can see already whitening on the horizon the dawn of a brighter day. One thing is certain, one thing cannot be denied, that the relations which have existed between the two countries for the last fifty years, especially for the last twenty years, still more for the last twelve years, and which almost came to a crisis a year ago—those relations have been a blot upon the civilization of the two countries. They have amounted practically to a proclamation of noncommercial intercourse between the two countries, so far as legislation could bring that about. Another thing cannot be denied, that the man who raised the Conservative party to the highest pitch of power and influence, the man whose name is still revered, though his example is not followed, Sir John A. Macdonald, deprecated and dreaded that situation. He did all that man could do to change it and improve it. To that end he made many sacrifices, and to that end he made his last appeal to the Canadian people.

One other thing cannot be denied, that at this moment, amongst the thoughtful men of the American union, the feeling is growing up that the policy which they have pursued towards us for the last fifty years has been wrong, that it has been injurious to themselves as well as to us, that it is selfish and narrow; and they are prepared to retrace their steps and to enter with us into a mutually profitable commercial intercourse. Now, when we reach that stage, it is inconceivable that we in Canada should be told that this retrograde policy, long followed by the United States and which they are now on the eve of abandoning, should become the Canadian policy and that we should follow a policy of non-commercial intercourse with them. It is incredible, and yet we have heard that idea proclaimed again and again in this House. We are told that unless this retrograde policy is maintained Canada is exposed to danger, and we are threatened that unless this policy of non-intercourse is maintained we are doomed to annexation. Annexation! Annexation! Once upon a time there was a very strong annexationist movement in this country, and it received its first check when Lord Elgin brought back from Washington the reciprocity treaty of 1856. From that day to this the desire for annexation has dwindled and dwindled, until there is not a vestige of it left in any part of this country.

Once upon a time—this is also a matter of history—the conviction of every American citizen was that the Canadian confederation should become a part of the American union. Recent events have shown that there are still men in the United States who harbour that hope. But there are also men who are beginning to perceive that the republic, though its career has been glorious, has yet many questions to solve and many dangers to face; and many of them are beginning to recognize that the solution of their difficult problems would be seriously complicated, perhaps fatally impaired, if, in the territory of the republic, was to be included another territory as large as their own, with a people not yet as numerous, but destined to be as numerous as their own, with problems of their own also to solve, and whose union with the United States would only add to the complications which the American people have to meet. If my poor voice could be heard throughout the length and breadth of this country, and if, without any presumption, it could be heard also beyond the frontier, I would say to our American neighbours: flattering as may be to your pride, the idea that the territory of the republic should extend over the whole continent from the waters of the Gulf of Mexico to the waters of the Arctic ocean, remember that we Canadians were born under the flag of your ancestors, a flag under which perhaps you may have suffered some oppression, but which to us has been, and is more than ever, the emblem of freedom. Remember that if you have founded a nation upon separation from the motherland, we Canadians have set our hearts upon building up a nation without separation; remember that in this task we are already far advanced, that with our institutions, with our national entity as a people, and with everything that constitutes our national home we are just as devoted as you are to yours.

Remember that the blood which flows in our veins is just as good as your own, and that if you are a proud people, though we have not your numbers, we are just as proud as you are, and that, rather than part with our national existence, we would part with our lives. If my voice could be heard that far, I would presume to say to our American friends: There may be a spectacle perhaps nobler yet than the spectacle of a united continent, a spectacle which would astound the world by its novelty and grandeur, the spectacle of two peoples living side by side along a frontier nearly 4,000 miles long, with not a cannon, with not a gun frowning across it, with not a fortress on either side, with no armament one against the other, but living in harmony, in mutual confidence, and with no other rivalry than a generous emulation in commerce and the arts of peace. To the Canadian people I would say that if it is possible for us to obtain such relations between this young and growing nation, and the powerful American republic, Canada will have rendered to old England, the mother of nations, nay, to the whole British Empire, a service unequalled in its present effects, and still more in its far-reaching consequences.

Part II

The Liberal Revolt

The opening stages of the campaign against reciprocity were dominated by the Toronto Eighteen. On February 20 eighteen Toronto Liberals, manufacturers, industrialists and financiers, led by Zebulon Lash and Sir Edmund Walker issued a manifesto opposing the agreement. Together with Clifford Sifton, they injected into the campaign the statistical data, financial resources and organizational genius necessary for launching effective opposition to Laurier and the Liberal party.

The motives of the eighteen were as varied and complex as their numbers would suggest. The fears of many for the future of Canada as an autonomous nation within the British Empire were genuine and deeply felt. But the apprehension was undoubtedly based to a considerable extent on the assumption that their interests were closely tied to the continuance of the policies of economic nationalism which both Macdonald and Laurier had pursued. The identification of the Liberal cabal with the fledgling Canadian Northern Railway was particularly impressive. Of the eighteen, five were directly connected with the Canadian Northern or with its principal financial backers. And while Walker admitted that the growth of Canada would in time do away with the loss of trade diverted to the United States, he was quick to point out that the railways needed transportation of Canadian commodities to make them pay.

The most detailed account of the alliance with the Conservatives was contained in a memorandum, apparently drafted by John Willison, editor of the Toronto News, recording a meeting in Borden's office with Sifton, Lash, Lloyd Harris, Liberal M.P. for Brantford, and Willison. How much Borden gave away in the course of these negotiations is open to question. Apart from the agreement to consult Lash, Willison and Walker, about cabinet appointments,

64

the terms agreed to by the Conservative leader were ones he probably would have carried out in any case. Nonetheless, the memorandum is one of the most remarkable documents in Canadian political history. It clearly establishes the relationship between the Conservative party and the Toronto business community during the election campaign. And it sets the tone for Borden Conservatism for the next decade.

The campaign against reciprocity was carried on by the Canadian National League. Headed by Lash and Walker, the League was founded "to oppose the adoption of the proposed Reciprocity Agreement between Canada and the United States of America and to support such measures as will uphold Canadian Nationality and British connection, will preserve our Fiscal Independence and will continue to develop our present National policy of interprovincial and external trade, under which the Dominion has achieved its present prosperity." The pamphlets and articles prepared by the League were a major factor in the reciprocity debate. They supplied Conservative campaign speakers and country newspapers with a wealth of arguments and statistical facts. And they were undoubtedly responsible to a considerable extent for the fact that the case against reciprocity held together remarkably well as the campaign progressed and was repeated without glaring inconsistencies in different parts of the country.

One of the most quoted pamphlets was Arthur Hawkes' "An Appeal to the British-Born." Born in England, Hawkes had had a checkered career as a journalst and publicist since immigrating to Canada. On arriving in Toronto in 1905 he had become the editor of the *Toronto World*, the editor of the *Monetary Times*, then director of publicity for the Canadan Northern Railway. In January 1911 he founded the *British News of Canada*, backed apparently with Canadian Northern funds, "for the purpose of multiplying and strengthening the relations existing between British people who remain in the old lands and those who come to the new." Originally published in this journal, "The Appeal to the British-Born" was based upon Sir John A. Macdonald's 1891 election slogan, "A British subject I was born, a British subject I will die," and was directed to the quarter of a million British immigrants in Canada. How effective it was it is difficult to state, but it was the source of considerable concern for Liberals across the country.

Closely involved with the activities of the League was Clifford Sifton. Although his financial figures can easily be discounted, Hawkes' account of Sifton's role in the campaign against reciprocity from his perspective as secretary of the League provides an interesting insight into the League's operations. As Hawkes makes clear, Sifton's influence cannot be minimized. His speech in the Commons was one of the most widely circulated piece of anti-reciprocity literature. Together with "a foreward and afterword," carefully designed to remind the farmers that they had more pressing needs than reciprocity, it was sown across the prairies from one corner to another.

The Mail and Empire, February 20, 1911.

The Manifesto of the
Toronto Eighteen

We oppose ratification of the proposed reciprocity agreement with the United States of America:—

1. Because in the year 1897 the Parliament of Canada repealed the legislation then existing relating to reciprocity, and since such repeal neither the people of Canada nor their Parliament have entrusted the Government with any duty or authority to negotiate with respect to any agreement on the subject.

2. Because the present unexampled prosperity of Canada is the result of the policy which has been pursued in the development of her trade and of her natural resources. Because this has involved the expenditure of hundreds of millions of dollars upon railways, canals, steamships and other means of transportation between east and west and west and east, and the obligation to incur further great expenditures for the same purpose; and because further development along the same lines would be seriously checked by the proposed reciprocity agreement and the benefits of

the expenditures referred to would be to a great extent lost.

3. Because it is essential to the continued national unity and development of Canada that no trade relations with any country should be agreed to by Canada on any basis which would check the growth and development of trade between the various parts of Canada with each other, or between Canada and the various parts of the Empire; and because the proposed reciprocity agreement between Canada and the United States of America would seriously check the growth and development of this trade.

4. Because any present benefit to any section of Canada or to any interests or individuals therein which might accrue from the proposed agreement would be more than offset by the loss and injury which would accrue to other sections and interests and individuals, and because the result to Canada as a whole would be greatly injurious.

5. Because as a result of the proposed agreement the freedom of action possessed by Canada with reference to her tariffs and channels of trade would be greatly curtailed, and she would be hampered in developing her own resources in her own way and by her own people.

6. Because after some years of reciprocity under the proposed agreement the channels of Canada's trade would have become so changed that a termination of the agreement and a return by the United States to a protective tariff as against Canada would cause a disturbance of trade to an unparalleled extent, and because the risk of this should not be voluntarily undertaken by Canada.

7. Because to avoid such a disruption Canada would be forced to extend

the scope of the agreement so as to include manufactures and other things.

8. Because the agreement as proposed would weaken the ties which bind Canada to the Empire, and because the unrestricted reciprocity which would naturally follow would still further weaken those ties and make it more difficult to avert political union with the United States.

9. Because the disruption in the channels of Canada's trade which was caused by the termination of the reciprocity treaty of 1854 and the subsequent establishment of a protective tariff by the United States gave rise to a decided leaning in many minds towards annexation with the United States, and this at a time when Canada was mainly peopled by native-born Canadians and other British subjects, to whom the prospect of annexation was most unwelcome, and because Canada in a comparatively few years will have millions of newcomers, a large percentage of whom will come from foreign countries, and because if Canada should then have to choose between disruption of her channels of trade with the United States or political union with them the preservation of Canadian autonomy and Canadian nationality would be enormously more difficult.

10. Believing as we do that Canadian nationality is now threatened with a more serious blow than any it has heretofore met with, and that all Canadians who place the interests of Canada before those of any party or section or individuals therein, should at this crisis state their views openly and fearlessly, we, who have hitherto supported the Liberal party in Canada, subscribe to this statement.

B. E. Walker	Toronto
John L. Blaikie	"
W. D. Mathews	"
W. K. George	"
Z. A. Lash	"
W. T. White	"
G. T. Somers	"
Robt. S. Gourlay	"
Wm. Mortimer Clark	"
R. J. Christie	"
H. Blain	"
H. S. Strathy	"
L. Goldman	"
Geo. A. Somerville	"
W. Francis	"
James D. Allan	"
E. R. Wood	"
Jn. C. Eaton	"

University of Toronto Library, *B. E. Walker Papers,* B. E. Walker to J. H. Fulton, March 16, 1911.

The Eighteen and the Railways

                    Toronto, March 16, 1911
Dear Mr. Fulton,

      . . . . I should have to write a very long letter to explain all my objections to the Reciprocity proposals, but I think they are very well set forth in the speech of the Hon. Clifford Sifton made in opposition to his party, which I send under separate cover. He is by far the ablest man in politics in Canada to-day, and while it is the speech of a politician, it pretty well covers the ground. We have been trying to build up a nation on lines running east and west with a large and rapidly growing inter-provincial trade, and we need transportation of our commodities in order to make our three transcontinental railways pay, although of course the growth of Canada would in time do away with the loss of any carriage because of trade diverted to the United States. The measure appeals to the Canadian farmer and to the fishermen of the maritime provinces, but I fancy to few others. The farmer is already the most prosperous member of our community and has a market at the highest prices ever known for much more than he is willing to produce, so to say that he needs increased markets is ludicrous and untrue.

      The strongest objections are national, however. By diverting our trade to the United States and stirring up all kinds of entangling alliances with them, we are making our national problems infinitely more difficult, considering that we have only seven and a half millions of people against one hundred millions. As free trade in one article after another is established with the United States, so long as the trusts exist they will undoubtedly take under their wing the Canadian market for the particular article. If we had twenty millions of people the situation would be quite different. . . .

                         Yous sincerely

Public Archives of Canada, *J. S. Willison Papers,* Vol 105, Memorandum, undated.

An Alliance of Convenience

At the office of Hon. Clifford Sifton in Ottawa on Wednesday, March 1st, 1911, Mr. Sifton, Mr. Z. A. Lash, K.C., Mr. Lloyd Harris, M.P., and Mr. J. S. Willison met to consider the best steps to be taken to resist ratification of the Reciprocity Agreement with Washington, to influence opinion in the country, to accomplish the defeat of the Government, and to arrange a basis of co-operation with Mr. Borden, Leader of the Conservative party.

The four first named having fully agreed as to the course to be taken and the policy which should be pursued by a new Administration, in case a change of Government should be effected, their views were laid before the Leader of the Opposition by Mr. Sifton. In substance, Mr. Borden was asked to agree:

(1) That the future Government, while giving proper representation to Quebec and to the Roman Catholic element, should not be subservient to Roman Catholic influences in public policy or in the administration of patronage.

(2) That it should resist American encroachments and American blandishments and in fiscal policy, in the handling of natural resources, and in political relations should be staunchly and definitely Canadian in spirit and in policy and should be vigilant under all circumstances to preserve and strengthen Canadian nationality and the connection with the Mother Country.

(3) That Mr. Borden in forming a Cabinet should consult with Sir Edmund Walker, Mr. Lash K.C., and Mr. Willison, in order to ensure that his Ministry should be so constituted as to guarantee the effective adoption and application of this policy, and that there should be reasonable representation therein of the views of those Liberals who may unite with Conservatives against the policy of Reciprocity.

(4) That Mr. Borden should pledge himself to place the outside civil service under control of the Civil Service Commission.

(5) That Mr. Borden should agree to reorganize the Department of Trade and Commerce, place the Department in charge of a strong Minister without undue regard to party considerations, and establish a commercial consular service in foreign countries in order to protect Canadian interests and extend Canadian trade.

(6) That Mr. Borden should recognize the necessity of introducing into his Cabinet from outside Parliament a number of men of outstanding national reputation and influence in order to give confidence to the progressive elements of the country, and strength and stability to the Government.

(7) That Mr. Borden should guarantee the appointment of a Tariff Commission to investigate industrial conditions

from time to time and report recommendations to Parliament.

Mr. Borden, in reply to Mr. Sifton, declared himself in sympathy with all these representations, freely pledged himself to use every possible endeavor to give them effect, and even expressed his readiness to resign the leadership of the Conservative party if by so doing a leader could be got under whose direction these objects would be more certainly and more effectively secured.

Upon these assurances the Committee pledged itself to cooperate with Mr. Borden and to proceed at once to organize for the next general election.

Arthur Hawkes, "Sir Clifford Sifton and the Reciprocity Election of 1911", *The Manitoba Free Press,* September 21, 1929.

Sifton and Reciprocity

LIBERAL OPPOSITION

The Liberal opposition to reciprocity began to take shape after a great demonstration in Massey hall on March 9. It was decided to found an organization, of which Z. A. Lash was to be chairman, and I secretary. W. T. White was named as treasurer. He never treasured; but that made no difference in the event.

It might have been supposed that the eighteen who manifested by manifesto and carried a memorable meeting, would gather in phalanxed, reinforced might and form a militant association that would be as terrible as an army with banners. We had the banner, all right; but its most engaged officer never saw the army.

The only semblance of a meeting to devise ways and means he knew anything about was a lunch and after-meeting at the York club, at which four men were present. As the result of a long afternoon of hard labor the objects of the Canadian National league were formulated: "To oppose the adoption of the proposed reciprocity agreement between Canada and the United States of America, and to support such measures as will uphold Canadian nationality and British connection, will preserve our fiscal independence and will continue to develop our present national policy of inter-provincial and external trade, under which the Dominion has achieved its present prosperity".

The National league partook of the nature of its chairman, who was never addicted to team play. Its financial obligations, which, to the surprise of our most experienced friend, totalled only $24,600. and not $75,000. were always met by his personal cheque. If we had lost the election, Mr. Lash might have found difficulty in collecting from his early colleagues, for funerals close more pockets. than they open.

When Chairman Lash was salmon fishing on the Restigouche in May—a yearly devotion with him—it seemed proper to resort to the titular treasurer for certain advice. It could not be obtained. The treasury appointment had never been formally made; and the affairs of the league were beyond the ken of the manager of the National Trust, who had no further liking for being mixed up in public controversy. It was Home Smith who induced White in August to go on the stump.

Those who have had experience of political campaigning, whether by pen or tongue, know that ultimate reliance must be placed on a few constant, able men. The ideal committee, so spiritual a leader as Spurgeon said, consists of three: one of them sick and another absent. So far as I know, Clifford Sifton was not an official of the Canadian National league: but he was the rock on which the secretary most surely relied. He was there at every call. When others were in perplexity he was in his element.

At a conference at Montreal of unofficial leaders, the country was more or less definitely marked out for propaganda purposes. The veteran, inveterate handler of undisplayed wires in the East, Sir Hugh Graham, of the Montreal Star, was there; and, as Sifton said, very adroitly led Lash into undertaking the financial responsibility for sowing the good seed throughout the west. Sir Hugh—still several years from the Atholstan barony—was earnestly devoted to corralling the Nationalists of Quebec; and though all through the campaign his power could be felt, it was not megophoned from watch towers.

Sifton's declaration in the Commons against the pact was the loveliest music the Conservatives had heard for many moons. They had mercilessly assailed him as Minister of the Interior, even after he had left the government. They would gladly have hailed him as a potential Moses. He knew too much to be hampered by that snare, which they thought was a compliment—as, indeed, it was.

During a somewhat extensive experience nothing has ever been more truly intriguing than to watch the Borden strategists as they discussed prospects with their old adversary. You have sometimes seen the silent, luminously wistful tribute of the confiding eye, when the mouth is still. The truth was that the Conservative party, as then at Ottawa half-embattled, was without the tradition, as it had been without the hope of victory until Liberals rebelled, where the Conservatives at first feared to denounce.

When the reciprocity agreement was proposed some Conservatives believed it would ensure the Liberals another twenty years' office. The only difference between them and some Liberals was that the Liberals fixed the cinch for thirty years.

Once the battle was in array, no hesitation was shown on either side. If there were Conservative accessions to the Liberals we heard nothing of them—they certainly were not eminent. The Liberal defections, even from Toronto, produced results. Never since the more militant Reform days had Liberals of Toronto been so significant.

It was expected that the campaign would be long. The parliament was not three years old, and seemed likely to accept the agreement and postpone the conclusive fight until the next year. That made it all the more desirable to saturate the people with propagandist material, which was the pre-eminent job of the Canadian National league.

Though Sifton had decided not to become a candidate again, he was anxious to get his views before the people who had been electing him ever since the summer of 1888—now twenty-three years ago. We arranged to reprint the Hansard report of his speech, with any additions he cared to make, and to send it out with another pamphlet, the scope of which we agreeably discussed. Under the title "The Road to Washington", I wrote a pamphlet which assembled a formidable amount of evidence of the extent to which our neighbours expected to pull us into their orbit, and out of the stream of inter-Britannic commerce. The classic instance of this naked ambition was President Taft's prophecy that the Agreement would make Canada an adjunct of the United States—a deliverance which Laurier used to declare, privately, was wholly asinine. It was only when United

States comment was collected that the prevalence of their annexationist contemplations was realized. Never did a statesman have more abundant reason than Laurier to seek salvation from his friends.

This pamphlet did not suite the distinguished chairman of the league. He used its quotations from speeches and articles and wrote another pamphlet entirely. It is half the battle to get a title that can bite; and "The Road to Washington" was a broadside in itself. But when a chairman who is financial provider writes a pamphlet there is no question as to who is publication boss and when, in the evangelists' rostrum he dons the counsel's robe, he will use the lawyer's language.

SLOW WARMING UP

We printed "Reciprocity With the United States", with its three subtitles, all set out on a stiff cover; and sent a copy to Sifton, asking how many he wished to go to Brandon. Two days later, in Ottawa, he asked me to write again, under the title we had formerly agreed upon; to print as large a first edition as I thought wise; to say nothing about it; and to send one to each person on the Brandon voters' list, with his own speech. Which was done.

Things were slowing down; and Sifton went off to Europe about the middle of May. Lash was off fishing; White was off the job; and, with what seemed to be a general apathy, I was almost off hope. At Montreal I saw Sifton on the eve of his sailing by the Laurentic. We spent the evening on board where, also, I met his father, to whom his attitude was one of deep filial respect. I told him I was depressed by the apparent lack of interest; the laggard movement among our allies;

and the seeming indifference of the country, indicated by the fewness of responses to invitations to co-operate with the league.

"Don't be in the least discouraged", he replied. "You don't know political Canada as well as I do. Things are always slow to warm up, even when they seem to make a swift start, as they did in this thing during the winter. Whatever you do, don't worry—it will be all right. You will see when the fight comes it will be eighteen seventy-eight over again. I'm as sure of that as I am that we're here. Go ahead doing what you think is best, till I come back in September. Drop me a line occasionally on how things are going".

We didn't have to wait till September to see him again. "The Road to Washington" had been put into circulation; and something new was projected, the earlier story of which it is proper to tell, personal though it be, because it makes more distinct the Siftonian stimulus that ensured its success as a factor in the election—I mean "The Appeal to the British-Born", of which it is still occasionally said that I shall never live it down.

APPEAL TO BRITISH-BORN

"The Appeal to the British-Born" was written as a newspaper article, about as long as two solid columns of the Free Press. Anybody reading it now would find it a Canada First document. . . .

It was proposed to re-print this article as a pamphlet, circulate it as widely as possible; and to carry on a speaking campaign among Old Countrymen who it was estimated (closely, as the census proved) had a quarter of a million votes. More than half of them had come to Canada since the 1908 election, and could vote, whereas no other immigrated men arriving since that time had the franchise. The privilege carried responsibility; and required information.

Especially in Ontario, it was figured, that Old Countrymen were numerous enough in every industrial centre to decide the day if there were otherwise a fairly even division of opinion, and if they voted practically unanimously. In the west it was plain that a considerable percentage of the organized farmers, including leaders, were Old Countrymen. The scope for the Appeal was, therefore, peculiarly potential towards an election whenever it came. Several tryouts were made at quiet meetings, about which interesting stories could be told. Each of them demonstrated the soundness of our size-up.

Somewhat reluctant consent to printing the pamphlet was given; and quite reluctant permission to spend a hundred dollars in testing the sentiment to which the Appeal appealed. Copies of the pamphlet were sent to all Conservative members and candidates; with requests for their opinions.

The reaction was not inspiring. A good old Conservative, since gathered to his grandfathers, wrote from Ottawa that the language of the Appeal was above the heads of my countrymen. One who showed appreciation and sent a list of several hundred names, was Arthur Meighen— when the election was really on. Another who let me know that he saw political country as we did was Mr. Monk, soon to be Mr. Borden's terribly harassed minister of works.

A PLAN GOES AHEAD

Early in July word was received of Sifton's unexpected return home. Two days after his arrival he was in Toronto. When we met, he said: "The government will call the election within three weeks. I know the signs". No doubt he knew more than the outward and visible signs; but he was not given to telling all he knew. Reciprocity was at last being fought —filibustered, perhaps, in the commons, and, as the event proved then, and in the naval conflict two years later, in political strategy the advantage is nearly always with the assailant—when there is something to assail.

"At Ottawa", he said, "they don't seem to know what to do. Nobody in the opposition has ever run a national campaign. Perley is quite new to it; and hasn't any idea of how he'll be swamped by all sorts of requests as soon as the campaign gets under way. He has no notion of how to delegate territorial responsibility. We'll be campaigning in less than three weeks, though. How have you been getting on?"

The answer was that we had been getting on so-so—the trouble was really what it had been in May. That neither surprised nor annoyed him. He said that in an election you must do the best you could with inexpert help and must not expect many people to be full of brains. Given a sketch of what we had done, he was good enough to say it was a great amount of work. We were carrying on a distribution office at Ottawa—franking is a blessing to both sides, even if it may be a vice in disguise. The demand for literature was growing. "The Road to Washington" was overhauled in the call for the more forensic stuff. Lash was wrestling with another delivery. (It was later finished as "Home Market and Farm").

"You sent me "An Appeal to the British-Born," he said, shortly. "Have you got a copy with you?"

I produced one. He tapped it on the table.

"Do you realize that's the best thing we've got? he asked, in his quick, incising way, when he was ready for action. "Do you know what I think you ought to do? You should make a separate campaign among the Old Countrymen right away. Don't wait for anybody, but go ahead; not with meetings called by Conservatives, but quite independently—keep clear of them—run a separate campaign. What do you think?"

I told him we had been preparing for that all summer, but had received little encouragement. If he'd get Lash to authorize whatever expenditure was needed, we'd proceed fast enough.

"All right," said he, "I'll see Lash today. Can you be here at 6 o'clock?"

At 6 o'cock he said Lash had agreed to what was proposed, so it would be all right to go on organizing without waiting for the election to be announced. We talked awhile; how well I remember it. We were on a chesterfield, he with his hand to his ear, for in 1911 he could still carry on a conversation without a tube. He smote my knee:

"Do you mind if I give you a piece of advice?"

"Give me two," I answered.

"Don't ask Lash what you should do. Decide what you want to do, and do it. Use your own judgment. Tell him afterwards what you've done. That's all. Good-bye; good luck."

SIFTON IMPERTURBABLE

Seventeen days afterwards, on Saturday, the 29th of July, the government announced dissolution to the House of Commons.

How many speeches Sifton made during the campaign I don't know. We met occasionally as our trails crossed. The Rev. Mr. Macdonald, the flaming editor of the Globe, had tried to blister Sifton, who was used to that sort of thing.

The last time we met during the fight was on the final Saturday and Sunday before the polling. In the afternoon he spoke in the armories at Windsor and at night at Chatham. We travelled to Toronto together.

Until the Windsor meeting I had never seen Sifton on the platform since the night in June, 1888, when he and Macdonald competed in the little schoolhouse back from the Assiniboine, in North Brandon. It was specially interesting to observe the changes nearly a quarter of a century of legislative life had wrought in a man who was almost twice the age at which he had won his first election.

The armories contained over 3,000 people, many of whom were standing. The day was very hot and, as always, in such conditions, the crowd took some time to settle down even after the meeting began. As a speaker to a great audience Sifton had several obvious disadvantages which militated against the advantage of a more than average physical size, and the easy confidence born of long practice in which, as he freely testified, small meetings in country schoolhouses had heavily contributed.

Canadian audiences years ago had the idea that a political speaker's main business was to rage and tear. They expected to hear the other fellow accused and abused, and assumed that the measure of success was the noise it evoked.

Sifton sought none of the effects of the orthodox partisan. He was laden with arguments, founded on and buttressed by facts. He reasoned as impersonally on the platform as he did with a book before him in his library. His voice was nothing to rave over; though it carried well, in spite of its unmistakable suggestion that it belonged to a man whose hearing was not good. He was minus that great intensifier of eloquence which was so potent an aid of so marvellous an orator as Gladstone —his countenance was immobile while he dispensed light and wisdom.

But Sifton had a faculty which is denied to many statesmen whose fame exceeds their desserts—his audience increased its interest while he spoke. This was due to the sheer weight of his matter and the clarity with which it was marshalled. That was the case on the hot Saturday afternoon at Windsor. He was preceded by the candidate for a neighboring riding from whom the gift of tongues had been withheld, but on whom the virtue of perseverance had been bestowed.

The audience was restless when Sifton rose. He began without any attempt to quiet it by vociferous plentitude. He was as imperturbable as Bryan was when I saw him at St. Paul starting a speech to 20,000 people on the fair grounds, and taking his ease with observations that meant nothing in particular, until the zone of quiet around him steadily spread, until silence and his own voice ruled the scene.

Somebody interfered to dispel the Windsor unease. Sifton stopped him; and went on. Soon the noise subsided, and the speech continued to its logical end. Though he had a sheaf of notes, he never looked at a page, but held them tightly behind his back. He was as gestureless as John Bright, to whom he need not otherwise be likened.

Bright was a prophet of righteousness, with a nervous, passionately-inspired command of the Saxon tongue which could be envied but not emulated —a political seer, but not a departmental administrator. Sifton was a unique administrator, a business man who always spoke with acuminous practicality, and cared nothing for the outward beauty of articulation. He was indifferent to many things for which lesser men labor when they meet the public. He inspired confidence, without striving to provoke enthusiasm.

At Windsor, which may be taken as a typical meeting of his section of the campaign, these qualities operated as a sort of run of his intellectual and political mine. The same forces were at work in all his public deliverances.

The contest issued in a Conservative majority of 46, of which 60 were obtained in Ontario. Sifton's perception of the potentiality of the British-born vote and of reaching it independently was, like all wisdom, justified of its fruits. You cannot go through an election campaign without more rather than less identification with your allies. In many minds, there was little difference between the appeals of those who, while not professing the same party allegiance, were broadly advocating the same views. But we preserved our independence as well as our identity, and audiences were constantly urged not to tie themselves to any political party. We criticized the Mail and Empire for carrying as a daily golden text at the head of its editorial pages, something that John A. Macdonald said in 1844, and the leading Conservative journal reciprocated by never mentioning meetings which were attended by hundreds and sometimes by thousands of people.

SIFTON WAS DYNAMIC

The Sifton dynamic in this election campaign, as I knew it, is now faithfully set down for the first time. His influence on Conservative headquarters was outside my purview. I am sure he gave invaluable counsel whether or not it was followed. The natural vehicle of his approach to public opinion was through the league that chiefly vocalized revolting Liberal sentiment. His insistence on "The Road to Washington" being published was more than justified when we made up our records. It was issued weeks after the one which Lash always spoke of as "our pamphlet". It was distributed only on demand. A hundred and fifty thousand more copies of it were called for than were printed of any other.

The distinct identity of everything we did was maintained throughout the campaign. The experience and directive force on which I continually relied came from the man whom I had first seen in action in North Brandon, so many years before. It is natural, therefore, to agree with Laurier's statement to the representative of The Detroit News that it was Sifton who mainly defeated him in 1911.

Clifford Sifton, "Reciprocal Trade with
the United States", *Campaign of 1911
Against Reciprocity*, (Toronto: Canadian
National League, 1911).

Foreword and Afterword

[Since delivery of the speech . . .
which I delivered in the House of Commons on February 28] there has been
much further discussion of the subject
which has served to confirm the conclusions previously reached. A few of the
important points connected with the subject as it affects Western Canada are
summarized herewith.

The argument that the Canadian
North West farmer would get a better
price for his wheat seems to be abandoned. It is clear that there was no
foundation for it. It is also clear that the
effect of the Treaty would be to assimilate
the trade to the American wheat trade and
largely lose Canadian control of the
traffic, thus making it impossible to keep
the grades pure or to effectively regulate
the business.

FOUR WESTERN NEEDS

The pressing needs of the North
West are:—
1. The construction and operation

of the Hudson's Bay Railway by the
Government.
2. The establishment of a proper
commission to control the grading and
transportation of wheat and put the export wheat in a pure state on the English
market.
3. The establishment of a sample
wheat market.
4. The development of a steady and
reliable market for animal products by the
establishment of chilled meat industries
and the extension of meat packing industries.

The cities and towns of Western
Canada can be built up mainly by the
industries which are natural to a great
agricultural region, namely, milling, meat
packing, etc. They are absolutely essential to the prosperity of the country, they
furnish profitable employment on a large
scale, cause great growth of the cities and
towns, which, in turn, make a great home
market. Winnipeg should in fifteen years
have in and around it five hundred thous-
and people. Other towns and cities should
grow in proportion. The market for farm
produce thus furnished would be enormous. The by-products of the industries,
especially milling, are valuable, and, in
fact, necessary if mixed farming is to be
made profitable.

TRUST WILL DOMINATE

The express object of this Treaty is
to facilitate the sale and exportation of
the raw products of the farm by the shortest channels to American markets. Permanent argicultural prosperity seems to
be quite impossible if this system is followed. There is little doubt that it will
result in the young cattle being taken to
the corn states for feeding purposes. It
looks as if the meat trust will dominate

the country, dictate prices and ship back its finished products. The trust itself will be absolutely removed from Canadian control.

In Ontario, at the present time, through the establishment of industries, the pork packers pay better prices to the farmers than are obtainable south of the line. Similar markets can be built up in the West.

BARLEY NOT IMPORTANT

There does not seem to be any sufficient foundation for the idea that there is a profitable market in the United States for any large amount of Canadian barley. The total production of American barley for all purposes in 1909 was 140,000,000 bushels. A comparatively small part of it was No. 1 malting barley. It is the demand for good malting barley which keeps the price up. If there was an unlimited demand for barley at present prices the western American farmers would increase their own output, but they apparently limit the output in obedience to the law of supply and demand. If any considerable proportion of Canadian North West farmers went in to barley and shipped it to the United States the market would go to pieces at once. It would be a good thing for the brewers, but would not help the farmers.

As a matter of fact, when you analyse the effects of the Treaty it appears everywhere to result in a good thing for some American Trust or Railway, while the advantages to Canada and Canadians are largely illusory.

The whole basis of the commercial and industrial growth of the West is its grain and cattle. If they are given away to be worked up at a profit south of the line, how is it expected that the country is going to be developed as it should be, and permanently retain its prosperity?

DUTY WOULD HAVE STAYED

The statement that the United States can take off the duty from wheat and cattle themselves, if they wish to, is fallacious. The American millers and packers would like to do it, but the farmers of the Middle West and North West states know that it will injure them and turn into their markets the products of the Canadian North West. There would be no chance of success at present for a bald proposition to take the duty off wheat and cattle going into the United States. The only reason it is seriously considered is that it is combined with other concessions contained in this Treaty. If the Treaty drops it is unlikely that for some time to come we shall hear anything of free wheat and cattle. By that time our country will be sufficiently developed to stand on its own feet. That is exactly why the large commercial interests of the United States are pushing this Treaty. The plain fact is that the great trusts of the United States want to get at Canada and exploit it and by this Treaty we are helping them to do it.

The young men of Western Canada who expect to live there and see their country prosper and afford them an opportunity of making a livelihood ought to stand together and fight against this proposition.

There are just two possible policies for Canada, one is Commercial Union with the United States, and the other is Commercial Independence. We are making our choice now.

If we decide for Commercial Union we shall henceforth be dominated by the United States to the entire exclusion of British interests.

Arthur Hawkes, "An Appeal to the British-Born", *Campaign of 1911 Against Reciprocity*, (Toronto: Canadian National League, 1911).

To the British-Born

I am going to appeal to the patriotism of every man, woman, and family of British birth in Canada—to demonstrate the depth and strength, the intelligence and endurance of our belief in the two countries to which we belong by parentage and by choice.

No great company of people on the globe to-day are situated as we are. By the hundred thousand we have crossed the ocean, changed our habit of life, enlarged our experience, widened our outlook, increased our possessions, and seen our children's feet set in wider places than our own ever knew—and we have done it without bating one jot or tittle of our tie with the Old Land; without sacrificing a single worthy sentiment which pervaded our youth. We have broken nothing in order to build anew.

EASY WAS THE CHANGE

We have come from the islands of the sea to this continent and have flourished in Provinces as widely spread as the babel-tongued countries of Europe. We have done it with as little violence to our inmost traditions as would have distiguished a move from the North to the South of England—not as far as from Montreal to Toronto, or from Winnipeg to Regina.

We have followed the citizenship of the Kingdom with the citizenship of the Dominion more easily than you can transfer a vote from Glasgow to Greenock. We have seen Justice, the hallmark of a free and enlightened people, wearing the same aspect here as it wears in the Old Home. We have found many things better than they were in the days of our childhood.

Some of us have once turned back, thinking the Old was better, but we have returned to the Younger Fold of the Flock from whence we came, glad and thankful to be again partakers of the Newness of Life which doth here much more abound.

And with it all there is no diminution of your affection or mine for the Land We Left. It takes on a different, a clearer, quality—it must do so when we have enlarged our own quality. It is like a mature, reflective family man's love for his parents, which makes him glad to visit his Old Folks, and more glad to get back home among his Young Folks.

And yet again, how little most of us know about the Land We Left or the Land We Live In! When I started for Canada over twenty-five years ago I had never been north of London. The look of Sheffield, the aspect of the rugged country of Longdendale, with its immense reservoirs; the cotton mills of the Irwell Valley; the peat moss between Manchester and Liverpool; were as strange to me as Saskatchewan is to the Prince Edward Islander. I was dropped off a train in the heart of Assiniboia one night; and for years I saw nothing but prairie. I used to read about Nova Scotia and Ontario and British Columbia, but did not know them.

THE LAND WE LIVE IN

That must be the case with most of us. But the limitations of creating a livelihood and founding a family in an entirely new country only intensify one's love for the country where so many great things are being done by just average, everyday, honest, people; and make us want to know more about it, and its future splendour. If we may love Canada so much, knowing her so little, how should we love her if we knew her from sea to sea?

The Land We Live In bears knowing—why, do you think? Because of its unmeasured Geography? Because of its natural appearance in the middle of February? Not at all; not at all. Get somebody to dump you down in the bush, or on the bald prairie, with enough food to last you to the next meal but one, and you won't break out into song about the country as you are left with only blue sky to keep you warm.

It is her People that have made Canada. And—think well on this—it is people just like you and me who have done it. Out of solitude—a community. Out of wealthless toil—prosperity. Out of vacancy—a nation. Out of a lone frontier —the bulwark of an Empire, the Envy of a Republic.

And how was it done by just such people as we are? They could scarcely tell. Most of them didn't comfort themselves with the reflection that they were laying a foundation for a virile, British nationhood. They were doing it just the same.

A COUNSEL OF DESPAIR

But, even to those who did walk by faith, what time they wielded the axe, and zig-zagged their plough among the stumps, the horizon was bounded by the Lakes.

Afar off, inaccessible, dangerous, were vast plains, buffalo-covered, Indian-haunted, unexplored, save by a few traders. It was hard enough toiling to keep a British Province in health alongside a Republic that tried to tempt allegiance by placing savory messes of pottage out of reach. In 1849 public and private men in Montreal openly, sorrowfully, besought their fellow-Canadians to ask to be annexed to the United States. It was a counsel of despair, for which it is easy to blame them until you know how hopeless the fight for prosperity seemed.

The cry for annexation, for a friendly wiping of Britain out of the heart of North America, failed, and the scroll that was prepared for the story of a nation's birth was saved so as by fire. It was saved not because of Britain's love for Upper Canada and Lower Canada, but because of the love of men in the Canadas for Britain. They knew, deep down in their souls, that Canada possessed Britain in a far more magnificent sense than Britain possessed Canada, and that out of their tribulation rich fruits would spring. That is even more splendidly true to-day.

NATION WAS BORN

But look—there was coming to birth a nation within a nation, such as no epoch had yet produced. Like many other births, it wasn't a very pleasant experience. Some of the midwives of Downing Street were more bother than use. But it came out all right. The Republic that had counted on the disjointed fragments of British North America falling into its hand, saw the disjointed fragments unite into a confederated Dominion. And, in a few years, the Republic noticed the Dominion spread from the Atlantic even to the Pacific; and behold something had happened in the history of Empire which nobody had predicted. There was a great access of affection for the distant Mother State.

More unpredicted things happened. Again a few years and it was possible to take a train alongside Atlantic tidal water and stay in it until the heaving bosom of the Pacific lay beneath the car window— a thing which the Republic has not accomplished to this day. Canada had "arrived."

To traverse fertile plains was comparatively simple; but this British people, this handful who could not be put outside the Empire by the supercilious indifference of Downing Street or by the calculated coolness of Washington, bridged a wilderness of a thousand miles, such as had never been crossed with rails. It was an insurance against the political strangulation of Canada; a guarantee by Canada that British dominion and British trade routes should be unbroken between Europe and Australia and Asia.

CANADA WAS TRANSFORMED

Wisdom was justified of her children. Canada this day is not the Canada I first saw in 1885, either in mind, body or estate. Then they were wondering whether it really was a country. Then it was permissible to think of it as a poor relation of the United States. Then it was little observed by the Empire of which it was the most noteworthy portent.

What was the matter with it? Lack of people—that's all—plus a lack of faith that People would come and Capital would come; and Fertility would come into its own.

But all things come—faith comes if it is given the least chance. Did it ever strike you how amazingly true it is that whatsoever a people soweth, that shall it

also reap, and that the nation reaps from the sowings of men of faith who back their faith with works?

Remember those who heralded a United Canada that would stretch from shore to shore; remember those who risked everything of their own, and of as many others as they could lay hands on, because they were impelled by a faith that overcame wildernesses; remember the thousands who chose to suffer the afflictions of the backwoods rather than remain in luxury with those who had foresworn the Flag; count, however incompletely, the elements of privation, of courage, of foresight, of unconquerable enterprise, that men like you and me threw into the crucible wherein the mould of Canada has taken its shape, and you will see that they were bound to produce two effects outside the Dominion—one on the United Kingdom, the other on the United States.

FAMOUS POLITICAL SENTENCE

In the United Kingdom there was a Great Indifference to Canada. Statesmen who were Statesmen unfeignedly believed that her destiny was with the Republic— which is a fine encouragement for the rest of us to be statesmen by right of our own thinking. The indifference disappeared—wonderfully disappeared. You might be cynical and say it was purely a matter of advertising. You would be wrong. There is more behind the advertising than the lure of a hundred and sixty acres of land, miles away from the railroad.

There is the integrity of British Institutions, the appeal of the British Character, the guarantee of the British Flag—the things that were secured by the devotion of men long since dead, thousands and thousands of whom lived in obscurity and died in little clearings encumbered with debt. Sir John Macdonald wrote the most famous sentence in Canadian politics, "A British subject I was born, a British subject I will die." He only wrote what thousands of men and women had lived and clung to and hallowed in backwoods that have been transformed into landscapes worthy of the Weald of Kent. The blood of the martyrs became the seed of the church. The devotion of the pioneers cemented the foundation on which has been reared the structure under which you and I have found shelter, and a good content; and to which we came veritably as to a second and a better home.

TARIFF WALL THAT WORKED

The effect of the rise of Canada on the United States has been, in a way, more remarkable than the result produced in Great Britain. The people "down there" regarded Canada generally with indifference, and often with amusement until the physical works which were the outward and visible expression of the inner spirit of the Canadian people were seen to afford great opportunities for trade and agriculture.

One method of increasing the young nation's chance of success had been to answer the United States tariff with a tariff which compelled the building of branch factories on the Canadian side of the border. It was remarkably successful. In the West there was illimitable land, fertile and cheap, to which farmers from the United States were welcomed. They settled on it in thousands. They found the Canadian-British exposition of justice, of civic administration, of the best amenities of life, more pleasing than in the States they had left, and tens of thousands of them took the oath of allegiance to the King. A further miracle had happened—men who came under the British Flag, vowing that the Stars and Stripes would ever be the all and in all of their patriotism, found a new and larger patriotism where the Canadian-British method was at work.

The increase of agriculture and manufactures brought increase in the channels of trade—the blood which keeps communities in life and health. More railways were built and more were undertaken. Every citizen of the United States who came to see us marvelled at what he saw, and went and told others. At last those who had held Canada of no account understood that there was a new Power in the North. They coveted what they had before disdained. "Why," they said "three hundred millions of capital has gone from the United States into Canadian factories, and hundreds of thousands of our people have gone to Canadian farms. A great trade is growing by leaps and bounds up there. We must get after it."

DEMAND FROM THE STATES

There began a demand for exchange of products which Canada, when faith in her destiny was small, had tried vainly to secure and had mercifully been preserved from obtaining. The indifference was on the other side of the line now. A President had lost ground in the Republic, and was beset by rebellion in his own household. He was minded to try on Canada—the Canada of 1910; the Canada which had become the most flourishing, the best-regarded partner in the peerless Empire—to try the commercial fixings that would have suited her infancy, but which offer nothing comely for her self-reliant prime.

A few Canadians thought of commercial union, but it was a long time ago. The sacrificial heroism of those who had gone through the long travail of the backwoods would not be denied. Capital came, people came, from across the seas, the East had become the West, and the West had become the East. Commercial independence was achieved and a distinct nationality had come to pass. It may rest with you and me, the British-born, more than with any other element in modern Canadianism, to decide whether that nationality has come to stay in face of the scarcely disguised aspiration of our neighbors that their Flag and not ours shall float above our heads.

LIKE GETTING TERRITORY

For our neighbors have prospered and we are asked to accept a compact which reverses their former conduct towards us; which would destroy the artery through which East and West live a common, national life. We, who have grown independent of Reciprocity, are to become enamoured of the word and the thing we have outgrown.

Let me cite two out of innumerable evidences of their ultimate idea. Asked by the President to win their farmers to the scheme, the Secretary of Agriculture wrote, "These considerations lead me to the conclusion that the adoption of the Reciprocity Treaty would, from the national standpoint, be as much an act of wisdom as was the adoption of treaties in the past that have added to our own country more than half its present area."

And here is the aspiration for trade domination over Canada and Britain expressed typically in one of the most respected papers of the Republic, the "Minneapolis Journal."

"The path of reciprocity leads to practical, if not political union with Canada. The other path leads to a closer relation between Canada and Great Britain. It means the carrying out of a dream of British Imperial Federation, bound together no less by trade than by sentiment, with Canada taking the place of the United States as chief purveyor of food products and manufactured articles to Great Britain.

KEEP DISTINCT INDIVIDUALITY

"To-day England is our best customer, and Canada is our third best customer. But our foreign trade wanes, and that of Canada grows. If we push Canada into England's arms, the trade arrangements between the two will tend more and more to shut us out.

"How long will our trade with these two customers last if reciprocity fails? Our Canadian trade must fall off, as the East and West channels of her commerce are scoured by use. And Canada will more and more supply English needs in our stead."

They must increase, we must decrease. That is the direction of their ambition. I know the United States whose people have no warmer admirer than I. In the blemishes of their Government they have no keener sympathizer. Their way is not our way—it is neither Canadian nor British. We are neither of the United States, nor exactly of Britain. We have a distinct individuality which we believe is better than either. We are free from the woes that spring from the United States sowing its wild oats. We are not encumberd by those handicaps which the long centuries have placed upon the land of our nativity.

CAESAR IS OURSELVES

We have complete command of ourselves. Uniquely we posses the Old land as well as the New. Its traditions, its story, its achievements in widely-sundered parts of the world— these things are ours richly to enjoy without the faintest sense of alienation. According to the speed of history, the last decade has produced an amazing readjustment in the inter-imperial influences which more than the mere mechanics of Parliaments, Conferences and Courts, are re-creating the Empire in which we were born and of which we are a motive part. We are fast coming into the front rank of inter-dependent States. I can conceive of no calling more noble, more full of the dignity of the fruitful years than this calling to create a new nation while we help to re-fashion a venerable and glorious Empire.

Once the thrilling appeal was to Caesar. The appeal is to Caesar now. And Caesar is ourselves.

Part III

The Conservatives

The Conservatives started out on the hustings where they had left off in the House. Downplaying the economics of reciprocity, party leaders hammered away at the political implications of closer ties with the United States. Tory strategy apparently was to concentrate in Ontario where party organizers were confident of a major breakthrough, to leave Quebec to Monk and Bourassa and to pick up seats in the West.

"The atmosphere that confronted me," recalled Robert Borden of the Conservative caucus the day following the introduction of the reciprocity agreement, "was not invigorating; there was the deepest dejection in our party, and many of our members were confident that the Government's proposals would appeal to the country and would give it another term of office." One Conservative, however, who did not share the pessimism which pervaded the party was James P. Whitney, the Premier of Ontario. A "sane Imperialist", proud of the institutions of the British Empire, and distrustful of the excesses of American democracy, Whitney immediately perceived the threat which reciprocity posed to Canadian independence and the Imperial tie. In an exchange of letters with Borden, he articulated his concern and pointed the way to the basic position which the party was to adopt in opposing the agreement.

Once they were back on their feet, the Conservatives pinned much of their hope on provincial organizations in Ontario, Manitoba and British Columbia. Particularly crucial was Whitney's well-oiled machine in Ontario. Although it had failed to make significant headway in the election of 1908 or in the by-elections which followed, party leaders were confident that it would carry them to victory the forthcoming campaign. On April 17 A. E. Kemp, the party's chief strategist in the province and M.P. for Toronto East, J. S. Carstairs, secretary of the

Liberal-Conservative Association and Dominion organizer, Frank Cochrane, Whitney's minister of lands and mines, and Dr. J. D. Reid, M.P, for Grenville, met in Toronto to assess the prospects for the party in Ontario. In a memorandum to Borden two days later, Reid reported that such was the strength of the Conservatives' constituency organizations and the weakness of the Liberals' organization that the party could expect a major triumph regardless of the issue that precipitated an election.

The party was not as fortunately situated in some of the other provinces. In New Brunswick the Conservatives were bucking a long tradition of Liberal success, and with four of the province's thirteen constituencies controlled by the French Acadian vote, Laurier Liberals enjoyed a considerable advantage. In a long memorandum to William Price, M.P. for Quebec West and a party organizer, O. S. Crockett, the Tories' chief organizer in New Brunswick, summed up the situation. Unlike Ontario, the New Brunswick Conservatives did not get the candidates Crockett felt were necessary for electoral success, both Pierre-Armand Landry, the farmer M.P. for Kent, and Max Aitken, later Lord Beaverbrook, declining to become candidates. The memorandum, however, provides an interesting glimpse into the nuts and bolts of party organization.

Borden outlined the basic planks in the Conservative election platform in a manifesto which he delivered on August 15. It was a general statement of the party's opposition to reciprocity, a point by point refutation of Laurier's manifesto, and a list of promises should the Conservatives come to power. Included on the latter were three of the measures proposed by Sifton as "pressing needs" in the North West, the Hudson Bay Railway, state control of the terminal elevators, and the establishment of chilled meat industries. Together with a

pledge to return to the Prairie provinces their natural resources, they represented a major effort to counter the political appeal of reciprocity with the western grain growers.

Closely involved with Tory strategy in the West was the Premier of Manitoba, Robert P. Roblin. While his Attorney-General, Robert Rogers, set the provincial organization in motion, Roblin led the Conservative forces on the campaign trail. In a major address at Beausejour on August 26, he sketched in the details of Borden's programme, and provided conservative candidates across the Prairies with the basic arguments of the Tory campaign.

A major factor in the Conservative campaign was the nation's press. Led by the Montreal Daily Star, the Ottawa Journal and the Toronto News, the Tory press became increasingly hostile to the reciprocity proposals as the campaign progressed. Sir Hugh Graham's Daily Star was particularly vocal. Whatever the merits of freer trade, reciprocity was for the Star a dangerous policy, anti-Canadian, anti-British and anti-Empire. Weeks after weeks of bitter attacks culminated on September 16 with an editorial entitled "Under Which Flag", spread across the entire front page, flanked on the one side by the Stars and Stripes and on the other by the Union Jack. It is impossible to estimate how many voters a newspaper can affect but the Canadian Annual Review for 1911 came to one conclusion: "It is not very often in the history of a young, or indeed of any country, that a single newspaper wields a powerful influence in the overturn of a government and the defeat of a political policy. Such, however, was the record of the Montreal Star in 1911."

Borden's final "message to the Canadian people" was issued from Halifax on September 19. In what the Conservative leader believed to be the best of his appeals, he pinpointed the central issue in his election campaign. "This compact, made in secret and without mandate, points indeed to a new path. We must decide whether the spirit of Canadianism or of Continentalism shall prevail on the northern half of this continent." Canada had rejected formalizing the bonds of the British Empire during the Laurier era; Borden was equally determined that she oppose a continental system dominated by the United States.

Public Archives of Ontario, *Sir James Whitney Papers*, R. L. Borden-Whitney correspondence, January-March, 1911.

Approaching the Battle

Ottawa, Ont. January 25th, 1911
Private
Dear Sir James,—

The Prime Minister has stated that Mr. Fielding will tomorrow announce the result of the tariff negotiations at Washington. I would be glad to have, in confidence, your views thereon as soon as possible after the announcement.

Yours faithfully,

Toronto, January 27th, 1911.
Private:
Dear Mr. Borden,

I have received your letter of yesterday.

I have not been able to give the subject any consideration, in fact I have not been able to do more than to glance hurriedly at the President's message and Fielding's speech, etc. I may write you again within the next two days, but I will say now roughly, and not as a considered opinion, how the matter strikes me to-day.

The British Government are as one man opposed to what I call sane Im-

perialism. The Canadian Government is also opposed to it—though not quite in the same way—and Sir Wilfrid Laurier will be found always putting a drag on any advances towards strengthening the bonds between the Mother Country and the Over-Seas Dominions.

Mr. Fielding has never been loyal to Confederation, and from childhood up his political vision was apparently bounded by the New England States and the City of Boston. I heard an admirer of his say once that before he came into Federal politics he never considered anything of more importance than the desirability of getting a hake of fish and a bag of potatoes into the Boston market on the most favourable terms. I am afraid too that this friend suggested that the ideas of a good many other people down in the Maritime Provinces were limited in the same way. However, this is beside the question.

With these two Governments then in the attitude I have indicated we have the unmistakable desire—and I think I may say the intention—of the United States to bring about political union. It seems to me that, having regard to the surrounding conditions and the situation generally, a perusal of Mr. Taft's message must bring that conviction home to the mind of any impartial reader of it. I believe that two years ago the people of Canada, outside of Quebec, were practically united in favour of sane Imperialism. Since then, in order to help the British Government, the Toronto Globe has gradually led its readers away from that idea, and with the situation as it is here, with the cold shoulder turned to us by Great Britain, the making of commercial treaties with the United States, and other Nations, will soon together bring about a condition of affairs when the people of the British

Dominions in North America will begin to entertain the idea that they may as well drop off the parent tree.

Events move rapidly these days, and I do not consider fifteen years too short a time to give for the development of this idea. This may sound pessimistic and in fact it is pessimistic, because that is the way I feel on the subject.

It struck me also, although I may be mistaken in this, that the principal advantages, if there are any, accruing to Canada by the new arrangement go to the Maritime Provinces and the disadvantages to Ontario.

Yours faithfully,

Ottawa, January 30th, 1911
Dear Sir James,

Thanks for your forcible and cogent letter which expresses very clearly what has been my own idea on this question of reciprocity. I should be glad to hear from you again if you have any further suggestions.

Faithfully yours,

Toronto, January 30th, 1911.
Private.
Dear Mr. Borden,

What I wrote you the other day was, of course, rather crude, and put together very hastily. However, it embodies my idea or at least my fear of what the result will be. Trade reasons govern in the end; and with the British Government turning the cold shoulder to us and the Canadian Government leading our people astray, I fear that in these days of hasty changes and conclusions we may come very rapidly to the conclusion that anything like sane imperialism is not to be ex-

pected. When we come to that conclusion it seems to me the rest will be easy.

In haste,
Yours very truly,

Ottawa, Ont., February 4th, 1911
Dear Sir James,—

. . . When ever you arrive at any more definite conclusions as to the final effect of the reciprocity proposals, I would be glad to hear from you again. Personally I think they are likely to be of immediate advantage to several portions of our community but not of permanent advantage. From the national standpoint I entertain absolutely no doubt. President Taft truly said in his message that Canada is at the parting of the ways. The proposal is that Canada should enjoy wider markets in the United States to which the rest of the Empire will not be admitted. If these wider markets are so advantageous as to justify this step, complete commercial absorbtion will must be still more advantageous. This of course means the addition to the American Republic of eight or ten new States comprising the Dominion as it exists to-day. Assuming these proposals to be advantageous from the economic standpoint (and that I would contest) the question is British connection plus good markets and a stable fiscal condition against abandonment of past effort and of past ideals followed by absorbtion into the great neighbouring nation.

Faithfully yours,

February 14th, 1911.
Private
Dear Sir James:

The future destiny of this country, both commercially and politically, will probably be settled within the next two years. It is perfectly idle to believe that the present instalment of free trade will, if it is carried, measure the trade relations between the two countries for any considerable period. Those who are deprived of protection (such as the fruit growers, market gardeners, etc.) will join the farmers of the West and free traders generally in an effort to destroy the protection accorded to our industries. The ultimate conclusion is not only logical but inevitable. If the preservation of Canada to the Empire is worth fighting for, men who can exercise powerful influence over public opinion ought to make their voices heard. The battle which confronts us will be no child's play, I could point you to two sources in the United States from either of which this government can easily get a campaign fund of one million dollars if it will make certain pledges.

If the business interests of the country believe that this crisis can be met by a few casual meetings and an occasional vigorous protest, they are living in a fools' paradise. We have got to fight and fight hard.

At the first reasonable opportunity I hope you will turn loose your vocabulary upon this damnable proposal.

Believe me,
Yours faithfully,

Toronto, February 23rd, 1911.
Dear Borden,
. . . *Re Reciprocity.*

We have considered the question of a resolution here and have deferred action for a few days. I would like to bring one point to your attention, namely: Suppose that the new House of Representatives, whether it meets in extra session or not, lowers the tariff on a great many articles on the list of foods which are not included in this Agreement, what will be the effect with reference to our present attitude? I have no doubt that the Democrats and insurgent Republicans will be prepared to go, and will go, further than the Reciprocity Agreement goes. Now, if they do that, how will it affect the wisdom of our attitude with regard to Reciprocity?

I am sorry that I have to write you so hastily. Kindly drop me a line by return post if possible.
Yours faithfully,

Ottawa, February 24th, 1911
Dear Sir James,—

Your letter of yesterday has just reached me and I hasten to give you my views on the points suggested:

1. The New House of Representatives may adopt the Reciprocity Treaty without amendment or addition in which case the proposals will again go before the Senate for its concurrence. In that case the present situation will not be altered.

2. Or, the House of Representatives may enact a general tariff bill to which the present proposals will be attached as a rider. In other words provisions with respect to Canadian imports contained in the pending proposals will be made part of a general tariff bill. The situation in that case will be undoubtedly altered; but at present we cannot forsee or even conjecture to what extent or in what way. It does not occur to me that our present attitude would probably be affected by any such contingency.

3. Or, the new House of Representatives may disregard this Treaty altogether and enact a lower tariff applicable to the imports from Canada as well as

from all other countries. In that case the present Bill pending in the Parliament of Canada would become inoperative and unnecessary.

4. Or, the new House of Representatives might enact a lower tariff with provisions for further reduction to all countries desiring to enter into reciprocal relations. This again might affect our attitude but we cannot know in advance to what extent or in what manner.

5. I do not pretend that the above enumerations exhaust all the possibilities which the future may develop. It strikes me, however, that our present position is strong and unassailable for the following among other reasons:

(a) Our development under the trade policy of the past thirty years has been not only satisfactory but wonderful.

(b) The conditions under which that progress has been attained have been stable and certain while the new proposal is altogether unstable and uncertain.

(c) The task of creating interprovincial trade and binding together our Provinces by ties of interest as well as of sentiment is rendered difficult or impossible by these proposals.

(d) These proposals cannot logically stop at the point now fixed. The farmers and particularly the interests injuriously affected will justly claim that if agriculture can stand free trade, manufacturers must be prepared to do the same.

(e) Thus the logical conclusion of such a policy is complete free trade and a Washington made tariff. From an economic standpoint this may be of advantage; from a national standpoint it is suicide.

(f) If the proposed policy should not reach its logical conclusion it will create friction, irritation and unfriendly relations between the two countries. That has been the experience in South Africa.

(g) Tariffs prepared in secret by diplomatic [sic] methods are unsatisfactory because their authors cannot possibly understand all their consequences, and as no amendment can be made the most potent and well founded remonstrance or protest is useless.

(h) Thus fixed tariffs created by diplomatic understanding have always proved unstable. Lord Selburne in a very able memorandum demonstrated that from experience of South Africa. I intend to quote from his memorandum when I next speak. See my remarks on page 4142 unrevised Hansard, enclosed you by this mail. The probable unstability is an exceedingly grave danger from a economic standpoint. After five years of reciprocity we may have to begin where we started thirty years ago.

(i) I appreciate the fact that the United States can lower its tariff and greatly affect our economic and possibly our national future. That is a danger always present but from which we have been happily relieved by the attitude of the United States in the past. While recognizing their power and influence in that regard it would be madness to combine with them and pay them for exercising it to their own advantage.

This memorandum has been very hastily dictated on the spur of the moment and no doubt is open to forcible criticism. However, it is the best that I can give you and I shall be glad to have your views with regard to it.

Believe me,

Yours faithfully,

Public Archives of Canada, *Robert Borden Papers,* OC 27A, J. D. Reid to Borden, April 19, 1911.

The Ontario Organization

April 19, 1911

Confidential

Memo. for Mr. Borden

In accordance with your wishes we visited Toronto on Tuesday last. Had a meeting with Mr. Kemp, Mr. Cochrane and Mr. Carstairs, all present together and discussed the Ontario situation. Hon. Mr. Hanna was not in the city. Mr. E. N. Smith telephoned he could not be present.

1. We took up the different groups as has been before you, and each person agreed to undertake and look after the constituencies as mentioned therein, to arrange for proper candidates and any other necessary organization.

To sum up the whole Province as we all agreed in case an election were brought on before redistribution we came to following conclusion, viz:—

At present we have fifty seats held by Conservatives. Of these we consider that 36 were absolutely sure of returning Conservatives. These seats were Dundas, Grenville, Leeds, Frontenac, East Hastings, West Hastings, East Peterboro, North Renfrew, South Lanark, Carleton, North Ontario, Durham, Victoria & Haliburton, South York, Centre Toronto, East Toronto, North Toronto, South Toronto, West Toronto, Peel, South Simcoe, Dufferin, East Hamilton, West Hamilton, Lincoln, Haldimand, Norfolk, East Elgin, West Elgin, East Middlesex, East Lambton, East Grey, South Waterloo, London, Parry Sound and Muskoka.

The remaining fourteen seats we believe the Liberals will make a vicious attack on as the majorities were not large. They are South Bruce, East Huron, West Huron, North Grey, North Essex, West Algoma, East Algoma, Nipissing, Centre York, Halton, Lennox & Addington, East Northumberland, North Lanark and North Simcoe.

However we firmly believe that the present representatives in every case but four are sure of being elected, and we only concede four seats we are likely to have a chance of defeat.

In the matter of the Liberal representatives they now hold 36 seats. We concede to 14 of them, seats we cannot win. They are Ottawa, Russell, Prescott, Kingston, North York, East Kent, West Lambton, South Essex, Brantford, Welland, South Huron, North Waterloo, South Wellington.

The remaining 22 seats we believe a vicious attack should be made on them and we believe nearly all of them should be won. They are North Middlesex, North Bruce, South Grey, South Perth, North Perth, North Wellington, West Kent, West Middlesex, South Oxford, Prince Edward, Glengarry, Stormont, Brockville, West Northumberland, West Peterboro, South Renfrew, South Ontario, Thunder Bay, East Simcoe, Wentworth, Brant, North Oxford. Every effort will be made at once to further the getting out of candidates and furthering any more organization in these 22 counties than may now be going on.

In order that you may understand the position in these 22 Liberal constituencies which we must attack we give you the following information.

West Middlesex   Jas Cobban has been already nominated and a good man.

North Middlesex   No one chosen, but Leo Stanley has agreed to run when time comes. Best available man.

North Oxford   John Shaw could win. He is manager of a furniture co. and will run if the President of the Company who lives in Hamilton will allow him.

South Oxford   Dr. Coleridge has already been nominated. A good man. Will win.

Brant   J. W. Fisher M.P.P. can win and it is practically understood he will run.

Brantford   Harris, Liberal. Nothing done yet on Conservative side.

Welland   Same as Brantford.

North Perth   Hugh Morphy, a good man will be nominated in June.

South Perth   Dr. Steele, a good man, will be nominated in June.

North Wellington   W. A. Clark has been nominated, a good man.

North Waterloo   Dr. Lavkner, M.P.P. it is thought could win, but hard to make any arrangements yet in this county.

South Wellington   No man in sight yet. Difficult to get a man. An outsider suggested.

East Simcoe   Unless Wm. Bennett retires he will be the candidate and the feeling is he cannot win.

Thunder Bay & Rainy River   No man chosen. If when dissolution takes place it is thought Mr. Carrick M.P.P. can win if he will run. If not only a candidate to prevent acclamation will be put up.

West Lambton   Unless Mr. Hanna urges Mr. Kittermaster to run he will not, then LeSuer will run and we lose.

South Huron   No man in sight.

North Bruce   Hugh Clark M.P.P. has agreed to run and will win.

South Grey   R. J. Ball has been nominated and a good man. Should win.

South Essex   Dr. Fred Parke has been nominated.

West Kent   Neil Watson is the best man and would run if Clements were out of the way, but he will not put up any fight to get him out of the way. We will not win this riding if Clements does not back down.

East Kent   No one in sight yet.

Wentworth   If E. D. Smith refuses then Cel. Graften or Gordon Wilson M.P.P. will be the man.

Brockville   We have four good men ready to run. The best one will be chosen at the proper time.

We agreed to meet at any time in the future or from time to time and consider the situation as it may be when we meet.

University of New Brunswick Library, *O. S. Crockett Papers*, Oswald Crockett to William Price, May 10, 1911.

The New Brunswick Organization

Fredericton, N.B.
May 10, 1911

Confidential

Dear Mr. Price:—

Pursuant to your request for a report upon the situation and prospects in the different constituencies of New Brunswick we submit the following:—

This Province has 13 seats in the present Parliament, viz,—Restigouche, Gloucester, Northumberland, Kent, Westmorland, which may be spoken of as the north shore group; Victoria (consisting of the two Counties of Madawaska and Victoria), Carleton, York, Queens-Sunbury, and Kings-Albert, which may be spoken of as the St. John River group; the two St. John seats—the City of St. John and the City and County of St. John and Charlotte in the southern corner and bordering upon the State of Maine. Of these seats our Party hold at present only 2, viz,—St. John City and York, the other 11 being held by Liberals. . . .

It is pretty certain that the Province will lose at least one seat by the coming re-distribution, and if the election is deferred until after the re-distribution is made there will be but 12 seats. The general expectation is that Restigouche will disappear as a constituency and be joined with Madawaska County and that Victoria County, which with the County of Madawaska forms the present constituency of Victoria, will be joined to the County of Carleton. It is proposed now to take up the organization of the Province upon this basis.

Of these 12 constituencies 3 of them, viz,—Kent, Gloucester and Restigouche-Madawaska, will be swung by the French Acadian vote which numbers over 75 in each one of them. About half the population of Westmorland County is also French Acadian and a large proportion of the population of Northumberland County.

In all of these constituencies the Liberals owe their successes in the last two general elections at least to the effect of the Laurier cry upon the French Acadian voters. The campaign of Mr. Bourassa during the past year or two is said to have taken hold of many Acadians in this Province and to have destroyed to a large extent the confidence previously felt in Sir Wilfrid, so that we believe that in the coming election with a proper campaign, a much larger Acadian vote can be polled for Conservative candidates in all of the Acadian constituencies than at any time since 1896.

It has been suggested that if we could get a prominent Acadian leader recognized as such by the Acadian population of the whole Province to stand as a candidate in one of the Acadian constituencies the effect would be to almost completely nullify the influence of the Laurier cry. With this in view and recognizing such a one in the person of Hon. Judge Landry, of the Supreme Court Bench, Mr. Crockett during the Easter adjournment talked the matter over with His Honor and feels convinced from the interview he had with him that if the Party is prepared to provide sufficient means to properly organize the Province and especially the Acadian constituencies and arrange for the general circulation of at least one of the French Acadian Journals published in this Province in the Acadian constituencies, Judge Landry can be prevailed upon to enter the field as a candidate in Westmorland and throw himself into the fight in the other constituencies named. If he does so we are convinced that Westmorland, Kent and Restigouche-Madawaska can be carried for the Party and probably Gloucester and that his candidature would also affect many Acadian votes in Northumberland County.

We may say that Judge Landry occupies a unique position among the Acadian people of the Maritime Provinces. He is unquestionably the foremost man of the race and is regarded by the Acadians of the three Provinces with the most implicit confidence. He has now been 18 years on the Supreme Court Bench and is entitled to retire with a superannuation allowance. If he is to be got into the fight it is necessary that arrangements should be made for our campaign without delay, as once he makes up his mind in the matter he wants to retire from the Bench as soon as possible before the active campaign begins. We may say that we consider his candidature the key to the situation in all of the constituencies included in the north shore group with perhaps the exception of Northumberland County. Without him we might possibly carry Kent County with Mr. Robideaux, a bright young Acadian lawyer, as our candidate. . . .

With reference to Northumberland we had an interview with Mr. Butler, the Secretary of the Liberal Conservative Association of the County, during the Easter recess. Mr. Butler stated that he had spoken to Mr. Max Aitken, M.P. when the latter was in Newcastle on his return from England with a view to his accepting nomination for the County and that he was encouraged to believe that Mr. Aitken would entertain the proposal. We may say that a rather awkward situation exists in this County at the present time and has existed since the last federal election. Hon. Donald Morrison, who was elected in the general provincial election of March 1908, as one of the four representatives of the County, and who afterwards became speaker of the Legislature, was nominated by a Conservative Convention as the candidate for the House of Commons. He resigned the speakership and his seat in the House and contested the election. Mr. James Robinson, Ex-M.P. had aspired to the nomination and after the selection of Mr. Morrison is claimed by our Party friends in the County to have done all that he could to defeat Mr. Morrison. Hon. John Morrissy, Chief Commissioner of Public Works in the New Brunswick Government, who is a Liberal, also supported Mr. Loggie and is said to have used the patronage of the Provincial Government in Mr. Loggie's behalf. After the federal election a Provincial by-election was necessary to fill the vacancy in the Provincial House caused by Mr. Morrison's resignation. The Conservative Party of the County held a Convention to nominate, and did nominate, a candidate as a supporter of the Hazen Government. A Liberal Convention was called at the instance of the leader of the opposition, Hon. J. W. Robinson, to nominate a Liberal candidate. Mr. John Burchill was nominated and Mr. Morrissy supported him as a Liberal and opposed the nominee of the Conservative Convention. Mr. Burchill was elected by a small majority and is now opposing the Provincial Government of which Mr. Morrissy is still a member. We mention these unpleasant facts to give you an idea of the mix-up which exists in this constituency. Mr. Butler's opinion was that there was no man in the constituency who could be nominated who would unite the factions which existed but that all would unite upon Mr. Aitken and that he and he alone could carry the Country for the Party.

With respect to the St. John River Counties, we are in hopes that the Provincial Government will perfect arrangements to have the St. John River Railway, which extends from Victoria County down the river to the City of St. John, under construction before Fall. If the Government succeeds in this it will have a considerable effect in Victoria-Carleton, York, Queens-Sunbury and Kings-Albert and ought to insure for us all four of the above named Counties.

In any event we believe that Carleton-Victoria can be carried if proper support is given the Party there. It has been practically settled that Mr. B. Frank Smith, a Merchant of Florenceville, who opposed Mr. Carvell in 1905, will be the candidate. He is a vigorous, energetic man of marked ability and a splendid platform speaker and is very popular, and in addition to this has back of him perhaps the best organized and most enthusiastic Party in any County in the Province. But for the extraordinary means which were used against him in 1905 he would undoubtedly have been elected then.

York is generally considered safe for the Party, though no doubt a great effort will be made again to capture the seat.

In Queens-Sunbury Col. McLean has been busy since the election of 1905 and has undoubtedly strengthened himself very materially by the extraordinary attention which he has paid to the constituency. The constituency, however, is normally Conservative and political lines are drawn very tightly. While it is a hard seat to win we believe that with the right candidate and with effective organization and systematic work the seat might be captured. It was undoubtedly lost the last time through inefficient organization on our part. We discussed the Queens-Sunbury situation with Premier Hazen, who represents the County of Sunbury in the Provincial Legislature, and with the other three representatives of the united Counties in the local House. They were all of the opinion that Dr. Caswell of Gagetown would be the strongest candidate and could win if properly supported.

In Kings-Albert it seems to be taken for granted that Mr. G. W. Fowler, Ex-M.P. will be the candidate, though he has recently stated he will not run. If he decides not to run the names of two or three other strong men have been considered by the leaders in the County, and our friends there claim that any one of them can win.

St. John City and St. John City and County—This is the home of the Minister of Public Works who will, no doubt, strain every nerve to carry both seats. It is very important that every possible effort be made to defeat his purpose. The Party in St. John is very strong and has stuck together under the most adverse circumstances. The result here will depend to a considerable extent upon whether or not the people feel that the Government will be defeated. If the people believe that our Party will win in the country generally the prestige of the Minister himself will

not save him. At the last election not-
withstanding we were without any press
support whatever, our Party succeeded in
carrying the City seat and keeping the
Minister's majority down to nearly 400.
The Minister has since provided immense
expenditures for the port of St. John, but
we believe that the Liberals have lost
ground as a result of the reciprocity pact,
which is particularly unpopular in St.
John and there is no doubt that with
proper support we can do as well in the
coming election as in 1908.

Charlotte—We cannot yet state definitely who will be the candidate. Mr.
G. W. Ganong, Ex-M.P. is generally
spoken of and would admittedly make
the strongest run. It is expected that
within a week or two there will be a
caucus of leading men of the Party to
take up the organization of the County
and that by this time there will be some
statement from Mr. Ganong as to whether
he will undertake the fight or not. If he
does not the nomination will probably go
to either George J. Clarke, speaker of the
Legislature, or to Mr. Frank Murchie,
both of whom are influential men.

We believe that we can safely say
that the reciprocity issue will strengthen
us in all of the New Brunswick constituencies with the possible exception of
Charlotte, where we are informed the
fishermen are favourable to the pact and
that a number of farmers having pulp
wood to sell to a mill on the American
side of the line will be influenced against
us.

You will see from the above that if
Judge Landry and Mr. Aitken consent
to stand as candidates in Westmorland
and Northumberland there is not one of
the 5 seats in the north shore group that
should not be carried for the Party. If
Judge Landry will not stand we fear we

will have to count Westmorland and
Restigouche-Madawaska as Liberal constituencies with a hard prospect for us in
Gloucester and a good fighting chance in
Kent, while Northumberland as stated
above, depends entirely upon the candidature of Mr. Aitken. If he runs we will
win. If he does not we will not. A
vigorous fight must be made in the four
river Counties and in the City and City
and County of St. John and in the County
of Charlotte as we think there is not one
of them which cannot be carried if the
Party goes into the contest with the determination to win.

This Province, we regret to say, has
been shamefully corrupted in past elections. We have stated above the odds
which the Conservatives had against them
in the election of 1908 and we believe
that the same means will be employed by
the Liberals to at least as great and probably greater an extent in the coming fight
and that to cope successfully with them in
the matter of systematic organization and
effective campaign work there should be
a fund of at least $150,000 for these 12
seats.

We believe furthermore that in New
Brunswick as in the other Provinces of
the Dominion, no time should be lost by
the party in perfecting its organization in
the various constituencies and that the
result of the election will largely depend
upon what is accomplished during the
present summer in this direction, and in
the influencing of public opinion on the
reciprocity question by a systematic circulation of literature and the holding of
public meetings in the rural districts. The
provision of a fund of say $10,000 at the
present time for these purposes would we
believe have more effect than the expenditure of four or five times that sum when
the fight is actually on. These things can-

not be accomplished in New Brunswick unless a fund is provided for the purpose. Our Party here is enthusiastic but unfortunately we have not very many rich men among them and if we were to start by passing the hat around to defray organization expenses we fear it would have a serious effect in destroying the confidence which now exists that the party at the present time has the backing that will insure success.

Yours respectfully,

Robert Borden in *The Daily Mail and Empire,* (Toronto), August 15, 1911.

An Appeal to the People

To the People of Canada:—

When Parliament was suddenly dissolved on the 29th of July, I issued a short statement touching the circumstances under which that dissolution had taken place. It now becomes my duty to indicate the issues which present themselves for decision.

In resisting the Government's proposal for reciprocal trade with the United States, we have been met with the cry that the majority must rule. Under our system of Government the minority in Parliament is in some sense the guardian of the people's rights. It is clear that the late Parliament never received any mandate to surrender to the United States the complete fiscal autonomy with which Great Britain endowed this Dominion, a consequence which follows from the reciprocity compact. With a firm heart we have taken the stand that the people and not a temporary Parliamentary majority shall give the answer which must determine the future destiny of the Dominion and of this empire. That position needs no apology and we offer none.

Nearly 50 years ago, Canada began her work of nation building in the face of difficulties which seemed insurmountable, but which did not daunt her spirit. On the West she flung her boundaries to the far Pacific and on the north beyond the Arctic Circle. She undertook the wardenship and development of a territory greater in area than the continent of Europe. She did not shrink from holding the border for nearly 4,000 miles along the northern frontier of one of the most powerful and aggressive nations of the modern world. Her faith and her courage were unsurpassed, but not greater than the success that has attended her endeavors. In the midst of that success, the Government, without public consideration or discussion, have undertaken to commit the country to a treaty which completely alters the conditions and the policy under which our country has grown so rapidly and so surely to its present splendid stature.

THE PACT ARRANGED

The objections to that compact are profound and abiding. They may be thus summarized:—

It tends to segregate and separate the provinces of Canada which confederation aimed to unite, and it thus destroys the very meaning of our confederation.

It shatters the ideal and the hope of reciprocity within the Empire. The President of the United States has avowed that the main purpose with which he sought the treaty was to prevent consolidation of the British Empire.

It brings Canada to the parting of the ways, turns her from the path of Canadian unity and British connection and leads her along the way to Washington.

It reverses the policy of Canadian nationhood, which sought to bring together the provinces of Canada by intercourse and commerce over East and West lines of transportation; and it stultifies the unexampled sacrifices of half a century which the Canadian people have cheerfully made for that high purpose.

It is a direct and serious menace to our internal lines of water communication and to our ocean shipping, as well as to our Canadian Atlantic ports, that have been constructed and equipped at such enormous cost to the country.

It makes Canada a commercial appanage of the United States, and virtually surrenders the control of her destinies.

It interlocks our finance system with that of the United States, and fetters the power of Parliament to alter our tariff according to the just requirements of our people.

Its duration is nominally within the control of either country, but actually within that of the United States alone. The conditions of its abrogation would involve so many delicate and difficult international considerations that the stronger party would eventually dictate the terms.

Its tendency and aim are complete commercial union between the two countries, to the exclusion of the rest of the Empire.

OPENS OUR MARKETS

It opens to the United States our home market, which consumes 80 per cent. of our animal and agricultural product. It also has the effect of opening that same market to the twelve foreign countries and to all the British possessions, for which we obtain no reciprocal or compensating advantage. Sir Wilfrid Laurier is sending to these foreign nations a polite invitation to forego and renounce this right to enter our markets. The suggestion that they are likely to be thus considerate and unselfish is so foolish that it requires no answer.

It abandons the policy of improved trade relations with the British people, our best customers, and centres our hopes on the American people, our strongest competitors in the markets of the world.

It makes an absurd pretence of bringing relief to the farmer by exposing him to the competition of the world in everything that he sells, and by continuing the existing burden of taxation on everything that he buys.

It threatens the existence of our fishing bounties, and takes away our power to give such encouragement to any industry affected by the agreement.

It will destroy the distinctive character and reputation of our staple products, which will henceforth be merged in those of the United States, and will be known as American rather than Canadian products.

It exposes our natural resources to the depredations of the gigantic trusts, which have already secured control of those of the United States.

It will assist those trusts to exercise an undue influence and pressure upon Provincial Governments for the purpose of forcing them to abandon the wise policy of conserving our natural resources and of converting them into finished commodities by the labor of our own people.

It will give to American trusts a power, an influence, and a control in this country equal to that which has been exercised so remorselessly and unsparingly in the United States.

It will for the most part reduce the

prices which our producers will receive for their output, while the control of the trusts will prevent any reduction to the consumer.

It will discourage the higher and more progressive methods of agriculture by which the product of the farm is turned out in finished form, and the fertility of the soil maintained and preserved.

It will encourage the export of our raw materials and unfinished products for manufacture abroad instead of at home.

It will establish conditions and relations, from which it will be extremely difficult and even impossible to retreat except with the consent of the United States, or under terms dictated by her.

And finally, it is at the best a rash and perilous experiment, inconsiderately and unwarrantably undertaken, in a period of unequaled development and prosperity after Canada had long since outgrown the conditions under which such a policy was once thought desirable.

THE PRIME MINISTER'S MANIFESTO

The address of the Prime Minister may fairly be taken as indicating the position of the Government party in this contest. Let me examine it briefly.

He attempts to represent the opponents of the treaty as casting doubt upon the loyalty of the Canadian people. There is no foundation for such an insinuation. The loyalty of the Canadian people is undoubted. But no people can escape the consequences of their own acts, and if Canada places itself under the commercial control of the United States its political importance if retained will be a shadow and not a substantial reality.

Three chief contentions are put forward by the Prime Minister. He says, 'At all times during the last forty years it has been the constant effort of all political parties in Canada to make with the United States an arrangement for the free exchange of natural products between the two countries.'

I absolutely deny this proposition. It has been repeatedly shown, both in Parliament and on the platform, that the Prime Minister by his own utterances during the last ten years has repudiated and denied such a policy. The repetition of this statement in his election manifesto is made with cynical disregard for the known facts.

One quotation from his utterances will suffice:—

'There was a time when we wanted reciprocity with the United States, but our efforts and our offers were put aside. We have said good-bye to that trade, and we now put all our hopes upon the British trade.' (Imperial Conference, May, 1907.)

The Prime Minister next refers to the supposed advantages of the 'free American market.' In Parliament we repeatedly demanded from the advocates of the treaty a detailed and systematic statement of these advantages covering the whole agricultural, industrial and commercial situation in Canada; but our demand was not complied with. The main facts have, however, been made clear in other ways. Looking at the result of the whole discussion, I assert that the Government and its friends have totally failed to make out a case. The disadvantages of opening up our farmers' markets to the United States, to the whole British Empire, and to twelve other countries, far outweighs any possible advantages to accrue from allowing free entry of our farm products to the United States.

FIRST STEP TOWARDS ANNEXATION

Lastly, the Prime Minister's endeavors to rebut the argument that the reciprocity treaty will lead to annexation. Whether it will do so or not no man can tell. But it is beyond the possibility of doubt that the leading public men of the United States, its press and the bulk of its people believe that it will so result and support it mainly for that reason. I could fill pages with quotations in proof of this assertion if it were necessary. The plain fact is that in entering upon this treaty the people of the United States believe that they are accomplishing the first step towards annexation. My position is that we cannot safely ignore the pronounced views of the other party to the compact, and that sooner or later we shall have to reckon with them. Surely this is a view which will commend itself to all reasonable and thoughtful citizens.

But there are issues which also merit attention. The Government has twice refused any investigation of the expenditure on the National Transcontinental Railway, which is assuming startling proportions. This refusal has been persisted in, although outrageous misappropriation of public money has been charged by engineers of high position on the works.

Shortly after the election of 1908 the Prime Minister was invited by the leading Liberal journals throughout the country to clean the Augean stables of certain great spending departments. The cleansing process has not commenced. Scandal after scandal was unearthed in the last two weeks of the recent session, and not a tenth has yet been told.

Since the last general election the Government has entered upon a new line of policy in regard to naval affairs, which is of far-reaching importance. The policy adopted was not debated before the people during that election, and it bears all the earmarks of a hasty and ill-considered scheme. In my judgment, our duty to the Empire cannot be properly or effectively fulfilled by such a measure. I hold that the plan of the Government contemplates the creation of a naval force that will be absolutely useless in time of war, and therefore of no practical benefit to Canada or to the Empire. It will cost immense sums of money to build, equip and maintain. It will probably result in time of war in the useless sacrifice of many valuable lives, and it will not add an iota to the fighting strength of the Empire. The more it is considered, the more does it become evident that the whole naval plan of the Government is an unfortunate blunder.

The remarkable inefficiency and lack of business capacity manifested by the Government in connection with the Quebec bridge and other great public undertakings should also receive the grave consideration of the electorate.

The Liberal-Conservative party gives its pledge to carry out the following policy if returned to power:

(1) A thorough reorganization of the method by which public expenditure is supervised. The increase in what is known as ordinary controllable expenditure from $21,500,000 in 1896 to nearly $74,000,000 in 1911 is proof of extravagance beyond any possible denial.

(2) The granting of their natural resources to the Prairie Provinces.

(3) The construction of the Hudson Bay Railway and its operation by independent commission.

(4) The control and operation by the State of the terminal elevators.

(5) The necessary encouragement

for establishing and carrying on the chilled meat industry.

(6) The establishment of a permanent tariff commission.

(7) The granting of substantial assistance towards the improvement of our public highways.

(8) The extension of free rural mail delivery.

(9) The extension of civil service reform.

(10) The granting of liberal assistance to the provinces for the purpose of supplementing and extending the work of agricultural education and for the improvement of agriculture.

And lastly, we pledge ourselves to a course of policy and administration which will maintain independent and unimpaired the control of our own affairs by the Parliament of Canada; a policy which, while affording no just cause of complaint to any foreign nation will find its highest ideal in the autonomous development of Canada as a nation within the British Empire.

THE ISSUE

In the past we have made great sacrifices to further our national ideals. We are now face to face with a misguided attempt to throw away the result of these sacrifices.

The true issue is this. Shall we continue in the course which has led us to our present enviable position of prosperity and national development, or shall we at the moment of greatest success and achievement, lose heart and abandon the fight for national existence?

Upon this momentous issue, I appeal to the people with the utmost confidence and in the strong belief that their verdict will be for the unity and not for the disintegration of Canada; for the strengthening and not the loosening of the ties which bind this Dominion to the British Empire.

R. P. Roblin, *The Winnipeg Telegram*,
August 28, 1911.

The Campaign in Manitoba

[Beausejour, 26 August, 1911]
"I notice that Sir Wilfrid and those
who stand for him in the province of
Manitoba, undertake to say that the only
issue that the people of this province
have to consider in this election is
whether the reciprocity pact, as made
between the United States and the government of Canada, shall become law or not.
I can understand both Sir Wilfrid and his
friends in Manitoba desiring that no other
issue shall be discussed by the people of
this province. I propose, however, that
there shall be other issues—that all matters and things pertaining to the welfare
and interests of the people of Canada, as
well as the people of Manitoba, in particular, shall be submitted to the electorate
on the 21st.

SIR WILFRID AND MANITOBA

"As an evidence that Sir Wilfrid
trembles in his boots at this moment for
fear his attitude, unaccountable, unreasonable, unjust, unpatriotic, unstatesmanlike

in so far as the province of Manitoba and
her relation to the Dominion of Canada is
concerned will be remembered against
him, he is undertaking to hedge, to
qualify, to make a promise, so it is alleged, that justice will be done us, even
though his hand be unwilling and his
heart embittered as of old against us. I do
not wish to question the honesty, the
sincerity, or the veracity of Premier Sifton of Alberta, who came to the city of
Winnipeg and there announced that he
and Premier Scott had arranged the basis
of settlement for Alberta, Saskatchewan
and Manitoba, by which the rights of
Manitoba that have been withheld from
us for so many years by Sir Wilfrid Laurier, were at last to be conceded.
"I have no doubt Mr. Sifton believed
what he said, but I do have doubts, and
I express them as the first minister of
Manitoba, in as strong a manner as is
possible, in any statement that Mr. Sifton
or any one else attempts to make on behalf of Sir Wilfrid Laurier, that he does
propose to deal fairly with the people of
Manitoba after the general election.

HAS MADE NO OFFICIAL STATEMENT

"Strange indeed is the attitude of Sir
Wilfrid if he is proposing to do what a
statesman and a patriot is supposed to
do, when he undertakes to speak through
the mouth of a stranger in so far as Manitoba is concerned, to tell the people of
Manitoba what he is going to do for them.
I declare tonight that not one line or one
word has been received or said to myself
or any member of the government of
Manitoba by Sir Wilfrid or anyone officially authorized by him, that any such
action will be taken. On the contrary, I
declare to the people of Manitoba that in
the last formal interview that I had with

the first minister of Canada and the Hon. Mr. Fielding, that Sir Wilfrid refused absolutely to consider the request of the legislature of Manitoba that she should have equality with either Alberta and Saskatchewan or the other provinces of confederation.

"This is the only official statement, this is the only record, this is the only thing on which to base a statement, and I, therefore, dismiss absolutely and without qualification Mr. Sifton's statement that he was authorized by Sir Wilfrid to promise the people of Manitoba that their claims for equality would be considered.

NOT BOUND IN ANY WAY

"Sir Wilfrid is not bound by what Premier Sifton says or does not say; he is only bound by what he said officially to the representatives of the province of Manitoba last winter in Ottawa, and I appeal to the people of Manitoba at this time to remember, that every vote that is polled for the Laurier candidate in the approaching elections is a vote polled for a subordinate position for this province in confederation; every vote polled for the Laurier candidate is a declaration on the part of the voter that he is willing to admit that he is not as good a citizen and is not entitled to the same consideration as a voter in Alberta or Saskatchewan, or Quebec. In other words, every vote polled for the Laurier candidate is a vote polled to shackle Manitoba; to cripple her enterprise, to handicap her future, to prevent the widening of her horizon and give her that place in the confederation of Canada that she should occupy by virtue of the industry, enterprise and patriotism of her people.

MR. BORDEN'S PROMISE

"On the other hand, we have the votes and pledges, and the assurances of the Conservative party from R. L. Borden down to the most humble member, that the attitude of Sir Wilfrid towards Manitoba has not only been arbitrary but positively cruel, and a menace to the permanence and solidarity of confederation. Further, that they will at the earliest possible moment give Manitoba justice, fair play, and equality with the other sisters of confederation. Now, this is a more important matter than some people may at the moment be able to recognize, and I want to say with a full knowledge of the facts, owing to the circumscribed condition such as Sir Wilfrid insists shall be created for us—that it will mean Manitoba will for all time, if Sir Wilfrid is returned to power, and have his way, make us not only the weakest member of confederation, the least influential, but will prevent us from that agricultural, educational, financial and industrial expansion that our geographical position and natural conditions warrant.

WRONGS MUST BE RIGHTED

"I appeal to my fellow countrymen not to be deceived by the soothsayer; I appeal to my fellow citizens not to be deceived by the man who has been false to his promises and who has shown by act and word his embittered feeling against us, but to stand for equality, insist upon our position as a member of confederation being equal to the others, and the only way to do this is to vote against his candidates—elect men pledged to support the leader and party who know that we have been wronged and are ready to redress that wrong. I shall not fail to raise my voice in warning to you as well as plead for my province upon every platform that I can reach, in order that this great wrong that has been done us for no reason other than personal enmity so far as I can see, may be discontinued, and that we may have our fetters broken, we may have the handicap removed, and that we may enjoy the same liberties and have the same advantages as are enjoyed by the other provinces of Canada. . . .

THE RECIPROCITY QUESTION

"I am not only willing but anxious and pleased to meet those who wish to discuss the reciprocity question, and to analyze it in its every feature, and ascertain just what it means to Manitoba as a province and to Canada as a whole. . . .

. . . Reciprocity is urged by certain people on the ground that it will not only bring us material advantage but that it will destroy and break down what they call the moneyed classes, the manufacturers.

DISHONEST AND UNFAIR

"Now, a more unfair, dishonest and absolutely untrue statement never was uttered by the most unscrupulous ward politician. I have before me a copy of the agreement. Every item is dealt with, and I challenge any man to take this agreement as published in the Grain Growers' Guide, and I have taken a copy of that sheet because of its attitude on this question, knowing that it would present the case as strongly as it could for the parties who talk as I have indicated. I say I challenge you to take that agreement and show me where one single protected interest in Canada has been attacked to a point that amounts to anything material.

They have reduced the duty on certain agricultural implements 2½ per cent., and on certain other things slightly, but of a character that does not affect the general national policy principle as crystallized into legislation in 1879 and fostered and perpetuated by Sir Wilfrid Laurier down to the present moment. The fact that they resort to these untrue statements is an evidence that they realize they have no case in so far as the merits of their own side of the argument is concerned, and they endeavor to create a feeling of falsehood against the class, who are absolutely secure and uninjured in the agreement.

PROTECTED INTERESTS

"Now, what are the great interests of Canada that are protected? Are they not the cotton, the sugar, the woollen, the iron, the steel, the brass, boots and shoes and the hundred and one manufacturing concerns that have been built up under the national policy, supplying to the people of Canada, articles that are required. Now take this list and look at it and point out to me one single industry that has been attacked in a way that is going to materially injure it. Let us take agricultural implements, the largest industrial concern in Canada. Is it attacked? Two and a half dollars have been taken off the duty of a binder valued at $100.00. Does the president and manager of the largest concern in Canada think and feel that he is injured? Not at all. Lyman M. Jones, who lived in Winnipeg many years, is the head of the Massey-Harris concern at Toronto. The Laurier government recommended him for knighthood and he was made Sir Melville Jones while I was in the city of London within the last two months. Why did they do that? Because they recognized that in Sir Melville Jones they would have one of the strongest bulwarks of defence in the reciprocity pact we have before us tonight for consideration, and they induced the King to honor him with a knighthood. He is, therefore, found battling for reciprocity as embodied in this proposition.

THE REDUCTION FALLACIOUS

"Now, let me illustrate what I mean when I say that the 2½ per cent. duty on binders and mowers amounts to nothing. The Hon. Mr. Paterson, the man who assisted Mr. Fielding in making this agreement, as minister of customs, has taken unto himself the power to say upon what sum you shall pay irrespective and independent of what you actually paid. In other words the Hon. Mr. Paterson says to me, if I buy a binder at Chicago for $80 when I get to Winnipeg with it he says you have got to pay duty on $100, although I have only paid $80. This is a concrete illustration and contrary in my opinion to law, but it shows you all Mr. Paterson has to do to help Sir Wilfrid Laurier, Sir Melville, and the agricultural people out is to raise the agricultural implement valuation $12.00 to make good the reduction of 2½ per cent. That is the kind of man we have to deal with, and I tell you farmers you do not want to be deceived by any men or organisation who have undertaken to deliver the farmers vote to Sir Wilfrid. . . .

INJURIES PACT WILL BRING

"Manitoba is an agricultural province. The sources of wealth to the people are confined almost exclusively to the soil. There are, however, many adjuncts to agriculture—grain growing is only one of the many sources that the occupant of the soil has for a material reward.

HORSE BREEDING

"In this province the legislature, the department of agriculture, and the Horse Breeders' association have for years been striving to raise the standard of horses grown in Manitoba. We are proud of the results of our labors. The visitor to any of the exhibitions held in the province is filled with wonder and admiration at the number and quality of our horses. We have encouraged them because the market for them was at our door. The demand was, and always has been, largely in excess of our supply, and a good horse weighing 1,600 lbs today as grown in Manitoba is worth anything from $300 to $350. One reason why we have been able to make the progress is because there was a 25 per cent. duty against horses brought from the United States where they were grown with less regard to quality than they were in our province.

"A number of years ago hundreds and thousands of horses were driven in from Montana and the States to the south of us and passed the customs on a valuation of from $15 to $30 each, a price necessarily that injured our horse industry. Therefore, the efforts of the various organizations of Manitoba, nobly assisted by Dr. Rutherford, the Dominion veterinary, the customs law was changed, and these cheap horses were largely prevented from coming in by conditions that the government made, that they could not profitably comply with. Therefore, in the last few years the remarkable progress that I have indicated. Even with the elimination of these cheap horses, diseased as they were in many cases, with glanders, that was scattered broadcast over our province, costing tens of thousands of dollars every year in the destruction of animals. We have been rapidly developing this industry, and our farmers are just beginning because it takes three or four years before you can perfect a colt for the market, to realize on their investments or their enterprise in this connection. At the present time even with 25 per cent. duty or $50 added and the freight from St. Paul or Iowa, whatever the point of shipment, car load after car load of horses are still being brought into the city of Winnipeg and sold every week in competition with those grown by our farmers.

"Now, with this pact in effect, down go the barriers that the government raised unquestionably in the interests of the industry a few years ago against the importation of cheap stock, off goes the duty of $50 to $75 on each horse, and our farmers have got to compete with this cheap and indifferent class of horses grown on the plains of Montana, which will make his investments and his enterprise if not unprofitable, will certainly be most discouraging. Now, why should we do that? Why should our farmers give up a market that will take all they have with this advantage and give it to a foreign nation. What do you get in return for it? I ask the advocates of reciprocity to tell me what they are going to give you farmers in return for this great loss. My answer is they get nothing whatever.

THE SHEEP INDUSTRY

"Take another article, sheep and lambs, a most important subsidiary to the farm, and I find, what? That a large firm of dealers in the city of Winnipeg only last week bought in the city of St. Paul 408 head of sheep for which they paid $3.60 per hundred pounds on cars in St. Paul. These sheep were shipped from the ranches in Montana and from the point of shipment—from Glasgow to St. Paul —plus commission and weighing charges deducted from the price named, it nets the farmer or grower on the Montana ranches $3.04 per hundred. At the same time I find the same firm buying a car load of sheep at Crane Lake, Saskatchewan, and I can give you the name of the man from whom they were purchased, and they paid $5 per hundred pounds to the grower of these sheep for the car load. In other words the farmer of the northwest received nearly $2 per hundred lbs. more for his sheep than did the man in Montana for the same article. Now, tell me if you can why the farmers of Manitoba should be asked to have the duty removed from sheep and lambs and be compelled to take $2 per hundred less for their sheep than what they are getting at the present time. This is a practical actual transaction, and is no theory, but it means plain dollars and cents to the farmers of the country, and I ask what do they get in return? They have the satisfaction of gratifying the vanity and ambition of two distinguished elderly gentlemen in the persons of Messrs. Fielding and Paterson who went to Washington and were overcome with the blandishments of Washington and signed away their financial interests as indicated in this statement.

THE PORK RAISING INDUSTRY

"I now take up hogs. What do we find in this connection. Today, according to the Winnipeg Free Press farmers hogs sell for $8.50 per hundred lbs. in the city of Winnipeg; according to the St. Paul Dispatch, the commercial journal of St.

Paul, we find that hogs sold on the same date in the city of St. Paul for from $7.10 to $7.55, or in other words in round figures we get $1 per hundred more for our hogs in Winnipeg than they do south of the line. Why should our farmers give up the dollar per hundred on their hogs in order than the United States farmers should have an opportunity to exploit our markets at their expense. Where is the honest, candid patriotic man who is loyal to his own home and family, to say nothing about the interests of his country who will have the temerity to say that it is in his interest that he should receive a small-price for his hogs in Winnipeg so that the American can have an opportunity of selling his here at a price greater than he can get at home.

OTHER FARM PRODUCTS

"Take poultry, eggs, etc. Eggs for instance. Eggs sell in the city of St. Paul at 16 cents per dozen according to the St. Paul Despatch of August 23, Here they sell for 25 cents wholesale, and if you go to buy them retail the consumer pays from 28¢ to 30¢. Why should we take off the duty on eggs and allow the American to have our poultry market and depress the price at the expense of our farmers? Is it fair that the farmer's wife and family who raise, nurse and care for the poultry should be compelled to take reduced price that reciprocity will force the farmer to take by virtue of the conditions that I have named? What farmer, if he has any regard for himself and his family can be found to vote for reciprocity in view of this fact. Last winter car load after car load, if not train load of eggs, were brought into this city from the south; the **freight** and duty were paid, and then they

were sold on the market here, our own farmers not producing enough to supply the demand, but for what they did have to sell they got the same price as the farmer south of the line, plus the duty, plus the freight, which would be from 5¢ to 7¢ a dozen. Now this is very material; it is very practical, and I think any farmers' wives and children, as I know farmers' wives and children are interested in this particular line when they are called upon to take the reduced price that reciprocity gives, will certainly have great cause for complaint. I cannot believe that any farmer will vote to thus reduce the value of the product of his own premises. The same applies to chicken, duck, and turkey, which we do not produce in quantities to supply our own home market, and which are brought in and pay a duty of 25 per cent, at the present time. Therefore, reciprocity means that every chicken in the farm yard, every duck, every goose, every turkey will be reduced in value 25 per cent, or one quarter of its total value whatever it may be. Is this not a serious question? Can the farmers afford to be carried away with the sentimental nonsense of two or three self-appointed representatives who are working for some reward in the way of political appointment on condition that they are able to deliver the votes of the farmer to Sir Wilfrid. Can they afford to vote away the value of the product of their own farms by voting for reciprocity. I certainly think not, and do not believe they will on the 21st so vote.

THE DAIRY INDUSTRIES

"Again take cream and milk, which certainly in the vicinity of cities and towns is a very important item and a source of very considerable revenue to the farmer, and we find that though so much encouragement has been given to the dairy interest that we are still unable to supply the demand and large quantities are brought in from St. Paul and Minneapolis, and pay the duty. Take for instance sour cream out of which butter is made. We find that our farmers were paid from 28 to 37¢ per lb. for butter fat, while in St. Paul it ran from 25 to 30¢ per lb., the latter being the highest. You will see, therefore, the danger there is to our dairy interest in removing the duty and allowing this in free. In Winnipeg milk sells today at 5¢ to 7¢ more per gallon than it does in the cities of Minneapolis and St. Paul. Remove the duty, take down the bars, and our farmers who rear large herds of cattle and who have been urged and persuaded and coaxed to go into this business will become discouraged, and the money they now receive for this commodity would be sent south of the line, and our dairies would languish and die. Will we support such a thing? I think not.

MARKET GARDENING

"Now let us take vegetables, and what do we find along this line? Potatoes, beets, carrots, celery, and all articles such as are grown by market gardeners—we find that in every case these articles are from 10 to 25 per cent. higher in our own province than they are in the states to the south of us, and the duties that run anywhere from 20 to 30 per cent. on these articles, which is a protection to the farmer and the market gardener, is not a barrier that prevents the importation of them even at the present time. On inquiry at one house in the city of Winnipeg whose name I can give if necessary, they told me that they had brought in this year already over 100 car loads of different kinds of vegetables such as we produce in Manitoba and are bringing them every day. Another gentleman or firm that I made inquiry of wrote me in reply to my inquiry and said on checking up his books he finds he paid over $5,000 last year for duty and freight charges on potatoes and other vegetables that he brought in from St. Paul market. Paid $5,000 in duty and freight, which would mean I suppose at least $50,000 of commodity value. Now these are only two firms out of probably 20, so I think I would be safe in saying that there are at least up to the present time 500 car loads of vegetables have been imported into Winnipeg this year, paying duties ranging as I say from 20 to 30 per cent. which goes into competition with our market gardeners. Now, what would be the condition of our market gardeners if the duty was removed and these people south of the line are permitted to ship their surplus stuff in here without duty. It would demoralise the business, it would discourage and break the heart of every struggling market gardener in Manitoba.

" 'Ah!' someone says, 'but would not those in Winnipeg who have to buy, buy cheaper?' Yes, it is true, and if the advocates of reciprocity would be honest and tell the facts, they would say that the introduction of the pact meant that everything the farmer has to sell would be reduced, and that the citizen of Winnipeg would be able to buy their chicken, their bacon, their milk, their vegetables at from 30 to 50 per cent. less than they are paying now. I would not have any quarrel with them, because they would state the truth, but my amazement is found in their dishonesty in trying to tell the farmer he is going to receive an increased price. These facts I have submitted cannot help but convince the farmer of the absolute dishonesty or ignorance, and I do not think it is the latter, of the men who are asking for the votes of the people for reciprocity on the ground that it is going to make for the material wealth of the individuals and of the nation.

WOULD DESTROY INTERPROVINCIAL TRADE

"I could go on further. Take bacon and meats of various kinds. I have a letter from one large concern doing business in the city of Winnipeg, in which he says under date of Aug. 24, that he has purchased and imported into the province of Manitoba since the 1st of April twelve carloads of what they call sweet, pickled meat, which covers bacon, lard, etc., at a cost of $46,077, and paid duty of $6,963. He says further that he also has brought from the provinces of Ontario and Quebec 41 carloads for which he paid $130,705, and he adds that if the duty on these meats were removed or partially removed, it would mean they would purchase all their requirements from the south instead of the east as at the present time. He also adds that if reciprocity had been in effect since the first of the year, he would have bought all his live hogs from the south at a saving of from $1 to $1.50 per hundred pounds. This means that our farmers would have to take that much less. The same applies to cattle and to everything in the market as well. I have gone over the various items that constitute the source of revenue to the farmer outside of cereals, and we find that as the home market is so much better than the United States market that even a madman crazed with the dope of the reciprocity quacks would not dare to do so foolish a thing in his own interest as to vote to allow all these articles named to be brought in free, getting nothing as a compensation in return.

GRAIN GROWING

"Now, as to cereals. I have not the time at my disposal today to deal with wheat, oats and barley, but I make this statement flatly, and without fear of contradiction, that within ten days after the people of Canada, have voted in favor of reciprocity, if such a calamity should overtake us, that the price of wheat at Duluth and Minneapolis will have gone down to the Port Arthur and Winnipeg price. I make that statement because I have an intimate knowledge of this grain business as a result of twenty years' experience. I further make it on the broad principle that the price of wheat in America is made on the markets of the world, and not by the manipulation of the option markets at Minneapolis or Duluth as at the present time. I know that the statement will be challenged, but I have simply to call witnesses in support of my statement, and witnesses that I am sure the advocates of reciprocity will not dare impeach, namely President Taft and James J. Hill. Both these men have made this statement, and both, as I have stated, are bound to make such a deliverance. That is not the worst of it. I make the further statement that reciprocity instead of being a benefit to the farmer in so far as the price of wheat is concerned will actually in practice result in them receiving a lower price than they do today."

The Montreal Daily Star, September 16, 1911.

Under Which Flag ?

The two flags than flank the caption of this article are twin standards of Christianity, of civilization, of progress throughout the world. Each of them is a flag of which a great people is justly proud. It is entirely true—as the advocates of Reciprocity say so frequently—that these flags stand for much the same principles, much the same ideals, much the same standards of living. Moreover, the nations which float them have much the same ambitions—both love power, prestige and prominence among the nations.

We do not print these flags in contrast to praise our own and belittle that of the United States. Our readers, who have followed the opinions we have ventured to express from time to time in these columns, know us well enough to be sure of that before we say it. We admire the American people. They have some institutions which we do not like as well as our own; but these institutions are not at all the consequences of their national character—they are the inevitable results of the stupendous and daring attempt of the founders of the American Republic to strike off at a single blow a Constitution and an entire system of government.

OUR FORM OF GOVERNMENT

Our advantage lies in the circumstances that our constitution and system of government is a growth—not a manufacture. If we had been making our own governing machinery, we might, for instance, have thought it a wise and democratic step to cause our judges to be elected. We might have argued that no stream can rise above its source and that the selection of the judges should be left to the people. But, fortunately, our judicial system was grown for us. Under the guiding hand of Providence, it emerged slowly out of the conditions which followed the development of the monarchical idea. The consequence is that our judges are still appointed—nominally by the Crown, but really by an Executive responsible to the people—and this system of appointment for life has given us a judiciary which is the envy of our American neighbors.

Another example of our good fortune is our sensitively responsible government. If our American neighbors had stayed "under the flag" they would have had it as well as we. It is not our virtue or superior judgment which has given us this boon and denied it to the Americans. It is the "accident" that they tried—very humanly—to make something quite different from the government whose rule they were fleeing. They feared to leave the executive and the legislative power all in the hands of one group of men. They distrusted their politicians; and we might have distrusted ours in the same way, had we had the chance. But fortune favored us. Our constitution was ready made for us. It was made by the slow, sure hand of development, under pressure of hard trials and great difficulties. And the work of experience proved to be better than the hasty "creation" of the American Convention.

We might go on citing other examples of this sort. But the sum total of it is that we have certain institutions and methods of government which we greatly prefer to those in operation across the line; and we propose to keep them. If we can preserve the independence and distinct nationality of Canada, we can keep them; but if we throw in our lot with "the Continent to which we belong," then we lose them and receive in their stead the very American institutions and methods which the American people admit to be inferior to ours.

RETAINING OUR IDENTITY

Now we want to say, with the full sense of the responsibility which attaches to such a statement, that we believe it will not be easy for Canada to retain its identity. Human nature must have changed and the teaching of history must be discounted if a nation of eight, or even eighteen millions, finds it easy to share a Continent with a nation of ninety or a hundred millions—and keep its feet. We must assume that the Americans are not ambitious—that they are not as selfish as other people—if we are to convince ourselves they do not and never will, covet Canada. Yet, if they covet Canada, they are ten to our one; and it is pure nonsense to talk as if it were like saying "good day" for us to decide to remain independent.

If we keep our national identity, we will have to defend it. A very little con-

sideration will show any thoughtful person how the crisis is likely to arrive. The United States and the British Empire are two great English-speaking powers. They are in much the position which Prussia and Austria occupied in the time of Bismarck. Just as Prussia and Austria were rivals for the hegemony of the German-speaking world, so Great Britain and the United States must presently be rivals for the hegemony of the English-speaking world. Austria was the greater power; but Prussia won. Great Britain is to-day the greater power; but shall the parallel be completed?

CANADA WILL DECIDE

Canada will have the casting vote. That is why our position is so critical—and so perilous. When we get—say—thirty or forty millions of people here, if we go in with the United States, the enlarged American Republic will then contain between 150,000,000 and 175,000,000 people. The British Isles will carry little more than 50,000,000. They and Australia and South Africa, will be isolated English-speaking communities, whose fat empire the hungry nation of the world will watch with watering mouths. It will be plain enough that the entire English-speaking race must then stand together, or fall separately into the maws of its rivals. But if this agreement of nations comes together and agrees upon a leadership, will that leadership rest with the 50,000,000 or with the 150,000,000?

On the other hand, if Canada, with its 40,000,000 stays by the Motherland with its 50,000,000, and finds ten to twenty millions more in Australia and South Africa, hegemony of the race will easily remain in British hands; for the

people of Britain, Australia, and South
Africa will be better equipped for war,
on a per capita basis, than we on this
peaceful Continent are at all likely to be.
That having been secured, the next step
beckons. Canada has by far the broadest
opportunity for development.

Our vast country will fill up. We
will grow from forty to eighty millions.
We will be the largest of the British
nations. Then the hegemony will come
to us; and a Canadian city will be the
capital of the British Empire.

Without the support of Britain,
Australia, South Africa and our "far-
flung Empire," we would always be overshadowed by the Americans. United
with these other British communities, we
will control and guide the destinies of
our race. It is this proud position that
we are asked to sell. We are invited to
declare now—before the competition has
fairly begun—that Washington and not a
Canadian city is to be the Anglo-Saxon
Capital. That is the issue which is at
stake in this election; and, compared
with it, the petty game of matching markets, at which the politicians are playing so
eagerly, shrinks into insignificance.

With this broader vision before our
eyes, perhaps one or two other things become clearer. Can we not say that we
have already seen at least two preliminary strategic "moves" in this impending
struggle for the leadership of the English-
speaking world? The first "move" was
sought to be made in Britain. A section
of her people proposed to bind the
Empire—and especially Canada and the
Motherland—more closely by means of
a system of tariff preference. That
"move," so far, has failed. The people
of the United Kingdom have refused to
make it.

TAFT WAKES UP

But the suggestion that it might be
made, has had its effect at Washington.
President Taft is engagingly frank on this
point. He tells his people that there are
"forces at work in England and Canada"
which seek to "separate her (Canada)
by a Chinese wall from the United States,
and make her part of an Imperial commercial band reaching from England
around the world to England again by a
system of preferential tariffs"; and that,
consequently, this is a "critical" time for
Reciprocity, and that "we (the Americans) must take it now or give it up
forever."

In this, we wholly agree with President Taft. His political prescience is un-
deniable. The basis for his conclusion is
not as broad as it should be, however.
There is another force at work far more
fatal to American Reciprocity than the
preferential proposal; and that is the
mounting growth of Canada. Give us a
few more years; and our people would
laugh Reciprocity out of court without
even a hearing.

But, in any event, President Taft
has made his "move" — the second
"move" in this great and world-shaking
game. He has offered Canada the preference over which Britain hesitates. We
are to have free access to his market; and
everybody else is to be taxed. It has a
most tempting sound. The life-long Re-
ciprocitarians in the Liberal Government
fell victims to it; and they were the most
astonished men in the world when they
found that the whole country did not hail
their "bargain" with delight. They
thought that all Canada was for Reciprocity in natural products.

It was, at one time; but now Rip
Van Winkles have no business in politics.

The world has moved in the last two decades. Conditions have mightily changed —and changed for the better. Now that the storm has risen, these men have tried to hide in the grave of Sir John Macdonald. But that grave has been closed for fifteen years; and is closed on a man who fought his last fight against a form of Reciprocity which he feared would rob him of his proudest possession—the privilege of dying "a British subject."

CONDITIONS HAVE CHANGED

Of course, every farmer knows that a preference in the United States is quite a different thing from a preference in Britain. The United States is an exporter of farm produce; the United Kingdom is an importer. There we have the thing in a nutshell. A British preference would be a bonus to every Canadian farmer; and it is, perhaps, just as well to remember that, in voting for Reciprocity, we are putting the possibility of that bonus away from us forever. An American preference is—to use an American expression —"an option on a fight." That is, we can send our farm produce into a market which has a constant surplus of its own growth, where it can "fight" for a chance against the home-grown article.

However, that is an economic question; and we are inviting your attention just now to the subject of our political future. We believe, for our part, that this is a greater matter than the rise and fall of markets. Whether our readers agree with us on this point or not, the men who have made history in the past have always been of this opinion. When the Empire Loyalists left their comfortable and oft-time luxurious homes in the new American Republic for the long "trek" into what was then the wilderness of

Canada, they did not do so in search of the dollar. It would have paid them better to stay and accept the American flag. They would have been richer, more comfortable, lived longer and given their families far greater advantages. But— right or wrong—foolish or sublime—they chose the Union Jack for their flag and followed it into peril, hardship, suffering and death.

THEY CHOSE THE UNION JACK

The Union Jack has been accustomed to fly over such sacrifices. "The flag that braved a thousand years, the battle and the breeze," has seen men die in its defence under every sun that shines and by every sea that has borne its ships. If British subjects had always counted the cost before they faced death under its folds, it would not be our flag to-day— it would not, in truth, be a flag at all. Wolfe dying at Quebec; Brock dying at Queenston Heights — the soldiers and pioneers and Empire-builders who have planted Canada where she stands, would have found more personal profit in other paths.

These signal names which fire our blood are by no means all of those who have made their real sacrifices to keep the flag flying which faces the Stars and Stripes at the head of this article. Literally thousands of Canadians who are alive to-day, or who have not been long in their graves, have known what it is to choose the smaller pay, the more limited chance in life, the narrower outlook, that they might stay "under the flag" and help build up a Canada of which their children and their children's children could be proud.

The blood-letting of the "exodus" has not long ceased. We have all seen our companions leave for the more dazzling lure of "American prosperity." They went to seek their fortunes where fortunes were being found. But we stayed by the ship. We may have been foolish—many said we were—but we had the faith in our country and a belief in the ability of our people to build up a mighty and lasting nation here on the northern half of this great continent. So we stayed. We took pence when we could have got dollars; and we chose the northern—the less brightly gilded—the more storm-tossed flag. Perhaps we were inspired by the feeling of that patriotic Canadian poet who wrote:—

THE MEN OF THE NORTHERN ZONE

Oh, we are the men of the Northern Zone–
  Shall a bit be placed in our mouth?
If ever a Northerner lost his throne,
  Did the conquerer come from the South?
  Nay, nay—and the answer blent
  In chorus is southward sent.
"Since when has a Southerner's conquering
    steel
  Hewed out in the North a throne?
Since when has a Southerner placed his heel
  On the men of the Northern Zone?
Our hearts are free as the rivers that flow
  To the seas where the north star shines;
Our lives are free as the breezes that blow
  Thro' the crests of our native pines,
  We never will bend the knee,
  We'll always and aye be free,
For liberty reigns in the land of the leal,
  Our brothers are round her throne;
A Southerner never shall place his heel
  On the men of the Northern Zone.
                              The Khan.

But now, at last, the tide has turned. The brothers who left us are coming home again. The hard, stubborn fight we have made to prove the essential pre-eminence of Canada has won. When we have secured the suffrage of the entire world in support of our claim that Canada is the land of greatest opportunity under the wide sky. We have routed indifference, we have conquered contempt, we have baffled jealous hostilities, we have convinced skepticism itself. We have filled our cities with industries; we have banded our half-Continent with railways, we have laughed at leagues of wilderness and leaped over mountains; and we have drawn to our prairies, and the fat fertile land of our older provinces, the sturdiest army of farmers in the world.

No one now doubts the possible future of Canada. We have made it sure. We are not a boastful people; but we may be forgiven if we boast a bit of our determination, our faith in the face of discouragement, our unyielding loyalty to our native land. We have believed in Canada; and she has justified our belief. She is the richest, most promising, most prosperous country in the modern world.

BELIEVED IN CANADA.

We have believed, furthermore, in our people. We have been confident that they would "make good." And they have. They are the possessors of El Dorado of the twentieth century; and they have proven their capacity to guide its development and carry it forward to its high destiny.

The capacity we have. Have we the courage? That is the issue to-day. Just at the climax of our success, we are asked by the shrewd nation which scorned us when we were weak and scouted us when we sought her favors, to give it all up—to abandon the ideal for which our fathers faced the bleak north—to share with her the rich harvest which we sowed in bitter hardship and cherished through long years of suffering and lonely sacrifice.

Shall we do it?

Shall we surrender just when the battle is won?

Shall we let the men, who deserted us in the dark days, now come in as full-fledged "American citizens" and take over the country they did not think worth living in?

Shall we give it to them to say that they have judged better than we have all along—that they cleverly escaped the digging and the planting, the dull days of rain and deadly days of drought, but that now they get a Prodigal's share of the feast? They will have reversed the parable. They went abroad and found—not a diet of husks—but the richest living, leaving the "lean commons," to us; and, now they come to us as citizens of a foreign country, expecting that the "fatted calf" will be served to them.

Shall we give up, too, the glorious future which beckons us—the chance that we will become the chief state in the British Empire and the most powerful nation in the world?

Shall we bring the sacrifices of the Fathers to naught?

Shall we re-tread the path, with apology on our lips and our price in our hands, that the United Empire Loyalists trod with stern lips and a priceless loyalty in their hearts?

Shall we admit to the refuge they found, and made sacred, the very flag whose intolerance they fled?

The answer to these questions will all be given on polling day. This is not a party election. It is a national crisis. We are, in truth, "at the parting of the ways." We will either continue to march on the highway toward national greatness with the flag of Canada floating in our clear northern air over our heads; or, we will turn aside toward absorption in the "great and glorious Republic," to the south of us, surrendering to a calculating smile what we have long defended from hostility in every form—armed invasion, tariff persecutions, bullying over boundaries, even insolent disregard of treaty obligations.

Robert Borden, *The Daily Mail and Empire,* (Toronto), September 19, 1911.

A Final Word

To the people of Canada:—As this campaign closes and the solemn duty confronts us of deciding, very probably for all times, the most momentous question ever submitted to the Canadian electorate, I declare with perfect sincerity to my fellow-countrymen that the outlook is full of hope. The keen attention which the people have given to the discussion of this question has made the few weeks of this campaign far more revealing than months of ordinary debate. Throughout this Dominion the electorate now understand that they are called upon to determine not a mere question of markets, but the future destiny of Canada, perhaps of the Empire.

Even upon the economic side the reciprocity compact is but a step in a greater process. On each side of the boundary line its advocates realize perfectly that in its final outcome this treaty undoubtedly means the commercial and fiscal union of Canada with the United States. The chief magistrate of the great Republic has warned us in language of striking and unmistakable import that the consummation of this treaty will forever prevent the consolidation of our Empire. With profound insight and clear vision he has made the memorable declaration that if Canada accepts this compact she can never become a part of that great Imperial commercial band, which, as he anticipates, will reach from England around the world to England again. We must make our choice between reciprocity within the Empire and reciprocity with the U.S. And let us never forget that Canada cannot become fiscally and commercially a part of the U.S. and remain politically a part—and an important part—of the British Empire.

Can there be any doubt that this compact will result in prematurely dissipating those abounding resources which we hold not alone for our own use and profit but in trust also for those who are to succeed us? Are we not bound in honor to transmit free and unimpaired to our descendants the marvelous heritage which our forefathers won, and held in the face of difficulties and obstacles today unknown? Will the young men of Canada willingly decree that so splendid an inheritance shall pass into other hands than their own?

The relations created by this compact will increase threefold the power of the United States over our commercial destinies. Less than two years ago, by the threat of prohibitory duties, they forced our Government to alter our tariff. Do not imagine that the spirit which compelled this unwarranted concession to our powerful neighbor will die on the morrow of its first great success. If we accept this compact we must anticipate a renewal of the attempt. Where is our guarantee that the renewed pressure will be met in any firmer fashion than before. We recognize our constant duty to maintain the most friendly relations with the great neighboring nation; but I ask you to believe that such relations can be best assured if we preserve in fullest measure our present fiscal independence and autonomy.

Above all, do not forget that the momentous choice which you must make is for all time. If the tariffs of the two countries are interlocked by this treaty be assured that the stronger party will always carry the key.

I believe that we are in truth standing to-day at the parting of the ways. This compact made in secret and without mandate, points indeed to a new path. We must decide whether the spirit of Canadianism or of Continentalism shall prevail on the northern half of this continent. To-day, Canada is the mistress of her destiny. She commands both the Atlantic and the Pacific; she holds the highway of the world. Outside of the United Kingdom she is the most important unit of the whole British system which extends beyond every sea and throughout every continent and governs no less than one-fifth of the entire human race. With Canada's youthful vitality, her rapidly increasing population, her marvelous material resources, her spirit of hopefulness and energy, she can place herself within a comparatively brief period in the highest position within this mighty Empire. This is the path upon which we have proceeded—this is the path from which we are asked to depart.

I do not believe that the spirit of the Canadian people will sanction any such departure. The response that I have met in every province fills me with the profoundest gratitude and the liveliest hope

as to the result. The same spirit animates Canada to-day as that which inspired the men who founded this Confederation. That spirit is one of faith in our country, our institutions and ourselves. It is inspired by imperishable memories of a past full of splendid achievement; it is crowned by the highest and most confident hope of a future, the splendor of which we can but dimly realize. It dwells equally in the sons of British pioneers and loyalists and in those of Canadians of French descent, to whose ancestors we owe a deep debt of gratitude for the loyal valor which preserved Canada to the British Crown. The sons of these valiant defenders of our soil profoundly realize that Britain's flag secures for them to-day rights and privileges which they justly hold most dear, but which will be endangered by the entangling alliance created by this compact.

This question is above all parties and all individuals. I appeal to Liberals as to Conservatives, and I speak to them not as a party leader but as a Canadian citizen, whose hopes are bound up with the hopes of his country. To all who are proud of her past, to all who hope for her future, I make an earnest and sincere appeal to rise above all party ties, to take heed of the higher considerations and to determine their course with a sense of the enduring results of their decision. I entreat them not to swerve from the straight path that leads to the making of a great nation. I beg them to cast a soberly considered and serious vote for the preservation of our heritage for the maintenance of our commercial and political freedom, for the permanence of Canada as an autonomous nation within the British Empire.

Part IV

The Nationalistes

The campaign took on a different complexion in the province of Quebec. In most of the French-speaking constituencies, Conservatives joined forces with the *nationalistes* and accepted Henri Bourassa, the *nationaliste* leader, as their chief spokesman. It is a measure of the rift that had developed between the French and English Conservatives that anti-Liberal candidates usually labelled themselves *Autonomistes* rather than Conservatives.

Bourassa and his *nationaliste* supporters are most often remembered for their views of the British Empire. But they were also concerned with social and economic problems, as Bourassa made clear in a speech which he delivered to the Canadian Club of Toronto in 1907. In fact when Bourassa resigned from his seat in the House of Commons a few months later, he did so primarily to concentrate on the problems of colonizing northern Quebec.

But it was the naval question which consumed most of his energy for the next few years. In the columns of *Le Devoir*, and at numerous political meetings, Bourassa conducted a campaign against Laurier's decision to construct a Canadian navy. The most important of these meetings was held in July, 1910 at Ste. Eustache. Before the church still bearing the scars of English bullets fired during the rebellions of 1837, resolutions summing up the *nationaliste* position, drafted by Bourassa and approved by F. D. Monk, were passed. Assembly after assembly during the next few months adopted these resolutions, opposing a policy which would involve Canada in foreign wars as long as Canada had no influence over British diplomacy.

What concerned Bourassa as an election became imminent was the danger that Laurier would divert attention in Quebec from the naval question to reciprocity. To counter this strategy, the *nationaliste* leader published a long, signed editorial in *Le Devoir* on August 2, 1911 warning his readers not to be distracted by the reciprocity debate. Four days later Monk issued his own manifesto at Three Rivers. And in an emotional appeal to the party faithful, he returned to the argument that had proved so successful in the preceding year during the Drummond-Athabasca by-election—that once Canada was involved in Imperial wars, conscription would soon follow.

The most detailed account of the attempt to form a third party in Quebec was provided by Bourassa in a series of reminiscences in *Le Devoir* in 1913. The accuracy of some of his statements, published after his disillusionment with the elected *Autonomistes*, is open to question. But Bourassa makes clear that the primary objective of the campaign was to defeat Laurier, and that the two protagonists in the struggle were not Borden and Laurier but Bourassa and Laurier.

Conservatives in Quebec had various reasons for supporting Bourassa, although most denied that any formal alliance existed. Charles H. Cahan, a Montreal lawyer and businessman, a former member and acting leader of the opposition in the Nova Scotia legislature and a future member of R. B. Bennett's cabinet, spelled out his position in an open letter to the *Montreal Herald* during the final week of the campaign. In a private letter to the Conservative leader following the election, Wilfrid-Bruno Nantel, M.P. for Terrebonne since 1908, and the Minister of Mines and Inland Revenue in Borden's new administration, was much more explicit.

Henri Bourassa, "The Nationalist Movement in Quebec", *Addresses Delivered Before The Canadian Club of Toronto,* (Toronto, 1907), pp. 56-64. January 22, 1907.

Nationalisme

. . . The Nationalist movement in Quebec is a strong and deeply rooted one, but there is nothing about it to be compared to the Irish Nationalist movement in the Old Country. The circumstances differ. Ours is not a movement based on any grievance against the national status of Canada. We have no hatred or distrust against Great Britain. We have a strong sentiment of love for Canada—not a Platonic love, nor a declamatory love of the pompous, heated spirit of election times. Our creed is that all the resources of Canada shall be developed for the people of Canada, that the representatives of the two great races should devote themselves unitedly to the development of our intellectual, moral and material advantages in the best of real Canadian sentiment.

I may state that the Nationalist movement in Quebec is not the movement of a political party. It is not a Nationalist party in the same sense as there is a Conservative party and a Liberal party. On the contrary, it is an attempt to establish a true Canadian patriotic spirit, a deep desire for the complete development of all the material resources and all the intellectual and moral resources that English and French settlement and civilization have rendered available to Canada. I repeat that the Canadian Nationalists are not a political party. I do not disguise the fact that if the Government refuses to adopt a reasonable attitude towards the reasonable desires of Quebec's younger generation, they may choose a proper occasion to give a concrete form to the movement. If, however, the existing parties in power and in opposition listen, instead of stamping the accusation of disloyalty on their movement, then they are satisfied. I can assure you that there is not in this movement any greed for power or office, nor is it as narrowly provincial as is painted. Its creed should constitute the creed of every Canadian. The whole ensemble of the movement rings Canadian. It is based on the only principles by which a true Canadian patriotism can be developed, a thing I venture to say is not now in existence. There is Ontario patriotism, Quebec patriotism, or Western patriotism, each based on the hope that it may swallow up the others, but there is no Canadian patriotism, and we can have no Canadian nation when we have no Canadian patriotism.

The younger men of Quebec take a pride in the belief that the movement should properly start in Quebec—not in a spirit of narrow parochialism. British civilization took birth in Quebec. There were first established the principles of British government. Their forefathers were the first to preach, to work and to fight for the best of British constitutional principles. They saw that it was possible and necessary to create a spirit of friendship and unity between the two races.

They were the pioneers of British self-government in America.

The great aim of the Nationalist movement is to encourage the growth of this real patriotism by developing Canada for the general benefit of Canadians. We wish to preserve our birthright, not as Frenchmen, but as Canadians. If I have time I should like to give you a few details as to our programme. It is a well-defined one, on economic, social and political lines. Development along all these lines general to the needs of Canada is the aim. We wish to develop the resources of Canada for the benefit of the Canadian people at large. We aim to keep the straight path between the two great calamities of communism and corporate domination. It may be well for private and corporate interests to take hold and develop the riches of Canada, but not at the expense of the people.

The Nationalist movement is equally opposed to monopolism and to socialism. Such great gifts of nature as our mines and our forests should not be made to yield big profits to the few to the exclusion of others. Some revenue from the mines and forests should, we say, go to the all, the people, to be spent shall we say in colonization, or some other worthy enterprise, the benefit of which the all will share. The interests of the lumber companies should be respected, and also those of the backwoods settler. As far as that part of the programme is concerned, you in Ontario are in advance of us, but we will not be long in following you up. On general principles we favor a reasonable and proper division of the land. We are opposed to the landed aristocracy, which prevents the helpful settling and upbuilding of our country and lets American speculators tie up and hold thousands of our acres.

We are only at the beginning of the era of water power development and electricity industry as yet. We have no conception of its future and its wonderful, its gigantic possibilities. Is this inheritance to be disposed of to corporation or individual? The people should retain their rights in their water powers. Let us study the policy which obtained in Switzerland and France, where the Governments made a classification of the water powers. Again, in this field, outside the party spirit, your Province has taken the lead. But the East will follow.

Go on; run the whole gamut of public utilities. Railways, tramways, telegraphs and telephones. Public utilities should not be left entirely in the hands of private corporations. We take, I submit, the happy medium position between the socialist and the corporation. We admit that at the present time it may be that we cannot undertake to operate every public service, but we should not sell for ever the public heritage of our descendants, who may be able to deal with them in a wiser and happier frame of mind. It may not at present be expedient to adopt complete Governmental ownership, but it is not well that the rights of future generations, who may be able to do so under a wiser and more efficient Federal Government, should be compromised. Let us keep the title of ownership.

We think specially of the railway policy. It may be the most important question before the country. Directly to the south of us lies the most energetic and aggressive railway country in the world, and is there not every danger that a combination of United States capital may secure almost unlimited power in the Dominion by the gradual acquisition of its railway systems? How can this danger be averted? By at least a modicum of

Government control. Canada should reserve the title of the ownership of the lines and allow to a company only the right of temporary operation. The geographical position of our country is such that it can only be preserved as a nation by a vigorous and advanced railway policy.

When I hear people comparing our railway policy to that of England I know that they have not taken thought. England is separated from all foreign countries. We have a frontier of 3,000 miles adjoining the most active railway, industrial and trade nation of the world. Would England be warranted in abandoning the protection of her sea to any foreign country to do it for her? American systems of railways have swallowed up the Mexican systems. Shall they do the same for Canada? Are we not becoming almost entirely at the mercy of American trade because we lack interest in our railway policy? Canada is a geographical absurdity, and it is possible to maintain and fortify Canadian unity only by a vigorous railway policy. Is it proper to leave in the hands of enterprising American companies the power to tap our West? I have no objection to the American interchanging with us, but they should be met by an intelligent railway policy.

I pass on to the tariff. This is a somewhat hard matter to define. The Nationalist idea is, at least in theory, free trade, but in practice this ideal we recognize is not at present attainable. We pretend to be moderate men. We seek a tariff inspired by devotion to the whole people of Canada and their interests, without considering that the whole people of Canada are included in the membership of the Canadian Manufacturers' Association. We wish to imbue the minds of the people of Canada with a strong and patriotic feeling. This country is worth while every citizen making some personal sacrifices for the general benefit. We want to be intelligent and practical. We want to act for the general good, whether from the imperial or national standpoint. . . . I believe in Canada preserving a dignified self-government, not in exploiting a false feeling of antagonism towards Americans, nor a servile feeling that would have us act at the mercy of our neighbors. Our tariff should be framed to encourage industry. We want no entanglement in Imperial tariff policy. We are strong enough, and solid enough to stand on our own bottom.

As for Imperial preference, we should look first to the interests of our own land. Trade with Britain should be promoted, but the only trade basis for the Empire must be that on which the Empire has been built up, the basis of individual rights and interests for every colony. There should be no entanglement in any Imperial tariff system which may some day cause Canada's interests to be sacrificed to those of Australia or New Zealand.

Regarding financial legislation, in general, we take the ground that more care should be exercised in the powers given by the State in the incorporation of companies. The seal of the State should not be used to legalize bogus charters to steal from the simple-minded Canadian or foreign investor. Every charter should be investigated and the good faith and capacity of the promoters tested. The Government should ascertain why a concern is to be capitalized at millions, when the promoters have neither the courage nor the wealth to deal in hundreds. Something should be done to put an end to "watered stock" and the obtaining of money under false pretences. The common sense of the nation should prevent financial directors acting on so many boards that they actually forget the names of the companies to which they belong. It should be a criminal offence for a man to belong to more directorates than he can effectually look after. A stock broker should not be permitted to speculate against his client. We want a deeper sense of duty and a deeper sense of honor in those who have the responsibilities of handling the trust of their fellow men.

And this should be extended to public administration generally. There is need for a true and real reform of the civil service of this country. Appointment and promotion should be taken entirely out of a sphere of politics. They should be made according to merit, on the recommendation of competent men, who stand as high as the tribunals of the country. In the judicial system also the same methods should prevail. Judges, though necessarily appointed by the Government, should be designated by some body in no way associated with the party system. The bar should be entrusted with the custody of its honor and held to strict account. The bar should have the choosing of men worthy of becoming magistrates. We believe, too, that appeals should be restricted to Provincial Courts of Appeal which involve only interests Provincial or municipal. That the Privy Council should be called upon only when the interpretation of the constitution of Canada is concerned or involved. Why should we keep such a court busy with our domestic quarrels? We should surely be able to look after these ourselves. It would be, I am sure, more satisfactory to have the offices of the highest tribunal confined to large constitutional cases.

In politics in general we want much reform. We are still in favor of the re-form of the Senate. We believe it should exist, and be different in constitution to the House of Commons. But we believe it should be more of the judicial bench of the country than the refuge for political wrecks, or worse, should be a committee of permanent intrigue and organization for financiers for speculation to which they would not dare to give publicity. It is suggested that the Chambers of Commerce, the Universities, the seats of agriculture, should have the designation or election of senators, along the lines of proportionate representation. The Lower House, perhaps naturally under existing conditions, approaches the matter in a narrow party spirit. It might be an improvement to allow the Provincial Governments to make the nominations.

And now for a word as to the immigration policy. We are all anxious to see the country develop and prosper, to welcome the best men of the various countries of the world. But it seems to us that the Government's policy has been directed too much towards securing quantity and not quality of settlers. This policy is unsound and unpatriotic. There should be somewhat radical means of analyzing. There should be an effectual stop to high financing in this matter. Men in high places should not be permitted to "develop" the West in the interests of land deals, in giving over to corporations immense territories to people whose aim is not national but selfish. There should be an end of paying any corporation so much per head for any kind of people they ship us. This is paying the premium to number rather than quality. The best immigration agent is a contented and prosperous settler, who writes home to his relatives. It would be far better for our country if instead of spending money recklessly to bring in everybody, the

Government would spend more in preventing those who do come in falling the prey of sharks and speculators in our own land. Less attention has been given to obtaining immigration from the people who are more akin to us, in England and France, than from those in less desirable countries. More money should be spent on the settler's welfare when he arrives, and less on inducing him to leave his old home. It is true that this policy might take a little longer to populate the North-West, but it would be done much better. And we must not forget that we are now building the permanent future of our nation.

Let us aim to keep the national status of Canada. Let us aim to the absorption of Canadians ideals and habits by the Americans who come to settle among us. We have growing up side by side an Anglo-Saxon civilization and a French-Canadian civilization. The latter are less liable, permit to say it, to embrace the Americanism than you are yourselves. You have little difference in language, in creed, in habits of living, in social intercourse. Toronto is more American than Quebec or Montreal. You must think seriously as to the future. If you do not cling loyally to the deep roots, the deep traditions of your past, you are in a dangerous position alongside of a country of eighty millions with all their forces of absorption. Let the good people of Toronto consider that point of view. The Nationalist movement in Quebec is the greatest guaranty of the permanency of Canada.

I have already spoken too long. I cannot in the brief time allotted pass over the whole scope of the political and social programme of the Nationalist movement. Does it appeal to the public spirit of Canadianism? It is not sufficient to talk; we must take a part. There can be no real reform if the public spirit does not prompt the movement. We must not be inspired from the party point of view, but from the national point of view. We believe in the party system, but we do not believe in allowing it to degenerate into party slavery. There is work and scope for a strong body of enlightened men who take the broad national patriotic point of view—men who are above the narrowness of mere partyism. It is well there are parties, it is well to have changes—often oftener than we do. There is less danger of corruption and maladministration when there are frequent changes of Government and public opinion makes its influence felt through the press and associations like this. We hope for the day when a strong public opinion will take the place of the party convention.

I trust I have said enough to show that the main object of the movement is to develop the national forces of Canada. Canada must remain a federation of Provinces and races. Unless there is room enough for the whole, there is not room for any. It is too late to make history over again.

Do not be misled as to the position of your French-speaking fellow Canadians in this movement. The French in this country were conquered by England and they have accepted the fact loyally. We must none of us sacrifice our ideals, but we must be broad enough to respect the Federal contract, to let the same golden rule apply to all Provinces and all minorities. In the much discussed educational legislation we never thought nor asked the Federal Government for special legislation. We had confidence, just as we knew the Protestant minority in our Province would never be troubled. In education we still maintain the British principle that the parents' will is superior to the State's will. There is no danger to British predominance in the two languages. You can never make of us good Englishmen, but you do not have to make us good Canadians. We claim a strong pledge— a pledge given by the Crown of England —and we know it will be respected by all British people. Alongside of the British sentiment we have the growth of the French civilization. That we keep up our traditions and develop them is no danger to the future of Canada. We are independent of the United States, even if we do not read English books and speak like they do in London. We are proud of our inter-Imperial relationship. The object of our movement is national, based on the plan that both races shall exist respecting each other. We have no distrust of Great Britain, but we believe in looking after the interests of Canada first.

We do not wish to impose our views upon you. Should the majority of the people say "Sacrifice your autonomy," well and good. But remember we are the oldest Canadians. We came here and fought the wild beast and hewed out the primitive homes. We have been loyal to the British flag and British institutions. It is due to the French-Canadians to remember that they alone of the thirteen Anglo-Saxon colonies did not raise the flag of rebellion. I say, then, that we have ac-

quired, morally and politically, the right to be heard. Because we oppose the Chamberlain policy we are not disloyal rebels—they have done that in England herself; because we claimed the right to condemn the Boer war we were not more disloyal than Morley, the British statesman, who likewise condemned it; because we opposed the contribution of Canada we were no worse than Sir James Bryce, now receiving special honors and responsibilities from the Imperial Government. We measure to the full stature of British citizenship, freedom of thought, of speech and of action. We believe we have acquired the right to speak as Canadians. By reason of having seceded entirely from European connection we believe ourselves in a position to judge, with a more Canadian view, all those problems. This is not detrimental to the autonomy of Canada. We are Imperialists in the true sense of the word. The principles which have built up the little Isle yonder are the principles which will build up Canada, and the only principles upon which the Empire shall endure. What was good fifty years ago is still good to-day.

That is the Nationalist policy. You have it briefly as I have given it. You may approve of it, you may condemn part of it, but, at all events, it is founded on true Canadianism by loyal British subjects.

Resolutions adopted at Saint-Eustache, July 17, 1910, *Le Devoir*, July 16, 1910.

The Nationaliste Resolutions

We, citizens of Canada, loyal subjects of H. M. King George V, declare ourselves ready to defend with our blood the soil of our country and the rights of the British Crown in Canada, as our fathers did in 1776 against the British subjects of His Majesty, in 1812, against the armies of the American Republic, and as we did in 1885 against our fellow-citizens in rebellion.

Firm in our belief in the greatness and efficiency of the principles of decentralization and self government, which have been, for half a century, solemnly proclaimed and acknowledged by both the authorities of Great Britain and Canada, we are opposed to any new policy, the result of which would be to draw us into distant wars, foreign to Canada, so long, at least, as the self-governing colonies of the Empire shall not enjoy with the Mother Country, and upon an equal footing, the sovercign power and authority which control the Imperial army and navy, treaties of peace and alliance, foreign relations, and the government of India and of the Crown Colonies.

We sincerely believe that such a policy of centralization and apparent imperial unity, in the accomplishment of which the new naval law is but an initial step, will generate within the empire misunderstanding, rivalries and conflicts which will threaten the peace and unity of the numerous countries and peoples of all races that are now so proud of their loyalty to the British Crown.

Having never been in the past a case of conflict for Great Britain and the Empire, we believe that a policy of peace and of moral and material development is necessary to Canada, to her growth and unity, and, thereby, to the glory and safety of the Empire.

Free citizens of a democratic country, we claim the right to express openly our sentiment upon this question, as well as upon any other that may affect the fate and the interests of Canada.

We acknowledge the right of the majority of the Canadian people to determine a new course in our relations with the other parts of the empire, provided such a step is taken in full knowledge of its consequences.

But we protest against any attempt to withdraw such a ponderous problem from the free consideration of the Canadian people at large, and of any of its various groups.

We disavow the declarations made in Toronto in December last by Hon. Alexandre Taschereau, provincial minister of public works, by which he fallaciously contended that the people of Quebec are ready to accept blindly any policy of naval defence for the Empire, and we blame the members of the Government and of the Legislature of this province, who by their vote, on the 2nd of June last, sanctioned those declarations.

We blame the federal government

and the majority in Parliament who have imposed on Canada the new navy legislation, thrown our country in the vortex of militarism, erstwhile so emphatically denounced by Sir Wilfrid Laurier, threatened the peace of Canada, and misappropriated for the construction of murderous weapons and the preparation of bloody wars millions destined to the development of our agriculture and means of transportation.

We censure as well the attitude of Mr. Borden and those of his followers who have urged the adoption of a no less nefarious policy.

We maintain that Parliament had no right to pledge the future of Canada to a policy which has never been submitted to the people upon whom shall fall the tribute of blood and the load of military taxation.

We approve unreservedly of the courageous and straightforward conduct of Mr. Monk and the few members of Parliament who, faithful to their trust, have demonstrated the dangers of that policy, and claimed for the people of Canada the right to express their will before their representatives bind them to such heavy obligations.

Henri Bourassa, *Le Devoir*, August 2, 1911.

The Nationaliste Manifesto

The situation created by the prime minister and the leader of the opposition is singularily false and narrow. Those who are not the slaves of any party should break down the barriers and place the battle on a larger ground.

Mr. Laurier is trying to lead the Canadian people into the trap in which he has already succeeded drawing Mr. Borden and his immediate followers. He speaks, in his manifesto, only of the reciprocity question. In this way he hopes to turn public attention from the many signs of pestilent gangrene infecting his administration: the scandalous acts of Mr. Pugsley—the embezzlements of the minister of militia in arms manufacture—the rottenness of the national printing bureau —the orgies and the frittering away of millions of the minister of marine—the Lanctot painting and the dirty linen by means of which the ministerial majority, headed by Mr. Laurier himself, endeavored to recover it—the $69,000 of Oliver and the millions thrown to Mackenzie and Mann—the common tricks and desperate means to which the ministers have had recourse in order to stifle the truth—the crooked history of the Farmer's Bank, to which Mr. Fielding granted his permission to carry on business after having been officially warned that the organizers of that institution had obtained their capital by fraud—the refusal to make public the names of the generous donors of a present of $100,000 to the minister of finance.

Mr. Laurier likewise thinks himself sheltered from any discussion of the diverse political problems which demand attention: agricultural and economic co-operation, supervision of over-capitalized financiers, regulation of railways and other public services, control of banks and credit institutions, immigration, minority rights.

Above all, he wishes to escape from the consequences of his vacillating opportunism in connection with Imperialist problems; he hopes to impose silence or to throw the veil of deceit over his actions in London; he wishes at all costs to have his Navy Act forgotten, and to shake off the shirt of Nessus which the electors of Drummond-Arthabaska fastened on his back.

On the other hand, Mr. Borden is making only a feeble effort to escape from the fetters that he has allowed to be placed upon his feet. Except for an energetic paragraph on the stifling of the Oliver enquiry, his manifesto passes over all the other scandals of the Laurier regime in silence. Before the vote of supply and the electoral redistribution he throws upon the Ministers the responsibility for the dissolution of the House. But he makes no declaration on the naval law, on Imperial problems, nor on any other political question except reciprocity.

There are various ways one can appreciate the two leaders' tactic: one can see in it, depending upon one's point of view and the way one looks at it, caution or fear, wisdom or blindness, skill or trickery. No one can see in it courage, strength, and comprehensiveness. The intelligence and the will of the Canadian people shall not be enchained in such narrow bonds.

In the province of Quebec in particular, despite the party degradation and corruption produced by patronage and the long sleep of the Conservative party, the old spirit of justice is not dead; the aspiration towards a high political ideal is re-born with each successive generation; it is impossible to arouse our people with a single material question and to concentrate their attention on the sole dilemma of choosing between the English and American markets for the export of Canadian products.

Each has the right to judge the value of the Taft-Fielding convention in his own way. One can, with plausible arguments, predict either that it will have unfortunate consequences or will result in much that is good.

But what no one can question is that the next parliament will be busy with something else. Whether the convention is ratified or rejected—or rather, the Canadian tariff is modified according to the terms of the convention or maintained in its integrity,—the world will continue to turn: it will be necessary to govern the country, to make laws, to resolve political problems which are more profound than reciprocity.

Many people pretend, and some sincerely believe, that reciprocity will lead Canada to political union with the United States. Other causes, older and stronger, drew Canada in that direction;

the regime of railways, excessive immigration and the anglicisation of the "West", lead us to it much more surely than reciprocity. What will the attitude of those who are newly elected be towards these national problems which parliaments in the past have not known or have wished to take up, and to which the leaders of the current parties have made not the slightest allusion—neither in their manifesto to the electors nor in the numerous speeches which they have recited during the past two years?

Do not the Canadian people have the right and the duty to know the opinions and particularly the intentions of the parties, the groups and the candidates who are going to ask them for a mandate, not only to rule on the question of reciprocity, but to legislate on all matters for five years?

The experience of the past teaches us that it is not wise to put one's trust in someone with an indefinite mandate.

Of all the questions that the Premier and the leader of opposition seem desirous of snatching from the judgment of the people, without doubt the most important is that collection of problems grouped together under the name of Imperialism, particularly the contribution of Canada to Imperial armaments on sea and land, the participation of the Canadian people in men and money to the Imperial wars where the fate of Canada is not at stake. . . .

At London Mr. Laurier declared that the English preference, which is after all only a form of Imperialism, remained the permanent basis of his economic policy, and that American reciprocity was only a secondary and contributory measure. He entered into an engagement with the Imperial authorities that will be cemented perhaps before long by millions of dollars expended and thousands of lives sacrificed in foreign wars just or unjust. . . .

These negotiations have been negotiated and concluded in secret. Sir Wilfrid waited until the last possible moment before producing the text of the treaties and the complete report of the deliberations. . . .

Then he brusquely dissolves Parliament without giving an account of the extraordinary mandate that was intrusted to him and for the execution of which the two Houses and all Parliamentary groups consented to a two months' adjournment.

Lastly he retires the two ministers who accompanied him to London, the heads of the two departments charged with the execution of the bellicose engagements, and he asks the Canadian people to think of nothing except Reciprocity.

Let it not be forgotten, the members elected on September 21 will not only have to adjust certain articles of the customs tariff in favor of the Americans. They will also have to judge the imperial policy of the government; the attitude of Mr. Laurier and his colleagues—disappeared at the Imperial Conference, and above all, to ratify or to condemn the engagements entered into by them at London without consulting the Canadian people.

That is the really important question that is above leaders and outside the confines of party.

In these circumstances the right line of conduct to follow is plainly marked: Bring out independent candidates—Nationalists, Liberals or Conservatives, supporters of Reciprocity or those who are opposed to it—men of honor and men of their word, who will rally round Mr. Monk to maintain in Parliament, and in the face of whatever government, the principles of autonomy laid down by the member for Jacques Cartier during the last year—men whose ideals are healthy and whose determination is firm, for they will have to settle the vital problems of the nation: Canadian autonomy, the preservation of national unity and the rights of minorities.

F. D. Monk, *The Montreal Daily Star*, August 7, 1911.

Another Manifesto

Three Rivers, August 6

I am very glad to come to Three Rivers to open the election campaign on behalf of a party which is fighting to defend the rights and the privileges which are dear to all good Canadians. . . .

The dominant question for us—the question to which Quebec attaches supreme importance, is the establishment of a Canadian navy, and I ask how is it that they are trying to hide that question from the people? We have never shirked the responsibilities of defending our own country, but the Laurier Government is seeking to extend those obligations by imposing upon the country the construction of a navy and the reorganization of the militia, which I tell you will carry us to conscription in a few years' time. In opposing this we have been told that we are leading a revolt, but there is nothing in our attitude which justifies such an accusation. The position we have taken, and which we maintain is that the country should be consulted upon these questions which involve such important changes

in our exterior relations. They will involve us in all the wars of the Empire, but have we anything to say in the foreign policy of the British Government? What do we know of the conduct of the diplomacy in relation that policy? The people, after all, are masters, and the Ministers of a Government are their servants. The time has now come when you will have to pass judgment. You are told, however, by Sir Wilfrid Laurier that the only issue is reciprocity. But there is something more than reciprocity, as I hope to demonstrate to you in submitting the main principles of our platform.

OUTLINES NATIONALIST PARTY'S PLATFORM

Our first principle is equal rights for all, which embraces, of course, the full recognition of the rights of the minority. That is the first principle upon which we are united.

Secondly, we ought to have a better system of immigration. The present system has resulted in many abuses in the past, and it is absolutely necessary these should be changed and reformed. Principally we ought to adopt a system which would give us a more effective control and opportunity to exercise a more just surveillance over the people who come out to this country.

Then our means of transportation should be adopted on more practical lines, and in this respect I attach first importance to the construction of the Georgian Bay Canal. I submitted a motion to Parliament calling for the execution of this project, but it was rejected by the Government.

More encouragement ought to be given to the agricultural and laboring classes through co-operative societies.

The banking system also needs reforming in order to give better protection to the deposits and savings of the people. How is it that the Government always puts off the consideration of amendments of the Banking Act which would permit of a proper inspection of the banks and assure the population against such losses as have been suffered during the past year? . . .

SAYS CANADA MUST REMAIN INDEPENDENT OF THE UNITED STATES

. . . Reciprocity is not so important as the question which we have discussed before you for the past six months, and we strongly object to it being submitted to the people to the exclusion of the question of the navy and other important matters. There was a treaty of reciprocity between the two countries before, but it was abrogated. Since then we have developed our own resources, and we have prospered. Are we now going to be pushed into a position of danger? In my own county we have manufacturers who are opposed to this reciprocity pact; we have farmers who are also opposed to it, and if I represent them in Parliament I also must oppose reciprocity. It is important for us to remain independent of the American people, independent of their ways and their influence which will be fatal to our prosperity and national identity.

PROTEST AGAINST ANY SUBSERVIENCE TO PARTY

. . . We stand before you in protest against this system of making everything subservient to party. Give us the encouragement that we have a right to expect. Knowing what we stand for, it is for you to elect to Parliament a group of men, men who are independent of party, men of principle and honesty, who will stand against all that is corrupt, but who will unite in all endeavors to conduct the affairs of the country in the right way of progress.

Henri Bourassa, *Le Devoir*, May 29, May
30, June 2, 1913.

The Nationaliste-
Conservative Alliance

THE CONSERVATIVES SEEK THE HELP
OF THE NATIONALISTES

During the session of 1910-11, two
of the pontiffs of the conservative San-
hedrin asked for an interview with me at
the house of a mutual friend. Here is an
exact summary of the interview. These
gentlemen were the first to speak.

"The Nationalists," they said "fight
as we do against the Liberal government;
but their attitude on the question of
reciprocity is very annoying to us. If we
were to unite in our efforts against reciprocity, we would probably come to
an understanding on the naval question
later, since we share your opinion to abide
by the decision of the people. If, in
Quebec, you place the naval law foremost, you will force the ultras of our
party to display their feelings of loyalty.
But if you make reciprocity a mere
secondary issue, the divergence between
us will grow wider to the profit of the
common enemy. Come the general elections, and candidates will be put in the

field who, although opposing the naval
act, will approve of reciprocity; others,
dumb on the question of reciprocity, will
oppose the naval policy of both parties.
This situation will be very embarrassing
for us. If we support these independent
candidates we will be accused of double
dealing; if, in these counties, we have a
third candidate, strictly conservative, the
ministerial candidate will pass in between
the two. On the other hand, what will the
Nationalists do in the counties where the
fight will be between Liberals supporting
the Government and conservative anti-
reciprocists?"

I gave them a decisive answer:
There can be nothing in common between
the Nationalists and the Tory party. We
are completely indifferent as to the fate
of one party or the other.

"We have given Mr. Monk and his
group our support because they have
pledged themselves to oppose the naval
policy of both parties as long as the
people were not consulted by plebiscite.

"Since the election of Drummond-
Athabaska, Mr. Borden has drawn closer
to Mr. Monk. He had virtually accepted
the idea of a plebiscite. It is the only
possible ground for an understanding. If
you are elected to power, you must consult the people faithfully, outside of a
general election, and avoid the numerous
conflicts it occasions. If the majority
favours the naval law or any other measure of contribution to the general defence
of the Empire, we will perforce have to
submit—although reserving the right to
continue spreading our ideas so as to
cause the people to reverse its decision.
On the other hand, if the majority decides
against the Act and against a contribution of any kind, you must equally accept
the verdict.

"The project of reciprocity in no

way changes the situation nor our attitude on what is, in our opinion, the most important question. In this agreement with the United States, we see neither all the good that the Liberals expect from it, nor all the evils predicted by the Conservatives. We are therefore rather indifferent as to its success or failure. We favour it in so far as it frustrates the schemes of the Imperialists.

"After all, whatever you do, this measure will necessarily become of secondary importance after the next elections. If the Government is defeated, the Customs agreement is obliterated. If the Liberals are returned to power and reciprocity causes a tithe of the evils that you predict, Sir Wilfrid will suppress it as he invented it. If, on the contrary, it proves to be of advantage to the country, we will accept it. We have known for a long time what to think of either party's consistency of principles.

"The naval question, on the contrary, will remain foremost. Intimately connected with the programme of the relations between England and its colonies, which is a live issue in the whole of the Empire, it will be solved only on that day when the Canadian people have made a decisive choice between the straight Nationalist solution and integral imperialism. You must not be surprised, therefore, if we refuse to be blinded by a cabinet that has introduced reciprocity to make the people forget the primary question of the navy and imperial relations.

"As we are not a party, we will put no candidates in the field, but we will support any liberal or conservative candidate, whether he is in favour of reciprocity or not, who will pledge himself to oppose any policy of direct or indirect participation in the wars of the Empire outside of Canada, or who, at least, will promise to reject any measure of that kind before the people have been consulted by means of a plebiscite. And in this we will consult neither the desires nor interests of one or the other of the parties.

"What we wish—and we make no secret of it—is to elect enough independent members to defeat the naval bill or any other project of contribution to imperial armaments as long as the people have not been consulted.

"It is up to Mr. Borden and his lieutenants to decide if they will let us elect the candidates we are willing to support, or enter into a three-cornered contest which will assure the election of the Government's candidates.

"In the electoral districts where the fight will be between a liberal and an "orthodox" conservative, we will let them fight between themselves."

Whether these gentlemen were satisfied or not, they made their report to Ottawa. I have reason to believe that the High Priest of the Sanhedrim accepted the situation, since the elections were made according to the conditions we had stipulated, as I will prove in my next article.

Some time after, two good authentic Tories—dyed in the wool, and of the deepest blue—renewed the attempt to forestall the Nationalists. They brought with them old stock in trade arguments as stale as they were devoid of convincing power, to prove that reciprocity was the only debatable question, and that the great conservative party, "that created Confederation and built the Canadian Pacific," was the sole one that could save the country from ruin. They received the same reply, but even more curtly.

These were the two only communications, direct or indirect, that we had with the representatives of the Conservative party. There you find the "hybrid, monstrous, immoral" alliance between the Imperialists and the Nationalists.

I may be wrong-minded; but I can see nothing in this which would make the Nationalists blush. Nor do the interviews I granted, on the eve of the election of 1908, to the Conservatives as well as to Sir Wilfrid Laurier personally, leave me any humiliating recollections.

In neither of these occasions—nor in any other one—have we lowered the flag, swallowed back our ideas, or sold our birthright for a mess of pottage, whether it came from grit or tory.

If Mr. Laurier and his clique, instead of shouting themselves hoarse and repeating nonsense "à la Lafortune" about the Nationalists whose support they had so long sought, were satisfied with saying that Mr. Borden and the Conservative party, in order to reach power, made overtures to the Nationalists and were compelled to submit to the conditions imposed upon them by our attitude, they would keep within the bounds of truth. If they added that once in power, the Conservatives had hastened to break loose from their agreements, and that they succeeded through the weakness and treachery of three of the ministers and of a dozen of the conservative members who have openly broken their pledges to the Nationalists and to the electors, they would still be right.

However, Mr. Laurier, always faithful to the maxims of Talleyrand, has a dread of the naked truth as equal to his of a naked lie. He must continually mix one with the other. Let us continue to unravel them.

THE AUTONOMIST PARTY

As the general elections drew nearer,

it became evident that the leaders of the Conservative party accepted the situation created by the nationalist campaign in the Province of Quebec.

The group around Mr. Monk organized under the name of the "Autonomist party", with its headquarters, its committees and its whole machinery entirely distinct from that of the Conservative party.

The Conservative party relinquished to the "Autonomist party" most of the electoral districts of the Province, only keeping the orthodox candidates—the English counties of the Eastern Townships, the counties of Argenteuil and Pontiac, and three districts of Montreal: St-Antoine, Ste-Anne and St-Laurent.

It was clearly understood that in all the rest of the Province, Mr. Monk would have the exclusive management of the election, that he could accept or refuse any opposition to his candidates, who were to be free to oppose the Naval Act and the "no less nefarious policy of Mr. Borden" if they wished; these candidates would be free to take whatever attitude they wished on the question of reciprocity, and would just the same receive all the support the Conservatives could give them. These concessions did not imply any reciprocal engagements; neither the Nationalists, nor even the "Autonomists" most sympathetic to the tories, had pledged themselves to support the Conservative candidates against those of the Government.

In spite of these favourable conditions, I did not at all deceive myself about the sincerity of a certain number of partisans around the member for Jacques Cartier. Without foreseeing treachery as cynical as that of Coderre, Blondin, Sevigny, Paquette, Rainville, I could see that compromises were already being prepared. The "Autonomist party" was being crowded with tories who had formerly anathemized Mr. Monk and the Nationalists. Their sudden zeal gave me no false hopes.

Moreover, I foresaw that Mr. Monk, who was ill and deeply afflicted, and who had been disgusted for a long time with politics and the parties, would not long delay his retirement.

He was the only one who offered the guarantees of respectability, constancy, disinterestedness and authority necessary to keep the "Autonomist party" in the straight path into which he had led them, and to prevent the schemers, helped by the weaklings, to surrender the army to the tory party.

The mere choice of this pompous appellation—the "Autonomist party"—already smelled of amalgam and reeked with ancient toryism. I did not demand that the candidates around Mr. Monk and myself take the title of Nationalists. My sincere conviction that Nationalism should not degenerate into a faction remained intact. It is still so. Moreover, I wished to see what would be the behaviour of our champions after the victory before asking them to wear our colours.

As soon as the campaign was resumed at the meeting in the Ontario Rink, on the 31st of May 1911, two months before the dissolution of parliament, I again emphasized the wide distinction between the Conservative party and ours. I explained thoroughly and at length the thesis I had sustained before Mr. Borden's delegates. This is how I summarized my attitude and that of the "Devoir":

"I will give my loyal support and the best of my efforts to any candidate, LIBERAL OR CONSERVATIVE, ENGLISH OR FRENCH, CATHOLIC OR PROTESTANT, RECIPROCIST OR ANTI-RECIPROCIST, who will

be determined, loyally and honestly, to give to Mr. Monk the support he deserves in order to secure the triumph of the ideas he has held in the House of Commons for the last several years.

"Le Devoir" and its editor are free, free of either Conservatives or Liberals, free or reciprocists and anti-reciprocists. "Le Devoir" was established as an independent organ, and an independent organ it will remain.

And because the "DEVOIR" is an independent paper and has an editor who claims to be free, they will support, at the next elections, Mr. Monk and all candidates, Liberals, Conservatives or Nationalists, reciprocists or anti-reciprocists, who will not allow themselves to be blinded by the beguiling promises of the Laurier Government, NOR BY THE GOLD OF MR. SIFTON AND OF SIR HUGH GRAHAM, but who will be candidates of the people for the defence of the rights of Canada against the schemes all of those who wish to sacrifice our autonomy for the gold of the Americans, or for the titles which the British Government can confer on our public men.

This language, I think, was quite plain, these declarations were acclaimed by the mass and hailed by Mr. Monk's staunchest followers. However, there did not seem to be the same unanimous sentiment and the same enthusiasm as before the Drummond-Arthabaska election. The "come-backs" of toryism, roused by the hope of victory and eager for their share of the spoils could hardly conceal their discontent. The embarrassment of the new supernumeraries could easily be seen under the fresh coat of "autonomist" paint with which they were daubed.

As a final test, I intimated in concluding my speech that I would probably confine my work, in the coming campaign, to the columns of my paper.

This was at first believed to be a sham intended to deceive the enemy. But when parliament was dissolved, I repeated my intention to remain with "Le Devoir". At this, there was quite a flutter in the Conservative ranks.

I still see and hear D. O. Lesperance, "highly excited", rushing from Quebec and beseeching me to take part in the fight so as to assure the election of the greatest possible number of the nationalist candidates, and he pretended to be one, in order to prevent the imperialists from dominating the Conservative party.

Mr. Monk asked me to reconsider my decision. Needless to say that his request and his arguments had more weight with me than the tremors of Mr. Lesperance. He pointed out to me the importance of pursuing to the bitter end the fight started the previous year and crowned with such success in Drummond-Arthabaska. He kindly stated that without my help he felt himself unable to manage the contest in the Province. He added motives of the most intimate nature. If it is remembered that about this time Mrs. Monk died after a long and painful illness, it will readily be understood that I could not resist the appeal of the member for Jacques-Cartier. I was the more loath to refuse since Mr. Monk had left me no doubt whatever as to his firm determination to continue the fight on the same grounds as in 1910.

After this interview, I published in "Le Devoir" of August 2, 1911, a kind of programme entitled *"Le vrai terrain de la lutte"* in which I insisted on the necessity of keeping the imperialist question in the foreground and of avoiding falling into the trap laid for its adversaries by the introduction of the reciprocity question. This article ended thusly:

Under these conditions, the way is clear: Let us bring up independent candidates, Nationalists, Liberals, or Conservatives, reciprocists or anti-reciprocists—men of honour and truth who will rally around Mr. Monk to support in parliament, whatever government may be in power, the principles of autonomy that the member for Jacques-Cartier has laid down during the last year— men with sound ideas and armed with a firm determination, when the time comes, to solve the vital problems of the nation: Canadian autonomy, the safeguard of our nationality and the rights of minorities.

Such was the subject of the numerous speeches I delivered in all parts of the Province, from Hull to Ste-Flavie. On the request of the Conservatives and "Autonomists" of Quebec, Armand Lavergne took charge of the campaign in all of the Quebec districts and managed it with as much firmness as ability. The magnificent results he obtained are well known.

THE CONSERVATIVES AND SIR HUGH GRAHAM SUBSIDIZE THE "AUTONOMIST" CAMPAIGN

So that there may be no doubt as to the part we were taking in the campaign, I published in "le Devoir" of the 3rd of August 1911, under the title — AVIS CLAIR ET PRECIS, a notice containing the following paragraphs:—

From the date of the meeting at Three Rivers, Mr. Bourassa will take no part whatever in any demonstration unless it is to support the independent candidates who pledged themselves to defend against all comers, or *whatever the party in power*, the principles laid down in common by Mr. Monk and Mr. Bourassa.

But when his name is used without his

consent, he will denounce the fraud, whatever be the consequences for the author of it.

All may rest assured that Bourassa will not play the part of a cat's paw nor that of a decoy.

Needless to add that in all the electoral districts given up to Mr. Monk and the "Autonomist" party by the Conservatives, the candidates accepted the common programme. Some called themselves "autonomists", others "independents" and a very few "Nationalists"—not one who styled himself a Conservative, and all insisted on having a speech from Lavergne and myself in their constituencies.

Mr. Blondin, not content with the magnificent meeting held at Grand-Mère, in 1910, nor with the inauguration of the electoral campaign at Three Rivers, in the month of August 1911, was imploring me to hold another meeting in his county.

Mr. Lesperance, who was profiting by the popularity of Lavergne, was reproaching me with near-desertion, because I was unable to go to Montmagny to speak in favour of the first of the Nationalists, as he styled himself.

Mr. Nantel begged a letter from me bearing witness to his sincerity and his independence.

Mr. Bergeron wrote to me to recall our common struggles in 1905, in favour of the Catholic minority of the Territories. He assured me that he was in perfect accord with my views on the naval question.

Young Lavallée, a former Liberal, wrote that the nationalist seed scattered in Bellechasse in 1908 was springing up, and that he took it upon himself to reap the crop.

In the counties of Bagot and Nicolet, the organizers of the "autonomist party"

caused the withdrawal from the contest of one of the most honourable and most prominent Conservatives of the Province, Mr. T. Chase Casgrain, to make way for the Nationalist candidates, Mr. Tancrède Marsil and Paul Emile Lamarche.

But the most pathetic entreaties and professions of faith came from Jos. Rainville and L. P. Pelletier.

I had already spoken at Verchères in favour of Rainville. But this valiant knight, on meeting poor worn-out Lavergne in the offices of "Le Devoir", hung by his coat tails to drag him to another meeting: "Armand!" he tearfully cried, "You know well that I am the only sincere one in that crowd! Do you not understand that I must be in the House of Commons to keep them from betraying us?

Mr. Pelletier, "independent candidate of both parties", who was calling Lavergne "his leader", kept the telephone ringing with his desperate calls: "Tell Bourassa that I implore him *on my knees* to come to Charlesbourg to speak for me!" Yes, on his knees!

Outside of the declarations of faith, speeches and party etiquette, there was the highly important question of electoral funds, that purulent sore of politics.

Mr. Monk was justly anxious on that account. He did not want the tory party to put the hook into his candidates.

On this point the Nationalists could offer no assistance. They were supplying the ideas, the enthusiasm and the popularity. But that is all they could give.

The organizers of the "autonomist" party had sized up the situation in this way: Amongst those who were both desirous and able to subscribe to the electoral fund of the opposition, there were some who shared the opinions of Mr. Monk on the naval question; others cared for nothing else but reciprocity; they were perfectly ready to help the candidates of either party provided they would oppose the tariff agreement; lastly, others had no other wish but that of defeating the government, whatever were the principles or the ideas of the opposing candidates, either on the naval question or on that of reciprocity.

These were the different classes of subscribers who, I believed, contributed the first funds. But when the fight was well on, the desire of the Conservative leaders to win at all costs overshadowed all other considerations; they did not hesitate to pour down into the cash-box of the "autonomist" party a share of their funds, without demanding in return any promise or any pledge whatever from the candidates, whether they were for or against reciprocity, who fought the government out of adverseness to the naval question and who denounced the "no less nefarious policy" of Mr. Borden.

When the "regular funds" were exhausted, Sir Hugh Graham came to the front. He offered to supply the lacking funds, provided each candidate gave him his personal note, payable in case of defeat only. Was his object in this to secure a hold on the candidates elected, who would sit and vote in parliament? I know that at least two of those who passed under his Candine Forks openly declared that they would not be bought. He paid without question.

Were other "autonomist" candidates more compliant or faint-hearted? Must we conclude that these underhand negotiations, of which I heard long after the elections, were the cause of certain defections? Was it in these intimate interviews that a few recognized adversaries of any imperial contribution began to realize that "something" should be done

for the mother-country and the Empire? Did the funds supplied by Sir Hugh Graham enlighten some of these "patriots" about the German peril? It is quite possible. But nothing transpired before the 21st of September 1911.

The fact remains that the funds of the Conservative party and the contributions from imperialist sources served to defray the election expenses of from 30 to 40 candidates, reciprocists and anti-reciprocists, who were denouncing the Naval Act and the "no less nefarious policy" of Mr. Borden, and who gave their solemn promise to vote against any government who would refuse a plebiscite on this question.

The best proof of Mr. Borden's change of front and of his desire to fall in with the Nationalists may perhaps be found in the manifesto he published, on August 15, on the eve of the campaign. Three fourths of this bulky document was devoted to reciprocity. The only paragraph relating to the naval question was a formal condemnation of the act passed during the previous session, and nothing more; not a word about the emergency, and nothing about the designs of the Conservative party in this matter; no distinction whatever between an emergency and a permanent policy.

Mr. Borden and his colleagues are today deliberately deceiving the people when they pretend that the leader of the Conservative Party had his declarations and resolutions of March 1910, in favour of an emergency contribution, endorsed by the people.

We were then perfectly right in stating, and still have reason to repeat, that the only direct mandate which the leader of the Conservative party solicited and obtained, was that of abrogating the Naval Act.

C. H. Cahan, *The Montreal Herald*, September 2, 1911.
Robert Borden Papers, OC 47, W. B. Nantel to Borden, November 28, 1911.

The Conservatives and the Nationalistes

Montreal, September 12, 1911
Editor, Herald:

I am in no alliance with Mr. Bourassa, "unholy" or otherwise; but I am avowedly and openly co-operating with him, so far as I can, in his opposition to the Laurier Government. . . .

I am co-operating with Mr. Bourassa in this campaign: First, because Mr. Bourassa is not in favor of the reciprocity pact. I have entered this electoral campaign as a worker in the ranks, because I believe that this reciprocity pact will, if adopted, prove most prejudicial to the vital industrial and commercial interests of Canada, and undermine the very foundations of our stability and strength as a political unit of the Empire. I know, and you know, and it would be a crime against our intelligence if we did not frankly recognize, that the whole strength of the movement for reciprocity in this country is due to the undoubted desire of Sir Wilfrid Laurier, of Mr. Fielding, of the Grangers of the North-Western Provinces, and of their most active supporters, to bring about free trade between Canada and the United States. Sir Wilfrid Laurier has repeatedly declared that the commercial and industrial interests of Canada and of the United States are identical; and that he and his party would never cease from their efforts until they obtain unrestricted recopricity, or absolute free trade with that Republic. Within the last few days, on a public platform in Montreal Mr. Fisher, a responsible member of the federal government in response to an interrogator, frankly avowed that he espoused free trade.

Political exigencies have temporarily prevented Sir Wilfrid and Mr. Fielding from going to the full length of their program; but I believe them to have been frank and sincere when in times past they freely disclosed the far-reaching results which they were then and are now still pledged to obtain. I believe that there can be no successful manufacturing development in Canada on the basis of free trade with the United States, unless that free trade is permanently and absolutely assured, so that large industries established in Canada, near the sources of supply of their raw materials, can be assured of having the United States as a permanent market for their manufactured products; and there can be no guarantee of permanency for any trade arrangements between Canada and the United States which are not based on the permanent political union between Canada and the United States. With Mr. Bourassa I am absolutely opposed to political union with the United States; and with him I am in favor of a policy of moderate protection which will ensure the establishment of manufacturing industries in Canada.

Secondly, I am co-operating with Mr. Bourassa in this campaign, because he insists upon wiping out thievery and corrupt dealing on the part of the federal administration and its political partizans.

The thieves, who hung on to and eventually destroyed the late Conservative Government of Canada, confined their operations to mere kindergarten practices as compared with the widespread, systematic and ruthless robbery that now prevails. Every business man knows that it is impossible to conduct legitimate public business with the present Government of Canada on an honest basis, and that if he does business at all it must be on a basis of gifts and graft. The Diaz administration in Mexico, so recently wiped out, was, in my opinion, and in my experience, a paragon of virtue as compared with the Laurier administration. Mr. Bourassa is an honest man, absolutely above reproach in his character and reputation. He is making, on every political platform in this province, splendid and successful appeals to the electors to support a clean, wholesome administration; he is the most efficient political force in this province, working for honesty and efficiency in federal affairs.

Thirdly—I am co-operating with Mr. Bourassa in this campaign because I accept the principle, first propounded by him and accepted by Mr. Borden and the Conservative party generally, that any permanent scheme of naval defence must be developed by a full and frank discussion, and a satisfactory re-adjustment of the political relations existing between the colonies and Great Britain, which must first be submitted for the decision of the Canadian people. The Laurier naval scheme is depicted by its author in Quebec as a strictly circumscribed Canadian enterprise, and in Ontario as broadly Imperial in its scope and operations. The scheme is deceptive and even farcical. Under our existing colonial conditions there can be no complete naval autonomy for Canada. The legislative jurisdiction of

the Canadian Parliament is limited to the territorial waters of Canada; and, beyond the limits of those waters, all Canadian ships are subject to the legislative jurisdiction of the English Parliament in which Canadians have no representation. Despite all exaggerated eloquence to the contrary, Canada, in respect of its legislative jurisdiction, is still a colony; the Merchants' Shipping Act, and the Naval Acts of the English Parliament, which still apply to Canadian ships and to Canadian seamen, are emphatic reminders of that fact. There are admittedly grave difficulties to be met and surmounted before we can provide for united action or any action between Imperial and Dominion units; but instead of making any statesmanlike efforts to meet these difficulties, which are rooted deep in our colonial status, Sir Wilfrid has resorted to the tricks of a political opportunist, and to the sophistry of a demagogue; he is avoiding vital issues by facing both ways for partisan purposes.

You ask "What is your policy on the naval question, Mr. Cahan?" It is not for me, a mere worker in the ranks, to develop a naval policy; but I sincerely believe that despite the violent denunciations against militarism by which Sir Wilfrid and his party allies have in times past inflamed the passions and misled the minds of the electors of Quebec, intelligent and broadminded Canadian statesmen can develop a policy which will meet with the approval of a majority of the Canadian people of every province of the Dominion; and I believe, with equal sincerity, that any such policy, when intelligently considered and accepted by a majority of the Canadian people will also receive the approval of Mr. Bourassa and his associates of the Province of Quebec.

Yours truly,

November 28, 1911

Dear Mr. Borden,

. . . I was never a Nationalist, and Bourassa knows it perfectly well. During the last campaign I had no Nationalist speaker to assist me, not even Bourassa. We had called a meeting to give him the opportunity to answer Laurier's speech in St. Jerome, but on account of illness he did not come, and Mr. Prevost and myself were obliged to take the meeting alone.

I have helped Bourassa in Bellechasse, and in the founding of his paper. I saw no other way to destroy Laurierism in Quebec; and for that purpose Nationalism was a good device. I wished to serve Laurier with the same medicine he gave the Conservative party in 1886, in the Riel affair, when he assisted Mercier to overthrow the Liberal-Conservatives of Quebec, through the Nationalism of Mercier, and so prepared his own way to Ottawa.

After all the Nationalists in Quebec are nothing else but dissatisfied Liberals, who were willing to abandon Laurier and turn Conservative without too sudden a change, but with plausible reasons.

Yours truly

Part V

The Liberals

The Liberal campaign was doomed from the start. Liberal strategy was to concentrate on the economic benefits of reciprocity—increased population, more trade, larger traffic for Canadian railways, higher land values and enlarged orders for Canadian factories. But as the election began, the party had clearly lost the initiative. The argument that the agreement would open a vast third market to the Canadian farmer was no longer useful, particularly in the cities where the consumer was convinced that increased farmer prosperity would result in an increased cost of living. Liberal spokesmen were forced to deal with the loyalty question, and this they found increasingly difficult in the face of the flood of propaganda from the Canadian National League.

The province of Quebec played a central role in the election strategy. As a practising politician Laurier realized that it was politically essential to preserve and protect his base of popular support. In a speech in Montreal at the end of October, 1910 he fired the opening volley in a campaign designed to prick the Bourassa bubble. It was an aggressive reply to Bourassa and his *nationaliste* supporters, defending his naval policy as a national duty, and denouncing the attempt to create an exclusively French-Canadian party. Throughout his address, it was Bourassa, not Monk, who became the focus of his attack, Bourassa's speeches which were quoted and countered, Bourassa's policies which were discussed and refuted. The lines were clear for the upcoming campaign.

Public meetings were held in virtually every constituency once the election had been called. These forums or "assemblées contradictoires" were unique to political life in "la belle province." Each party nominated a number of speakers to address the audience alternately. According to Charles

Power, later to become a member of Mackenzie King's cabinet, the meetings were valuable exercises in participatory democracy." There was much heckling, but I do not remember a speaker being denied a full hearing . . . The *assemblée contradictoire* not only provided an ideal training for parliamentary debaters, it also supplied a lively medium for the exchange of political views and for the clash of political philosophies. I am inclined to think that, as a result, more people retained a livelier interest in politics." The assemblée at Ste. Hyacinthe on August 13 was the largest and bitterest of these meetings in 1911 and set the tone for many which followed in the course of the campaign.

Outside of Quebec the most immediate problem was the province of Ontario where the party had been plagued with a number of difficulties for over two years. Part of the problem centred on Allan Aylesworth, the Minister of Justice, and the provincial leader of the federal Liberals. A brilliant student at the University of Toronto and then a leading member of the legal profession in Ontario, he had entered the cabinet in 1905 to revitalize the party and restore its prestige throughout the province. But he possessed few of the talents of a successful politician and had little interest in the intricacies of party management and organization. The question came to a head at the end of April 1910 when Hartley H. Dewart, a young Toronto Liberal, wrote an open letter to the Toronto *Globe* lamenting the state of the party's organization in Ontario and laying the blame on the Minister of Justice. Although Laurier refused to accept his resignation, Aylesworth let it be known he would not be a candidate in another election.

Lack of leadership and efficient organization heightened the task of selling reci-

procity. The difficulty was that few Canadians understood what the treaty involved and what its benefits might be. As the Minister of Labour, William Lyon Mackenzie King made clear at the end of June 1911 to George Graham, the Minister of Railways, and the chief campaign strategist in Ontario, the basic educational work of the Liberal organization had barely begun. The correspondence between Graham and Fielding provides an interesting insight into the preparation of campaign literature once the wheels were in motion. Yet it is important to note that at a time when the propaganda of the Canadian National League and its Conservative allies was flooding the country, the Liberal counter-attack was still on the drawing board.

The Liberals tried to return the debate to the economics of reciprocity once their campaign got underway. Canadians, they assumed, would approve the agreement when they understood what it involved and the benefits which would result from its implementation. In a private letter to one of his constituents on the eve of the campaign, King assessed the arguments for and against the reciprocity proposals. As the election unfolded, party spokesmen developed these themes. Laurier maintained that increased trade meant increased prosperity; rather than weakening ties with Great Britain, prosperity would strengthen loyalty and the bonds of kinship. And in the middle of August, Fielding issued a major statement in Halifax, detailing the benefits which the Maritime provinces would receive from reciprocity.

Party leaders, however, were unable to avoid the loyalty question. And as the campaign progressed they were forced to devote most of their energies to refuting the charges that reciprocity would break the Imperial connection by pushing Canada into the arms of the United States. Campaign literature was carefully designed to demonstrate the fallacy of this argument. In countless pamphlets statistics were compiled to point out that Canada already imported two and one half times as much from the United States as from Great Britain, obtensibly with little effect on her notional status. To the argument that reciprocity would deflect trade from the country's east-west transportation network, the Liberals replied the St. Lawrence was the shortest route to Liverpool in the western and mid-western states and would thus expect a vastly increased carriage trade with reciprocity. "People lived on figures," wrote Stephen Leacock in his fanciful description of the reciprocity campaign in Mariposa, "and the man who could remember most of them stood out as a born leader."

The Liberals also tried to focus attention upon the dangers of the "Unholy Alliance" between Borden and Bourassa. The union, they charged, would result in Borden surrendering the party to Bourassa and his *nationaliste* supporters. Led by the Toronto *Globe*, the Liberal press devoted column after column to the *nationaliste* leader's campaign, documenting their charges that a double game was being played, with Borden in Ontario protesting his loyalty to Britain while his allies in Quebec were "doing their treasonable utmost to inflame the minds of the French-Canadians against that very Imperial idea." Whether these tactics gained any votes is open to queston. By concentrating on Bourassa, the Liberals underlined the racial and religious question upon which they were also vulnerable.

Wilfrid Laurier, *The Montreal Daily Herald,* October 11, 1910.

The Challenge is Accepted

. . . the principal object which this situation affords to me, in my opinion, is to outline the political situation of our country. I come here to discuss with you calmly the questions which at the present time ought to occupy the attention of our people. We are evidently in the midst of a series of important events and the most remarkable fact at the present time on the political horizon is that the Conservative party, the Conservative party as we have known it, the party of Macdonald, the party of Cartier and Chapleau, is in process of disorganization, and that in a short time it will be fully decomposed, even if decomposition is not already accomplished. . . .

. . . in the province of Quebec . . . this disintegration of the Conservative party began a long time ago. As you know, it is a long time ago since the sensible elements, the healthy minds of the Conservative party separated themselves from this party and became part of ours. I say that they separated themselves from it. I ought to say, perhaps, that they were excluded from it, for, in fact, they were excluded by the violent section who ended by absorbing the organization of the party. This violent section, as you know it, comprises the pharisees of Canadian Catholicism—those who have constituted themselves without ostentation the defenders of the religion which no one attacked, those who handle the holy water sprinkler as though it were a club, those who have arrogated to themselves the monopoly of orthodoxy, those who excommunicate, right and left, all those whose stature is a little greater than theirs; those who only seem to have hatred and envy for motive and instinct; those who insulted Cardinal Taschereau when he was alive and who now that he is dead attack his memory; those who made Chapleau's life bitter; those, finally, whom the people with their picturesque language are designated under the name of Castors.

You are going to ask me perhaps by what name this new organization is going to call itself. You might say perhaps Nationalists; . . .

. . . they will be Nationalist, Conservative or Liberal, according to the complexion of the audiences they address, but at the bottom they are all 'castors'.

At recent meetings they called themselves anything they thought their audiences wanted in order to do most harm possible to the Government, and in order to do that they fell back upon assertions which were as absurd as they were false and false as they were absurd.

There is meanwhile one of their tactics whose foolishness I must expose, that is where at all their meetings they affirm that the Laurier of 1911 is quite different from the Laurier of 1902. . . .

I have come here to discuss this question and to show you where the change has been. What was the situation in 1902? In 1902 there was a convention, the Imperial Conference of London, at which there were present representatives of Canada, Newfoundland, Australia, the Cape of Good Hope and Natal. And at this convention a resolution was proposed by one of the members, Mr. Seddon, of New Zealand, as follows:

It is desirable that Imperial reserve forces should be organized in each of the dependencies of His Majesty across the seas for active service, in case of danger, outside of the said dependency or colony in which this reserve may be organized. The conditions under which this reserve might be employed outside of the colony in which it may be organized should be determined jointly by the Imperial Government and that of the colony at the time when that reserve is formed and to conform with the laws at that time in force regarding that reserve. The costs of training and armament of the said reserve should be paid in proportion and by a method of payment determined by the Imperial Government and that of the colony.

This motion, I need not tell you, had it been adopted, would have meant an entry into European Militarism. It was reported by the Imperial Government. The Secretary of State for War . . . proposed that all the powers, all the young nations who make part of the Empire, should build, equip and maintain a reserve force of the army which would be always at the disposition of the War Office at London.

At the same time the Secretary of State for the Marine demanded that the same powers should contribute a sum of money annually for the maintenance of an Imperial fleet.

There, indeed, was the entrance to militarism. But the Canadian Ministers who were at London, and I was one of them, opposed this demand of the Imperial Government in a categoric refusal; a refusal respectful in form, but absolute in meaning. But we did more than that. We placed before the Conference our policy, which we intended to follow, and at the risk of taxing our patience, in order to thoroughly establish our position, permit me to place before the project which I proposed then at this Imperial Conference.

After setting forth that we had already commenced our system of defence we continued as follows:

Actually the expenses which Canada will need for the defence of the country are restricted to the land army; the Canadian Government is disposed equally to meet the costs of the organization of a navy. On the sea coast of Canada there is a numerous population admirably qualified as a naval reserve, and it is hoped that shortly it will be possible to establish a service which will permit of giving the desired training to that population and utilizing its services in the defence of the country in case of need. Briefly, the Ministers repeat if it is impossible for them to give their support to the proposed measures they will give full accounts of the obligation of the Dominion to make larger and larger disbursements for the defence, according as the increase of the population and increase in enrichment of the country will permit. Their desire is that these disbursements be made so as to free the taxpayer of the metropolis of a part of the burden which he is actually supporting and they ardently wish that their plans for defence may be put into execution with the cooperation of the Imperial authorities, and according to the advice of experienced Imperial officers, so as to permit the practice of local autonomy, which has been so powerful a factor in the constitution of Imperial unity.

You will see by this note that we declared our intention to sustain the obligation incumbent upon all nations of defending their own territory, that we had already organized a militia, and that we were equally ready to undertake our naval defence, but that we would at all times follow and maintain the principle of our local autonomy.

Now, I have simply to call your attention to two things provided by this naval law. It simply decrees this, that the Government of Canada should organize another naval service, and that this service should remain entirely under the control of the Government of Canada.

Outside of this there is not a single word which would give to Great Britain that which she demanded in 1902—the organization of a war service to be put at the disposition of the War Office. Not one word.

. . . let us examine also this conference of 1907. At that conference was represented, Canada, Australia, Newfoundland, New Zealand, Cape Colony, Natal and another country, which in 1902 was at war with England, but which was then represented by the most valiant soldiers who had fought against England, the illustrious General Botha. At this conference, one of the representatives of Cape Colony, Doctor Smart, proposed this resolution:—

That this conference, recognizing the importance of the services rendered by the navy in the defence of the Empire and the protection of its commerce and the primary importance of furnishing and maintaining a navy in the highest possible state of efficiency, expresses the opinion that it is the duty of the dependencies overseas to contribute to the maintenance of the navy in a manner which ought to be determined by the local Legislature, whether in giving a sum of money, in establishing a local navy, or in furnishing other services in a manner which should be decided after an understanding with the Admiralty and according to the manner which would best suit the particular autonomy of each colony.

Reflect a moment on these words which you have heard! It is a proposition which had an obligation which was represented as imperial and of imperative necessity. An obligation on the part of all the dominions which compose the British Empire to adopt a common system of defence for the reason that each dominion, whether she should ultimately contribute to a local navy or make a contribution to the imperial navy, nevertheless, affirmed the principle of a common defence to which all parts of the Empire were obliged to contribute.

Now, gentlemen, for my part, I opposed with all my strength this proposition. And why? Because it was an obligation to recognize the beauty of contributing and that was an obligation which did not conform perfectly to our policy of 1902, and on my opposition the proposition was not pushed any further. And, if I saw there the salvation of our provinces and of our autonomy, that was the very policy that our adversaries had approved. . . .

Now this is what I have to say to you on the principal point. Here is the only question which is of importance in this debate: What is the reason we had for proposing and voting this naval service law? There, gentlemen, is a question on which superior minds can pronounce themselves, and which they can discuss, and I am here with you to discuss it.

The reason, gentlemen, why we have proposed this naval service law in 1910 you have found in the memorandum which I read to you just now when we said that we proposed to organize a naval defence according to the proportion in which we should increase in population and riches.

This law was proposed in 1902, in 1907, in 1908 and in 1910, eight years after it was first proposed. Eight years, gentlemen, in the life of a people is a minute; in fact, it is not a minute, it is a second. But in this minute, in this second, Canada has made the progress of a giant. We are in conditions far different from those in which we were in 1902. We have increased in population and in riches. Our population has increased by more than 30 per cent and our revenue has increased by more than 100 per cent. In 1902, our population according to the census of the previous year, was 5,375,-000. In 1910 I have no hesitation in saying that the population is at least 8,000,000 of people.

Our revenue in 1902 was $58,000,-000. For the fiscal year which closed on the 31st of March of last year our revenue showed a total of more than $100,000,-000. And this year, the year which finished on the 31st of March last, I do not hesitate to say will show a revenue of at least $112,000,000.

And now, gentlemen, here are the reasons, as I have said in the memorandum I quoted, why we have accomplished the work that we said we should accomplish in 1902. But there are others. There is another reason more peremptory and more definite. It is that we have increased morally as we have increased in numbers. We should have had some hesitation perhaps in 1902 in saying what I now say to you without any doubt what-ever and that is that we have become a nation.

Again, it is the duty of every power-ful nation to defend its territory. It is the duty of every nation which has a maritime territory to organize a naval defence. . . . This obligation is accepted by all the great Powers—by England, Germany, Austria, Hungary, France and Italy, and even by the Powers of the second order, according to their rank and extent of their territory. Sweden, Nor-way, Denmark, and even Portugal main-tain their armies and recognize that they ought to have a territorial defence and that it is their duty to maintain an organ-ized naval service.

At the present time there are two countries which do not maintain a navy. They are Switzerland and Belgium, and the cause of this—Switzerland is situated in the centre of Europe, she has not a single line of maritime frontier. Belgium has a maritime territory easy to protect, for she has only forty leagues of shore. Forty leagues—that is to say, not even the distance from Montreal to Sorel—and in these forty leagues she has a port of considerable importance, the port of Antwerp, which she protects not by means of a navy, but which she has sur-rounded by enormous fortifications at a cost of seventy millions of francs.

And, now, gentlemen, this is the position that we maintain, that each nation is obliged to provide for its national defence, and this position is so strong, so sane, and so practical that Mr. Bourassa thinks that the only means to combat it is to affirm that we are not a nation. In a speech which he delivered in Antigonish, Mr. Bourassa said—and I will quote his words—'That we are not a country that we are not even the small-est nation, that we cannot govern ourselves without having permission and that we are subject to the decisions of the British Empire'.

And this, after the struggles that we have sustained in order that we might have the right to govern ourselves. Gentlemen, according to Mr. Bourassa, we are no more than the Leaward Islands, Guiana, Jamaica, Bermuda, and all the other colonies which form part of the British Empire, but which are designated still under the name of Crown Colonies and which are governed by Downing Street.

When Mr. Bourassa stated that we are not a nation I retort that either Mr. Bourassa does not know or else that he forgets the history and traditions of our country. The reason why Mr. Bourassa pretends that we are not a nation is that we are still under the protection of England. It is true that we are under the political protection of England, but we are legislatively independent. . . .

Look for a country whose colony is able to make its own treaties of commerce; you will not find any. Look for a country where a colony who has obtained the right to have a responsible government for its own people, you will not find one. There is only the British Empire where such a state of things can be found and it is Canada which has been the pioneer of that new politics.

We have a population of eight millions; we have a territory which covers a continent; we have the power to make our own laws; we have the power to administer our own affairs; we have the power to make our commercial treaties and yet, however, we are said not to be a nation. Well, I say this to Mr. Bourassa: He and I do not often agree now, but there was a time when we were more in accord than we are at present, but yet we do agree on one point; it is, that we are in favor of the tie which unites us to the British Empire. We are loyal subjects of the King of Great Britain. Well, if we were in a position of inferiority such a one of not being a nation, since we have a population of eight million people, I should say we should be obliged to demand the revision of that tie which binds us to Great Britain, but that is not the case at all. The two things are compatible, but Mr. Bourassa has arrived at that penible necessity which culminates and belittles this country in order to prevent him assuming the obligations which the dignity of his country imposes upon him.

Here, gentlemen, we have the reason, the true reason why we have assumed this new politic; why we have decided like all the other nations, to have our own navy. Gentlemen, I am not here to judge my compatriots to say that my compatriots are of the opinion that we are not a nation and that we occupy merely the rank of one of the Crown colonies. If I were to judge so, I should be wrong. But if I have well interpreted the sentiment of my compatriots I have not the least doubt that the action which I have taken on the question of the navy will be accepted by all my compatriots as the right one. I have told you, gentlemen, the position of our policy. It is a question of high conception. I regret to say that it is apparently too high to be understood by those who are making war upon it. . . .

I said a few minutes ago, that it is the duty of all nations to be prepared to defend that territory. We have a military law, which has stood since the first day of the colony, which was continued through the French regime and which has been continued under the English regime, which was finally revised in 1868, by Sir

Geo. E. Cartier himself, and which has never since that time been submitted to any appreciable change.

An important disposition of that law is that all the male population between the age of eighteen and sixty years, is subject to military service in time of war. That disposition has remained dominant for nearly one hundred years, but there is another disposition which has created what is called voluntary service, and according to that voluntary service we have nearly three thousand men in the permanent troops, but who engaged themselves voluntarily.

We have nearly 50,000 men in temporary troops who have not abandoned the civil life, but who exercise from time to time and who served under the flag, if need be.

Three thousand men of permanent troops, fifty thousand men of voluntary troop distributed from Prince Edward island to the Island of Vancouver.

It is often said why this military force? We have no enemies, and for nearly one hundred years that we have had no war, the experience of all the people and in all ages has shown that the military force is absolutely necessary to the existence of a nation for the execution of the law.

As to the autonomy of the institution of a military force, that is to pay a tax of insurance to assure the security of the nation.

You insure your home, you incur a tax, not that you have serious fears that the house will be burnt, but because such a calamity is always possible.

You assure your life, not that you fear to die, but that such an event is always possible.

It is the same with nations. They must take some precautions against eventualities, the possibility of war.

I ought to recognize that the law was revised in 1868 by Sir George Cartier. Several objections were then raised, but these objections have long ago disappeared, and to-day I think I am not mistaken when I say that every one understands that this military service which we have is necessary to us, and I think that in the city of Montreal, every time the 65th Regiment is seen to march past with the flags, there are many hearts which beat with pride. I might say that there are young Nationalists—and I know one who have joined as volunteers. It was a fine thing, and we must congratulate him for it. Every year this young Nationalist puts on the beautiful uniform of the Canadian soldiers and for twelve days he learns how to use his weapon and take part in military exercises.

Then, gentlemen, why should a young Canadian not be permitted to wear the blue uniform of the soldier, since a young Nationalist is permitted to wear the red uniform of the soldier.

Why should not the young Canadian carry out manoeuvres on the deck of a boat, when the young Nationalist is doing his drill in the cow shed, to use an expression of Rabelais?

Gentlemen, there is a similarity in the two cases, the two services complete one another, we know the militia service, let us now examine naval service.

Let me tell you first of all that according to the law of the naval service, the service is purely voluntary, there is nothing compulsory about it. I know that young Nationalists who are now running around the country, who go from church door to church door, claim that according to the law of the naval service, the whole male population from eighteen years of age to sixty years of age, can be called upon to take their place on the man-of-war. One must assure these young people that their fears are totally without foundation. I am glad to tell them that, even if the country were at war—which God forbid, and which is hardly possible, if the country were engaged in war, even to defend its own territory they would never be called upon to serve. I should not like to scratch them, they would be left at home with the women and children.

One must excuse these young students for such language, but when men like Messrs. Monk and Bourassa, come and tell us such nonsense, it is really abusing the public and making fun of the public. It would be odious if it were not so comical. . . .

But there is something else. Everybody knows it is possible to take a man from the fields and place him in the ranks of an army, to put a gun in his hands and that he will be a good soldier. The French revolution was a striking example. In 1792 thousands and thousands of young men who had never handled a gun served under the flag to repel the invader, and these young people became the finest troops in the world, and in our own country in 1812 there was obligatory service. Young men were taken from the fields to serve under the flag, and these new recruits won the battle of Chateauguay.

Gentlemen, a soldier can be made with a man from the fields without preliminary apprenticeship, but to take a man from the fields and place him on the deck of a ship is simply absurd, and if Mr. Bourassa had reflected ever so little he would have seen that the suggestion has not even common sense. Then, gentlemen, was I not right when I said at the beginning of my remarks: "The

assertions with which our project is being fought are as false as they are absurd, and as absurd as they are false?"

Let us pass now to another point. We are told, and the statement is repeated, that our navy, according to the dispositions of the law, will be obliged to take part in all the wars of Great Britain.

However, it is with such insanities as this that they combat our marine project. The British navy has not been in battle since 1805, and if our navy were obliged to take part in all the battles of the British fleet, I believe that our young Nationalists might live in peace until they reach the age of Methusaleh before they would be called.

But is it true to-day that according to this naval law our fleet once organized would be obliged to take part in all the wars of the Empire? According to law the control of the Canadian marine would at all times belong to the Government of Canada. Clause 23 provides: 'In critical times the Governor-in-council may put the marine or any part of it at the disposition of His Majesty for general service in the Royal Marine'.

The Government, the Parliament, the people of Canada can put our marine at the service of the King, but no one else can do so, and anyone who says to the contrary to the express provision of this law simply mocks the public.

I refer to another argument of Mr. Bourassa's on which he bases his declaration that our marine would be obliged to take part in the wars of the Empire, when he said that when I presented this law Great Britain was at war. That is true. It is a consequence of our dependence on the British Crown. It is an international law that when a nation is at war all its possessions are subject to attack.

Of this we have a striking proof of the war of the United States with Spain. The United States declared war against Spain to ensure the liberation of Cuba, but at the same time they sent a spark into the Philippines and took them. They were at war with all the Spanish territories. It is the same thing with us. From the moment that Great Britain is at war we are exposed to attack.

Does it follow, then, because we are exposed to attack we are going to take part in all the wars of the Empire? No. We shall take part if we think proper; we shall certainly take part if our territory is attacked. Suppose that there was a war between England and Russia, and that Russia sent a fleet to attack British Columbia or the St. Lawrence; we should certainly have to defend our territory. Supposing that we should take part in the war it would be for the people and Government of Canada to decide the question. . . .

The arguments brought in opposition to this law are simply absurd, and when in a few years the horizon is cleared people will be astonished that men should be found of so foolish a spirit as to find a bugbear in this question.

When the Nationalists say that our young men will be obliged to serve on warships they say a thing which is absurd and false. No one will be obliged to join the navy who does not wish to do so. The young men who do join the service know that they will not be obliged to take part in all the wars of England, but they know that they can be called on by the people of Canada, when Parliament judges it to be apropos, to take part in England's wars.

But, gentlemen, if there are young men who wish to fight, to serve their King and country, who will say them nay? Why deny to the young men, who wish to enter the service to defend their King and country in this manner, the right which the Nationalists themselves declare: 'We do not want to go, and we do not wish that you should go either.' What kind of liberty is this? That they do not wish to go is quite in order, but when they seek to prevent me from serving my King and country they dictate to me in a manner which I will not permit. . . .

. . . the motive for which we have decided to organize naval defence is that we fear war. We have on the Atlantic and Pacific coasts thousands of miles of territory, which we are obliged to control for the protection of our citizens. I do not believe in war, I believe that war between civilized countries will become more and more rare. It is a hundred years since we have known war, and I hope that before long we and our neighbors will celebrate this hundred years of peace between us.

One of the reasons why war is becoming more rare is that democracy now takes part in the Government of civilized countries. I do not say that democracy is wiser or more impeccable than any other class of society, but that democracy detests war. But while war is becoming more scarce, it has not yet been done away with, and I say that while Canada is not obliged to take part in any war, it is our duty to take part in any war in which the supremacy of the British navy is in danger, and to do it with all our strength. That is our position.

Well, gentlemen, remark these words: They date from the commencement of their parliamentary regime; they are the words of the greatest statesman that French Canada has produced, Lafontaine. What he demanded was a union of the reformers of Upper and Lower

Canada in a spirit of peace, union and fraternity. That has been my political gospel, and I have never known any other. I need not tell you that I have the honor, as you have, to belong to the French race. I am the chief of a party of which the French race is a minority. I have never, thank God, had to hide my origin.

For 20 years I have had the honor to be chief of the Liberal party. When I was chosen in 1887 I represented to my colleagues in the House of Commons that they should choose a leader from the majority and that I had better remain a simple soldier in the grand army of the Liberal party. But my friends replied "No", the Liberal party knows no distinction of race or religion. We are all equal in this country. Gentlemen, our rights were in peril. But my English colleagues came forward and offered themselves in defence of those rights, and if the rights of our fellow citizens of English origin were to be imperilled I would address myself to you to defend those rights as you would defend your own.

I have been accused of being a traitor to my race. But such accusations do not concern me much. Examine the two questions on which at the present time I am accused of treason for very different motives. I am accused of treason in this province because it is said that I have violated the rights of the French-Canadians in permitting the immigration which is taking place just now to the North-west. But we have only followed the example of the United States, which in a century has become the most powerful nation in the world, because they have opened their territory to all those who have any ambition in the world. During a hundred years it was the American star which was resplendent in the firmament. I have the ambition that the 20th century

should be the century in which Canada should be the star towards which the world should turn.

We have peopled the Canada of the west, and for my part I desire that the immigration of the Province of Quebec instead of moving into the United States should be directed towards our western provinces. There are a million Canadians in the United States, but they should be in the territories of the new provinces. Cartier dreamed of making of Manitoba a new province of Quebec, but by reason of certain circumstances that noble dream has not been realized.

The reason why there was so much emigration from the Province of Quebec in the past was that there was only one kind of work apart from the liberal professions—agriculture. Those who could not live on the land were obliged to seek work in the United States. To-day however, they come to look for work at Montreal. Your population here has doubled in ten years, and to-morrow if you wish you may make a tour of all the new factories which have been opened within the past ten years commencing with the Angus shops of the C.P.R., and one after the other will tell you that their markets are in the Canadian west.

Then I am again accused of being a traitor to my country and the Empire because we are going, in a short time I hope, to open negotiations for a treaty of reciprocity with the United States. The first duty of a country is to work for its prosperity, and I submit that in this action we are doing that which is likely to bring an immense prosperity to this country. And if it is treason to work for this and I am ready to accept that reproach. In 1896 I sent two of my colleagues to Washington to negotiate a treaty of reciprocity. We were received with much politeness but could obtain nothing. At that time I said we would make no more pilgrimages to Washington. We have not made a pilgrimage to Washington again, but last year there was a pilgrimage from Washington to Ottawa. Since that time we have adopted a new policy of preference towards England. That policy has been a benefit to the commerce of the Dominion and we do not intend to abolish it.

On the other hand we must not forget that we are behind the United States in the matter of industrial development by at least fifty years. I believe it is possible to make a treaty with the United States which will not only be of great advantage to us but equally to the United States, and I would not have a treaty which was not at least equally profitable to one as to the other.

I have just returned from a long tour in the Provinces of the West and I believe that if to-morrow there was a general election we should be returned with an even larger majority than we have to-day. There would of course, be changes here and there but the total result would be as I say.

However, I repeat that the fortune which has favored us up to now might be unfavorable, but I do not believe it would. But we can wait for what may happen to us with every confidence. If it should please fortune to take from us that which it has given in the past I would not complain. Not a murmur would escape from my lips whatever might come.

There is one thing which they cannot take from me. They cannot take from me either my pride, my dignity or my courage. They cannot take from me this fact, historic now, that during the fourteen years of the Laurier Government there has been more harmony, more peace, more prosperity, more good feeling amongst the Canadian people than at any previous epoch of our history. My last word to the electors of Montreal, my fellow citizens of all origins and all parties of the province is that without undue worry about my personal feelings you should remain now and always faithful to those principles of progress, liberty, tolerance and justice which have assured that measure without precedent of unity, harmony, well being and prosperity which has marked our progress during the past few years.

The Ottawa Citizen, August 14, 1911.

"Assemblée Contradictoire" at Ste. Hyacinthe

St. Hyacinthe, Aug. 13—In its long and fruitful record of spectacular politics, the province of Quebec has never witnessed a greater gathering than that which took place here today when Henri Bourassa, the rising hope of the Nationalist party, crossed swords with Hon. Rodolphe Lemieux, the new minister of marine. Fully thirty thousand people from many parts of Quebec were present and cheered the respective leaders with all that exuberant intensity which belongs particularly to the French race.

There were repeated scenes of almost uncontrollable disorder. Time and again the speakers' remarks were drowned in the uproar of the rival camps, and it kept the police busy in maintaining a semblance of decorum. For probably the greater part, however, the meeting was orderly, though in turn Messrs. Lemieux, Bourassa, and particularly Armand Lavergne, had to put up with noisy interruption. At one time a panic was narrowly averted. The immense crowd started to sway backwards and forwards and crowded against the platform outside the drill hall from which the speech making took place. The frail railing gave way under the pressure and those near the edges were carried over, among them being the aged father of the new minister of marine. No one sustained injuries, but it was fully ten minutes before order was restored.

The old timers declare there has never been such a gathering since the days of the memorable Mercier. They came from all over, even Ottawa contributing its quota of a hundred. Sunday is the day par excellence for campaigns in Quebec, and while the townsfolk turned out en masse, six immense special trains brought thousands from Montreal and equal numbers from Sorel, Farnham, Sherbrooke, Drummondville, Levis and Quebec. Conspicuous in the gathering, too, were the farmers from the adjoining district, and, while not as demonstrative as the rest, they followed the speech making with evidences of keen appreciation of what was said and the importance of the issues involved.

For over four hours the immense gathering was addressed, legitimate political argument being combined with scathing denunciation and fierce invective. The warmer the talk, the greater the display of militant enthusiasm. While the surging mass was so **great that** thousands must have been unable to hear, it did not minimize the expression of rampant partisan feeling.

It is hard to say who had the better of it. The degree of the cheering was not necessarily a criterion. The most striking feature of it all was the fact that thousands stood and listened without any indication whatever of their party affiliation. The bulk of the demonstration came from the group of Montreal Nationalists on one side and the Young Liberal clubs of Montreal, St. Hyacinthe and St. Johns on the other. In lung capacity honors were about even.

Mr. Lemieux, usually very calm, was in fighting trim. Twice in turn, when Mr. Bourassa and Mr. Lavergne made signs to the audience, the minister of marine, shaking his fist in their face, and with evident temper, demanded silence or out they would go. The Liberals shouted wildly in approval, the Nationalists "booed," but there was no more trouble on that score. Twice did Mr. Lemieux give the lie direct to the Nationalist leaders. He accused Bourassa of being a disappointed office seeker. The latter denied it in part, and the minister called him a prevaricator. Even more aggressive was he when Armand Lavergne accused Sir Wilfrid Laurier and himself of having conspired with Judge Tourigny to dismiss the petition against Girard of Chicoutimi. This precipitated the biggest uproar of all, lasting fully ten minutes.

It was a Liberal meeting in its inception, called as it was in the interests of Mr. Beauparlant, the ex-M.P. for the constituency. The former member, however, is in a local hospital with appendicitis. He was visited yesterday by Bourassa. Beauparlant also had thrown out the challenge to the Nationalist leader, which was accepted as soon as it was known that Mr. Lemieux was to be one of the speakers. The minister of marine was supported by Hon. Dr. Beland, the new postmaster general, and Oscar Gladu, M.P. for Yamaska. With Mr. Bourassa were Armand Lavergne, probable opponent of Sir Wilfrid in Quebec

East, Tancrede Marcil, Omer Heroux, and a number of local celebrities in the cause. Mayor Payan presided.

There was not a great deal that was new in the main argument. The Liberals talked of reciprocity and the navy; the Nationalists directed their batteries on "la marine de guerre" and on Sir Wilfrid Laurier, denouncing him as a traitor to his race, a renegade, and as a rabid and repellant imperialist, the bete noire of Nationalism and its ideals. With them the navy is first, reciprocity is second. They do not object so much to "la marine de guerre" except that it is liable to take part in the wars of Great Britain.

It is obvious that the Nationalist leader has with him many of the young men. The aggressive element in his enthusiastic following today were those also who on September 21 will cast their first vote, while with them were many who have not yet acquired the privilege of the franchise. Conspicuous, too, were the young students, in whom especially the picturesque personality of Le Maitre and the racial character of his appeals strike a peculiarly responsive chord, particularly among those whose horoscope is limited to the province of Quebec. Whether it is an ephemeral development remains to be seen next month. There seemed all the indications of deep rooted intensity in the case. Election day alone will tell whether these young fire eaters are from the cities alone, or but the counterparts of a calmer but nevertheless predominant sentiment in the back townships.

In thousands the Jean Baptistes were here today, some of them joined in the wild hurrah. The most of them pulled at their pipes and listened. In the end, when young Gladu of Yamaska, with a voice that carries five blocks, wound up it was nearly all Liberal. The Nationalists were certainly outnumbered there, and the meeting broke up with cheers for Laurier, Lemieux and Beauparlant. It may have been but forgetfulness, but no one called for cheers for Bourassa, who at that time had left. The minister of marine was carried on the shoulders of his followers to his automobile. If he did not have the better of the argument, certain it is that he did not have the worst of it. Of the two he was the more aggressive, displaying much more temper than Bourassa. What the latter lacked Armand Lavergne, practically frothing at the mouth, made up. Up in Ontario inflammatory talk of the kind heard here today would engender a free fight and a considerable number of bruised pates.

HON. LEMIEUX OPENED

Hon. Rodolphe Lemieux, who was received with much cheering, expressed at the outset his pleasure in being in St. Hyacinthe, the old foyer of Liberalism, and said that though he is not old he had been 25 years a fighter in the cause. It was from the regretted Mercier that the young men of his days received their passport. The Nationalist organs had said he would not come for fear. For fear of whom? he asked. Mr. Bourassa it was intimidated. "I know well," he declared, "that the Nationalists have made of their fetish a second chantecler who crows at sunrise, but he has never caused me to fear or tremble. After a year of insults I have thought it my duty to defend, not myself, but the prime minister, my colleague, Mr. Brodeur, and the Liberals of the province."

At this point began the trouble. A group of the Nationalists started to make noise. Armand Lavergne made some signs. "No need of signs from you, Mr. Lavergne," stated the minister, amid cries of "Throw him out." Armand became tranquil and Mr. Lemieux went on.

ATTACK ON M. BOURASSA

"We Liberals have been called everything from idiots to aristocrats. That is how Bourassa describes his compatriots." Turning to the Nationalist leader, he shouted, "I have said, and I repeat in the presence of the insulter of the prime minister, of my colleague, you refer to us as overfed and salaried men. Proud aristocrat, you did not look with contempt upon the soft billets in former days. Pure among the pure, you wanted to be Canadian commissioner at Paris. You were ready to dislodge the regretted Hector Fabre, yes, Hector Fabre, whose father was the treasurer of the Sons of Liberty and Virtue. Strayed in the midst of so many vices, you wanted to succeed the late Mr. Beausoleil as postmaster of Montreal. Virtuous representative of the opposition, you also wanted to clothe yourself with the robe of deputy speaker of the commons. With your staff you were willing to take the direction of the herd of ministerial sheep. At that time you were willing to satisfy your cravings and accept a salaried position. You solicited and pressed for these three posts with their emoluments. The party gave you to understand that we would not dismiss an old man who had well served his country, that we would not entrust to a young man of 35 a position destined to a veteran. You were told that in order to properly conduct the debates of a deliberative assembly you lacked the essential quality of judgment. Profoundly disappointed, the seigneur of Montebello pointed his finger to the office of the prime minister and offered this threat, which has actuated his actions ever since —"Tell Sir Wilfrid Laurier and his colleagues that I am more dangerous from my seat as a member than from the chair of the speaker."

Bourassa said not a word to all this, while a pin drop could be heard. Mr. Lemieux went on to say that this took place at the opening of the session of 1905, some time before the presentation of the Autonomy bill. After consulting the debates of the house you will see that the re-election of a deputy speaker that year was delayed. The seigneur of Montebello hung around the office of the minister. He demanded his Castoria. Your humble servant gave him the unfavorable news from within. Since then I have learned to measure the depth of his hatred. His speeches and insolent writings ever since have been directed to the fall of Laurier. That is why he founded Nationalism. It is a new doctrine, not a new party. In spite of the small and mean things said by the Nationalists the name of Laurier will shine in history. It is in the solution of the difficult problems that the great Canadian has laid his political genius. Mr. Bourassa and the Castors with him have no merit other than that of raising popular passions and prejudices at a difficult period of our history."

Mr. Lemieux then referred to the dissolution of parliament, and said it was due to abuse by the opposition of parliamentary privilege. They had obstructed for six months the reciprocity treaty. The British and American governments had established the closure, and that reform now imposed itself on Canada. The Liberal party did not fear an appeal to the country on the trade issue.

The minister was proceeding to give the history of reciprocity when the crowd started to surge. The Montreal Nationalist crowd caused it in attempting to scatter in place of being concentrated. The railing of the platform was carried away and a stampede started. Two old men fainted. Finally, however, order was restored, and Mr. Lemieux went on to say that Bourassa declared reciprocity a secondary issue because of his desire to arouse national prejudice. The prime minister said he was attacked fore and aft. The Tories called him disloyal, the Nationalists branded him as an imperialist. These are the tactics of the "baby alliance," Mr. Borden, Mr. Sifton, Mr. Monk and Mr. Bourassa apparently taking different roles but all working to the same end. Their occult scheme is known. The pact of hatred is signed and sealed. Each of them demands his pound of flesh and the blood of Laurier.

LEMIEUX THREATENS BOURASSA

Dealing with the naval question Mr. Lemieux said it was the idea of Cartier. At this there was a Nationalist shout, and Bourassa raised his hand. "No need of interruption from you Monsieur Bourassa," shouted the minister, shaking his fist. "Sit down, or out you go." Mr. Bourassa smiled sarcastically but said nothing.

The minister challenged the Nationalist leaders to quote a line showing that the naval service is obligatory. The navy, he argued, was necessary, since Great Britain had withdrawn her fleet from the coast. He touched upon the imperial conference, declared that Sir Wilfrid Laurier had secured the national autonomy, and after referring again to the benefits of reciprocity, concluded by declaring "the Borden-Bourassa coalition a naval crime which will receive its chastisement on September 21st." Prolonged Liberal cheers followed.

GREAT BOURASSA RECEPTION

Then came Mr. Bourassa. As he arose, bowing and smiling, the Nationalists cheered themselves hoarse for two or three minutes and waved little flags and tricolors. His speech was shorter than that of the minister of marine.

"I am not going to trouble you with a history of the Lemieux family," was his first shot, whereat the Nationalists screamed. "Mr. Lemieux has told you I was a supplicant for office. I did not ask for the place of Mr. Fabre, nor for the position of postmaster of Montreal. I would have taken that of the deputy speaker only if allowed to maintain my liberty of thought."

"You lie when you say you did not seek these appointments," declared Mr. Lemieux, and then wild disorder started. The Nationalists cheered "Le Maitre," as they call him, the Liberals cheered Lemieux. This bedlam spent itself in about five minutes and then there was perfect calm. Mr. Bourassa spoke on reciprocity.

"I am favorable," he said, "to trade between Canada and the United States, but it is questionable if it is necessary to make this pact. It was the work of Mr. Taft, scheming to hold on to office. The Canadian government has rushed into it without consulting the people. Ah, messieurs, their motive is all too plain. They would have you forget their deeds, "marine de guerre," that, let it be understood, is the first and principal consideration. In 1908 did Laurier favor a navy? No. Now he adopts a law against our interests and against the interests of our children. The electors have not forgotten the Sorel painting case. You do not forget that in the midst of the Oliver enquiry parliament is suddenly and scandalously dissolved, despite the work of the honorable the Liberal whip of Quebec."

Cries of "Honte, honte," came from the Nationalists and this engendered more disorder, Mr. Bourassa's voice being drowned. When quiet came the Nationalist leader reverted to the navy.

ON THE NAVY QUESTION

"Does Mr. Lemieux," he asked, "think to shut my mouth on it by accusing me of seeking office? Mr. Lemieux claims to be a victim of a monstrous conspiracy. Because Mr. Borden has said in the West that the navy is not intended to serve Britain does not alter my opinion. The 'marine' of Laurier is above all an imperialistic creation. I do not go to Mr. Borden for a witness. Let me quote Mr. Fielding, who says 'When Britain is at war'—just or unjust, mind you—'it is the duty of Canada to assist' (Nationalist cheers).

"They quote the militia law of Cartier. That was exclusively for the defence of Canada. Once Mr. Laurier declared the law did not allow of troops going to South Africa and yet, in the face of our protests they went, despite law and constitution."

Mr. Bourassa made much of a letter written to him in 1903 by Mr. Lemieux, who, commenting on a resolution of the Montreal board of trade in favour of contributing to imperial projects, declared it to be a false principle. In 1907 Mr. Laurier proposed this imperialistic idea and it was stopped. I approved his case and voted for him. In 1909 he brings down this monstrous naval bill and passes

it despite the protest of a hundred thous-
and petitioners.

"Twenty-five thousand, to be exact,
a slight error," interrupted Mr. Gladu,
whereupon there was another hulabaloo.

"They threw the petitions back at
us," went on Mr. Bourassa, "and now
flaunting the picture of Laurier, they
would have us forget one more point—
the future of our children."

THEIR SONS AND WAR!

Liberal jeers interrupted the nationalist leader for some minutes. He waited
unperturbed and continued to say there
was a wide difference between the militia
and the navy. The former was for the
defence of Canada, the navy would take
its orders from Britain. "Suppose," he
shouted, "war is declared tomorrow.
Parliament would be summoned in fifteen

days, but meanwhile the navy with your
sons aboard, would be rushed to the
battle. I do not say that the law provides
for conscription, but I do object to participation in imperial wars in which
Canada has no interest or concern."
(Nationalist cheers).

"Do as you will with reciprocity but
remember in this fight the navy is first.
I ask you not to vote for Laurier, not to
vote for Borden, vote for any one who
will agree to support Mr. Monk in his
admirable efforts to protect our liberties.
I ask you to vote out of office those who
have sacrificed our rights, who have created this monstrous "marine" and who
have recklessly squandered your money.
I admire Mr. Laurier as a private citizen
—(cheers),—but it is our duty to punish
him for the betrayal in his public capacity
of our most sacred rights and liberties."
(Prolonged cheers).

Hartley H. Dewart, "The Political Situation—A Study in Cause and Effect", *The
Globe*, April 27, 1910.

Political Disorganization

It was a matter of surprise to no one
that the utter lack of coherence amongst
the Conservative leaders, when any large
political question had to be dealt with,
led to a demand for reconstruction and
the appointment of new lieutenants. The
surprise was that the demand had not
come sooner. Nor is it to be wondered
at that, having set its own friends by the
ears, the Conservative journal that was
mainly responsible for the faction fight
should turn its attention to the Liberals.
It was a clever endeavor to lead the
country to believe that there was real
disagreement on matters of policy in the
Liberal ranks at Toronto. Matters relating
to the internal affairs of the Ontario Club,
which has taken strong root as the social
home of our political friends, have been
magnified out of all proportion to their
political significance. It was inevitable
that in a club with temporarily limited
quarters but few could actually hear the
Ministers of the Crown. But the club was
surely doing an important political and
public service in providing the occasion
for utterances that could be read in the
public press throughout the whole Dominion. Similarly the attempt to inflame
the discontent of the disaffected few upon
questions of local patronage was made
to do duty and create an impression in
the public mind that individual Liberals
were as far disseevered on these matters
as were the Conservative leaders on vital
matters of policy.

While this misdirected criticism has
failed of effect, the present occasion when
our Conservative friends are making such
a diligent pretence at political house-
cleaning appears to me an opportune time
for expressing opinions which I know are
held by many active and loyal Liberals
who, like myself, have endeavored to
fairly gauge the present standing of the
Liberal party in the Province of Ontario
and who earnestly desire for it the best
things. This is no time for Pharisaically
thanking heaven that we are not as other
men are—politically. It is a good time for
stocktaking on our own account.

There are many reasons for confidence and satisfaction. Since 1896 the
Liberal Government at Ottawa has been
strong in initiating a policy of legislation
that has rung true on lines of national
development, with due regard for our
duty as an integral part of the Empire.
If there is one reason more than another
why the Liberal party has maintained its
hold upon the people of Canada, it is
because it has a policy that has appealed
to the national imagination and has been
justified in its works. The disruption in
the Conservative party is due to a lack
of coherent policy. There is no initiative
or constructive ability in dealing with
national issues.

Yet the Liberal party in Ontario to-
day, while strong in its constructive
policy, is lamentably weak in the matter

of organization. Take the district of which the city of Toronto is the centre. Of sporadic and spasmodic activity at election time we have plenty. Of the systematic organization that results in local educational work we have next to nothing. Victories cannot be won by shouting and bustling about for four weeks before an election. We need the organized and constant application of directed energies. Now with regard to the men who have done their best to galvanize the Liberal workers into an organization at election time and who have accepted office in the Toronto Reform Association, often against their will and at considerable personal sacrifice, I protest against their being pilloried now. They have done their best. The fault does not lie with them. They have done wonders in a centre of active (Conservative organization and society influence like Toronto).

Where then must the responsibility be laid? It must surely be laid at the door of those Ministers of the Crown who have failed to provide the directing power. A Commander-in-Chief, even if he be as brilliant and skilful as Sir Wilfrid Laurier undoubtedly is, cannot be expected to achieve the success that he should without able tacticians between himself and the men in the ranks. Hon. Charles Murphy and Hon. Mackenzie King have not had a chance to earn their spurs as organizers, but they will be expected to do so. It is a notorious fact that in the campaign of 1908 there was not a solitary Minister of the Crown in the Province of Ontario west of Brockville who was of the least value to the Liberal organization as an informing energizing or directing force. In the Toronto district our only representative in the Commons is the Minister of Justice.

None of our six senators can now be reckoned on in the matter of organization.

We find a different state of affairs in the Provinces to the east. Three Ministers of the Crown and even Senators not only perform their administrative and Parliamentary duties well, but also take charge of their districts, feel the pulse of the people, bring informed minds to the consideration of poltical issues and see that the latent forces of Liberalism are brought into a political organization that means something. Analyze the returns to the Province of Quebec and you will see that behind the personality of Sir Wilfrid there is the organized effort that spells out success in close ridings.

Constituencies in western Ontario can figure out this problem for themselves and make their own application. But I know that in the city of Toronto and surrounding ridings we have suffered and are suffering as a party because the Minister who is supposed to represent this district is not a political force or even a factor in organization. A district or even a constituency may be lost if featherweight advisers are the main sources from which knowledge of political conditions is derived. The local Minister should be at least the mouthpiece through which the political views or needs of the district are expressed. There are important views relating to the immigration policy, as it affects us locally, to be expressed. Large questions relating to the expenditure of moneys on public works have to be considered. Other departmental matters of importance require solution. The consideration locally that these matters have received and to which they are entitled is due in nearly every instance to the direct representations made by active Liberal workers to the Minister in charge of the department interested. Surely the public at large are justified in expecting the directing force of the Minister of Justice in these matters of local policy, just as much as Liberals are in matters of political organization. If our policy is sound and our views are right, as we believe them to be, the party leader who sees to it that organized effort and wise direction are brought to bear to achieve success performs a public as well as a party service.

I am not now entering into the arena to discuss the rightness or wrongness of the attitude of the Minister of Justice regarding matters that more particularly concern his own department. No one questions his pre-eminence as leader at the Bar of the Province or his comprehensive knowledge of the difficult problems of law it has been his duty to consider. The Minister of Justice can maintain and justify his opinions on these matters, stubbornly if need me, and no man better than he. But in view of his recent declaration that he is a "partisan" by which I understand him to mean a man of party views in the best sense, every party man has the right to ask why the

Minister of Justice does not give effective party service. I maintain that we have the right, both from the political and public point of view, on the grounds that I have pointed out, to receive effective direction in public matters and organizing ability in party business from those who are chosen the responsible Ministers of the Crown. I have hesitated for some time before expressing these views, but someone should speak out even at the risk of incurring hostile criticism.

The history of Canada even since Confederation is not without its political lessons. Sir John Macdonald retained weaklings in his Cabinet that no party could successfully carry after his decease. Even strong men in the Province of Ontario made the fatal mistake of failing to introduce much-needed new blood in time to avert a fatal ending. Politics, after all, should be like any other business in life. It is imperative that the fittest should survive. The country is entitled to the best service of the best men, and political prescience as well as sound executive ability is needed.

Public Archives of Canada, *George Graham Papers*, W. L. M. King to Graham, June 26, 1911.

six meetings each and made to go over the ground. It is better that the people should get the details into their heads before a fight. . . .

Yours sincerely

An Assessment of the Political Situation

Ottawa, June 26, 1911

My dear Graham,

You may have noticed that I have had a few meetings in different parts during the last fortnight. At all of the meetings reciprocity seems to have been received with favour, but I must confess I find everywhere the need of the people in different ridings being more fully informed as to just what the nature of the proposal is. The press and the speakers are taking it for granted that the people know the agreement, and that it is only its effect that needs consideration.

The truth is our strongest side of the case is the agreement itself, and it would be well, I think, to emphasize to everyone going out, the importance of its nature being fully discussed. The results then speak for themselves. There is a good deal of need for more educational work in Ontario, and as soon as the House meets, if we are likely to have a sitting of any length before adjournment I think it would be a good idea if every member who is worth anything in the way of speaking, excluding members of the Government, were given at least five or

Wilfrid Laurier, *The Globe*, July 29, 1911.

A Call To Arms

At all times during the last forty years it has been the constant effort of all political parties in Canada to make with the United States an arrangement for the free exchange of natural products between the two countries. In 1854 Lord Elgin, on behalf of Canada and the Maritime Provinces, negotiated with the United States a treaty for that purpose which lasted until 1866, and which within the memory of many still alive was of the greatest advantage. Ever since the termination of that Treaty all public men of any prominence in Canada, whatever their differences on other questions, have been unanimous in an attempt to again secure the free exchange of natural products.

Nor is this to be wondered at, seeing that in the industries—agriculture, fisheries, lumbering, and mining—Canada possesses advantages enjoyed by no other country on earth, and that upon the markets secured for the products of these industries depend the growth of our manufacturing and commercial interests and the prosperity of all classes in the Dominion. The latest attempt of the Conservative party to that end was made by Sir John Macdonald himself, who dissolved Parliament in 1891 for the purpose of submitting to the electorate of Canada the expediency of his again approaching the American authorities for the renewal of the Treaty of 1854.

In 1893 the intention to obtain Reciprocity with the United States, if it were possible, was made a prominent feature in the platform of the Liberal party, upon which that party attained power. In 1896, after the present Government took office, it renewed in vain this offer to the United States, but, meeting with no response, it declared that no further overtures of this nature would be made by Canada.

Within the last twelve months the President of the United States sent to Ottawa two Commissioners from Washington for the purpose of opening negotiations looking toward the lowering of the tariff barriers which have hitherto stood in the way of freer exchange of commodities between Canada and the United States. These negotiations in January last culminated in an Agreement between the two Governments by which the duties of each country on such products might be lowered or altogether removed.

This Agreement was strenuously resisted in the United States by various interests on the alleged ground that it was all to the advantage of Canada and to the detriment of the other country, but the view that it was mutually advantageous to both countries finally prevailed in Congress, and the Agreement stands today as an offer by the United States to Canada of that very measure of Reciprocity which for more than forty years has engaged the earnest and constant efforts of every leading Canadian statesman.

The present Conservative party in Parliament seeks absolutely to reverse the life-long policy of its great leaders in the past, declaring that it will oppose to the bitter end the very principles enunciated by both Sir John Macdonald and Sir John Thompson in the last election address upon which each of those statesmen ever appealed to the Canadian people.

Not content to debate this proposition upon its merits, the Conservative party in the Commons has adopted a system of organized and avowed obstruction to prevent any vote from being taken in Parliament by which the opinion of your representatives there could be expressed. Day after day, when the presiding officer has tried to put the question, he has been met by dilatory motions, by endless speeches, and by obstructive devices of every kind, each put forward on some specious pretext, but being in reality nothing else than an abuse of the freedom of speech of Parliamentary debate. Such pretences are simply a clumsy attempt to give some colour to the unwarranted and undignified obstruction.

To overcome that obstruction after a session which has already lasted eight months, would not only mean a continuation of the unseemly spectacle presented by the Opposition in the House of Commons since the resumption of its sittings on the 18th inst., but would also mean weeks and months of wasted time, and perhaps, in the end, the loss for this season to the Canadian producer of the free American market.

The issue, my fellow-countrymen, is in your hands, and to your decision His Majesty's Government in Canada are well content to leave it. It has been alleged by the Opposition that this Agreement, if consummated, would imperil Canada's connection with the Mother-country, and finally bring about the annexation of Canada to the United States. It is impossible to treat such an argument with any kind of respect, if, indeed, it can be dignified with the name of argument; for if it has any meaning, its meaning is that the people of Canada would be seduced from their allegiance by prosperity to follow the larger flow of natural products from this country to the other. Indeed, the very reverse would be the natural consequence, for the experience of all ages abundantly testifies that trade is ever the most potent agency of peace, amity, and mutual respect between nations.

Nor is that all. This Agreement, which in no way impairs our fiscal policy, which still maintains at topmast the proud principle of British Preference—this Agreement, by opening new avenues of trade hitherto closed, would further improve the friendly relations which now happily exist between this country and the Mother-country on the one hand and the American Republic on the other, and which it is hoped may at no distant day eventuate into a general treaty of arbitration, the effect of which would be to remove for ever all possibilities of war between the great Empire of which we are proud to form part and the great nation which we are proud to have as neighbours.

P.A.C., *W. L. M. King Papers,* King to J. Wilson, May 9, 1911.

Assessing the Issues

Ottawa, May 9, 1911

Dear Mr. Wilson,

As you asked for three reasons for and against, [i.e. the reciprocity treaty] I am citing as three main reasons for (1) the increased prosperity which will come to all those engaged in agricultural pursuits and, in consequence, to all other classes in the community through the opening of a market of 90 millions of people for the sale of their goods; (2) the prevention through increased competition of the growth of trust in Canada which seek to monopolize the raw materials of the country and products of the farms, as, for example, the packing trust which tries to control the hog market in Canada, with the result that bacon is sold for a higher price to Canadians than to people in England; (3) the fostering of a friendly feeling between the people of the United States and Canada through the avoidance of the kind of friction which tariff matters bring, a circumstance which is certain to help promote the peace not only on this continent, but between the British Empire and the United States.

The arguments against are of the nature of supposed fears rather than actual anticipated results. They are, briefly, (1) that the reductions of the tariff in natural products may lead to reduction of the tariff on manufactured goods, hence the opposition of manufacturers. This argument is likely to appeal mostly to the manufacturers, but not to members of the rural communities. (2) That freedom of trade may lead to annexation. This, of course, leaves out of account the fact that the Canadian people would have their own say in a matter of political affiliation with greater freedom of trade just as they have under lesser. (3) That there has been no special mandate from the people. This, of course, does not take account of the fact that all governments of Canada, for the last thirty years have been trying to get reciprocity in natural products.

Yours truly

W. S. Fielding, *The Maritimes and the Reciprocity Agreement*, Halifax, August 19, 1911, pp. 8-14.

The Maritimes and Reciprocity

A POLICY FOR ALL CANADA

Never was a policy submitted to the Canadian people which gave more widespread promise of advantage. The agreement offers the prospect of increased trade in every Province of the Dominion. While, for reasons already stated, an agreement for a general free exchange of manufactured goods would not be fair to our workers in those lines, there are few Canadians who do not believe that in most of our great industries—farming, fruit-growing, fishing and lumbering—Canada need fear no competitors at home or abroad. Enlarged markets for our products have been diligently sought by our Government. With this object in view we have subsidized steamers and sent commercial agents to distant parts of the earth. Would it not be strange if we failed to avail ourselves of the opportunity to share in the markets of ninety-two millions of the richest consumers in the world?

THE OPPORTUNITY OF THE MARITIME PROVINCES

To no part of the Dominion does this agreement bring greater hope than to the Maritime Provinces. While conditions have, we are glad to know, somewhat improved in these Provinces in recent years, it must be acknowledged that our growth and progress fall far short of what we ought to expect. The western country has been developing rapidly. We in the Lower Provinces recognized the conditions which have brought this about, and we have cheerfully borne our share of the large outlays which have been necessary to open up that country. We view with every satisfaction the progress and prosperity of our western land and will cordially co-operate in every movement for its further advancement. But we cannot be expected to be indifferent to the conditions that are nearer to us. Freer trade relations with the United States have been the dream of every leading Canadian statesman for nearly half a century. In the Lower Provinces particularly the importance of such better trade relations has been universally recognized. The Conservative policy of higher tariff was only accepted by its own friends because it was declared by Sir John Macdonald himself and by other statesmen of his party to be the best possible road towards obtaining reciprocity with the United States. The increase of our interprovincial trade and our trade with Great Britain is gratifying and we must see that every reasonable effort is made for their further expansion. But if, in addition to these, we can give our people that access to the United States markets for many of our natural products which they have been seeking for so many years, we shall undoubtedly bring new life and new hope and new strength to this eastern part of the Dominion.

The great industries of Nova Scotia, New Brunswick and Prince Edward Island are farming, fruit growing, fishing, lumbering and mining. Every one of these industries has been well considered and cared for in the reciprocity agreement.

THE COAL TRADE

Our chief mining industry is that of coal. Duties on coal and flour have usually been bracketed together in the past —one being treated as beneficial to the West, the other to the East. Under the agreement, there is to be a reduction of the duties on both coal and flour. I believe that I am justified in saying that our chief coal operators regard the coal situation under the agreement as a satisfactory one, inasmuch as the reduction of duty is not sufficient to adversely affect any mining interest, while there is a substantial advantage to the coal trade in having this question of the coal duty definitely settled. I have had something to do with legislation, both at Halifax and at Ottawa, bearing on our coal trade, which has been instrumental in bringing about the marked development that has taken place during the last twenty years, and I rejoice that in conjunction with my colleagues, I have been able to place the coal question in so satisfactory a position under the operation of this agreement.

THE FARMERS' INTEREST

The farming interests of the Maritime Provinces have always looked upon reciprocity as most desirable. We are glad to know that our home markets have steadily increased in recent years under the wise policy of development adopted by the Canadian Government. But there are seasons when access to the American market will be of the utmost value to all engaged in the agricultural industry.

THE FRUIT GROWER

To our fruit growers reciprocity offers the prospect of a most desirable market. Some of our finest fruits are tender and will hardly bear transportation to distant countries. If properly handled and transported to the markets of the United States, they will realize prices better than can be obtained in any other quarter. The American market for our small fruits, berries, &c., is an unlimited one. The privilege of sending these things into the United States without the intervention of tariff barriers will certainly prove advantageous to our producers.

LUMBER

The lumber industry in the Maritime Provinces is a very extensive one, and for some classes of our lumber the American market is the most convenient. Our own duties on lumber remain practically unchanged, but in the United States the duty on rough lumber is to be entirely abolished and a proportionate reduction is made on lumber in the higher classes. The very prospect of reciprocity has already added greatly to the value of our timber lands, and there can be no doubt that the lumber industry will be largely benefited by the adoption of the agreement.

THE FISHERMEN

Last, and perhaps greatest amongst the chief industries which I have mentioned, is the industry of the fisherman.

It would be amazing if any intelligent voice should be raised against reciprocity from the fisherman's point of view. There can be but few fishermen who do not fully realize the desirability of access to the American market. I have pointed out how the statesmen of the Conservative party as well as others have in the past strenuously sought reciprocity in negotiations along these lines. Free fish has always been regarded as a boon much to be desired. So desirous have many of our public men been to secure the free admission of fish into the United States markets that they have been willing to include in their negotiations the granting to Americans of the right to fish within the Canadian three mile limit—a right which we have not granted in our present agreement. It will be remembered that when, a few years ago, Newfoundland entered into negotiations with the United States authorities which contemplated the free admission of Newfoundland fish, the Canadian Conservative Government protested and urged that Canadian fish should be included in the arrangement. Even in the face of the duties against us, we export large quantities of fish to the United States. Free of duties, there is no doubt that our exports will largely increase. The proximity of the market will encourage the sale of fresh fish, the branch of the industry which is usually most profitable to the fisherman. Prominent fish merchants in the United States are ready to establish branch houses in the Maritime Provinces to purchase Canadian fish. Hundreds of young men leave our shores every year to go to the United States to fish in American vessels. Why? There is only one answer: The fish taken by the American vessel is admitted free into the American market, while fish taken at the same time in a Canadian vessel would be subject to the American duty. In the present condition of affairs, there is thus great temptation to our young men to go to the United States. Many of them, I am happy to state, while engaging in the fishing business, retain their allegiance to our Sovereign and return to their homes in the Dominion. Many others, unfortunately, find the advantages of the American market so great that they break their connection with Canada and become citizens of the United States. Under this reciprocity agreement, it will be possible for our young men to engage in the fishing business in our own vessels under the British flag and yet enjoy all the advantages which have hitherto drawn our population away.

In former years when Porto Rico was a Spanish colony, we had a large trade with that island. When Porto Rico was acquired by the United States we lost that trade. The reciprocity agreement gives us the opportunity to recover to some extent the trade of the island. Under the agreement Canadian fish will be admitted free into Porto Rico.

THE ANNEXATION BOGEY

Nothing more clearly shows the weakness of the case against reciprocity than the fact that our opponents have to resort to the device of waving the British flag and accusing the advocates of reciprocity of disloyalty. It is an old and well worn trick which will not deceive intelligent people. The glorious flag of the Empire was never intended to be used for so mean a purpose. Never were the people of British North America more loyal or more contented with British institutions than during the period of the old reciprocity treaty. It was in the very midst of that period that His late Majesty King Edward, then Prince of Wales, visited British North America and received everywhere such splendid evidence of the loyalty and devotion of our people. Sir John Macdonald, Sir Charles Tupper, Sir John Thompson, Mr. Foster and other public men of the Conservative party were not deemed disloyal when they laboured without success to obtain a reciprocal trade arrangement with the United States. It will be difficult to persuade anybody that the Canadian Ministers of to-day are disloyal when they have carried on reciprocity negotiations which have been crowned with the success that was denied to their predecessors. No Canadian who is trading to-day with citizens of the United States, in money or in merchandize, feels that he thereby in any way compromises himself as a loyal citizen of Canada and a loyal subject of the King, nor will any feeling of that kind be experienced by other citizens of Canada who will avail themselves of the larger opportunities of trade which we believe will be opened up to them by the reciprocity agreement. The pretence that the Canadian farmer, fisherman or lumberman who sells his products in the United States impairs his loyalty to His Majesty is an insult to loyal Canadians and will, I feel sure, be resented by them.

PEACE AND GOODWILL

Even if we desired to do so, we could not be indifferent to our commercial relations with the people of the neighbouring Republic. Touching each other as the two countries do along a border line of thousands of miles, the people of both should always desire the best relations in commercial and all other affairs. Irresponsible speakers and writers of either nation may feel free to indulge in foolish and, too often, offensive utterances concerning the other. But responsible Ministers in London, in Ottawa and in Washington, with the support of the best people in each country, will realize the importance of cultivating between Canada and the United States those friendly commercial relations which will make for both Continental and Imperial peace. It is in that spirit that our Government have welcomed the approaches of the authorities of the United States and have joined them in this effort to establish better trade relations between the two countries.

P.A.C., *George Graham Papers*, W. S. Fielding to Graham, May 24, 1911, May 30, 1911.

Election Propaganda

May 24, 1911

My dear Graham,

Availing myself of your kind invitation that I should offer suggestions concerning the preparation of literature, may I venture to invite your attention to the following?

While there are some questions of importance which may have to be dealt with later on, I think that at the present stage it is most important to have an abundant supply of literature dealing with the reciprocity question.

The speeches already prepared and being sent out are, no doubt, good enough in their way. But I feel that something more is needed.

It would be well that your bureau should obtain copies of all the literature that is being issued by the Opposition and see that pamphlets are prepared answering any point that seems to need answer.

Just now the Opposition seem to be concentrating their efforts towards persuading the farmers that they will have no market in the United States. A few weeks ago, the chief argument of our opponents was that our farm products instead of going to Eastern Canada and to England, would go to the United States, and that this would be most disastrous to our east and west railway lines. Attention should be called to this former argument and to the fact that it is now abandoned. The cry now is that the Canadian market and the British market are the best for our farm products, that prices are lower in the United States than in Canada, and that there will be no market in the United States for any of our farm products.

I think Mr. Fisher is gathering some information bearing on this point which would be helpful to you.

At the same time that our opponents are trying to alarm our farmers by the cry of American competition, the farming interests of the United States are strongly organized in opposing reciprocity on the ground that they cannot compete with Canadian products. The representations made by the American farmers to the United States Congressional Committee and the speeches of the anti-reciprocity Senators and Members of Congress should be carefully examined and quotations made to show this attitude of the U.S. Opposition. I think it would be well to gather, in good form, extracts, many of which have already been quoted in the debate, from speeches and other utterances of Sir John A. Macdonald, Sir Charles Tupper and others, in favour of reciprocity. The Opposition do not like us to do that. They constantly say the situation is changed. Certainly a change has taken place, but it is not one that helps them. If Canada was able to stand reciprocity in natural products in 1891, she is much better able to stand it now. I would have a pamphlet devoted to these utterances of former days, showing that reciprocity has been the policy of all parties, from the beginning of Confederation and even before. To show this very clearly, supporting the contention by many quotations from speeches and despatches, and to point out that the present opposition to reciprocity is entirely partisan, is, I am persuaded, a good line to take.

Besides speeches and pamphlets, I think much good might be done by smaller documents, of a very few pages, dealing with particular lines of business. For example, there might be one such document presenting the matter from the point of view of the farmer, another from the point of view of the lumberman, another from the point of view of the fisherman &c. Each of these documents might be widely circulated in the districts particularly interested in the subject treated. No doubt there are many other thoughts which will occur to one who settles down to a study of the question. I give you what comes to my mind for the moment.

Let me add that in any arrangement that may be made for the expense of preparing and publishing these things I am quite prepared to take a proper part in the way of contributing a fair share of the cost.

Yours sincerely

Ottawa, May 30, 1911

My dear Graham

Even though I am fortified by the urgent advice of colleagues and friends, I feel some hesitation about going away now when there is so much to do. Perhaps for that reason, more than under ordinary conditions, I feel that I should hesitate in offering advice to others as to what should be done. However, you have invited me to do so: so you must share with me the responsibility. I want to add

a word to what I have already said regarding reciprocity literature.

I think it would be good politics to have a small pamphlet issued devoted entirely to the history of the reciprocity question in a condensed form, with a view to showing that reciprocity in natural products has been the desire of all our public men for generations. The right man studying the question will find quotations in official despatches and in the speeches of public men of all shades of opinion. Particular attention should be given to quotations from Sir John Macdonald, Sir Charles Tupper, Sir John Thompson and Mr. Foster. An extract from a Speech from the Throne, only a few weeks before Sir John Macdonald's death, enables us to emphasize the fact that down to the time of his death he was always an advocate of reciprocity. A card issued by Sir John Thompson to the electors of Antigonish County, Nova Scotia in 1891 is particularly useful. All this might be prepared in a careful non-partisan way. I am persuaded that it will do good, especially among moderate Conservatives, who will be disposed to act with us. Our opponents do not like these references, and that is just one of the reasons why I think we should insist upon having this aspect of the question put before the country. A concluding part could deal with the argument that the situation has changed. It is true that the situation has changed. But it has not changed to the disadvantage of the advocates of reciprocity. If Canada in the time of the Conservatives was able to stand competition with the United States in natural products, she is much better able to do so to-day.

Another suggestion I venture to offer is in relation to cartoons. Sometimes that part of the business is overdone. But I am persuaded that a few carefully prepared cartoons may play an effective part in the campaign. I have not at this moment time to think out subjects generally, but one or two come to my mind now.

The character of Mr. Facing Both Ways, which is often used by cartoonists, can be most effectively used in this matter, taking Mr. Borden or any other leading Conservative as the speaker. For example: with one voice the Conservatives are telling the farmers that under reciprocity they will suffer competition and have to sell at lower prices. At the same time, their agents are going into the factories of Montreal getting anti-reciprocity petitions signed upon representations that the cost of food will be made higher.

On the same line, you could depict the anti-reciprocity people telling the railway men that the farm produce of Can-ada, instead of coming over our eastern railway for consumption and shipment to England, is to be consumed in the United States, thus destroying our freight routes. At the same time, our opponents are labouring strenuously to prove to the farmer that prices are lower in the States and that therefore no Canadian stuff will be carried over to the South.

Another thought that might be represented is that the American farmer, on his side of the line, is shouting that competition from Canada will ruin him, while the Canadian Tory farmer is shouting that competition from the United States will ruin him.

But I am sure that I have said enough and too much: so I will add nothing more.

Yours sincerely

The Globe, September 9, 1911.

The Unholy Alliance

Two flags have been hoisted in the present campaign for the election of members to the Commons. One is the Union Jack of Britain. The other is the Tricolor of France. Allegiance was pledged to both on the same day. The Liberal reciprocity candidate, speaking in the French language, spoke for himself and for all Liberals of whatever race throughout all Canada when he said: "We are all united as one under one flag, the Union Jack." For the Nationalists and their Conservative allies the authorized spokesman of political treason, waving aloft the Tricolor of France, shouted aloud: "This is the flag we are going to raise on high on the 21st of September. The red is for Prevost, still a Rouge; the blue is for Nantel, our Conservative ally; the white is for Henri Bourassa, our devoted leader." And what happened that day at St. Jerome is happening every day throughout Quebec.

This is indeed quite the most significant of all the incidents of this campaign. A band of young French-Canadians, every one of them a traitor to British ideals, led by a clever political aspirant, are encouraged to gather under an alien flag and to enflame their compatriots with the hope of political "independence," "an autonomous French State," "independent and unmixed," on the banks of the St. Lawrence.

For whatever damage Canada's political integrity may suffer from the organized disloyalty of Mr. Bourassa and his traitorous Nationalists, the full measure of blame must attach inevitably and inseparably to Mr. R. L. Borden. He more than any other man in Canadian politics had the power to defeat and destroy this anti-British Nationalism in Quebec. He more than any other man gave it its supreme chance. He encouraged it not only by his silence, but by giving place on his public platforms to its allies and spokesmen. In Quebec, Mr. Borden joined hands with the men who have joined hands with Mr. Bourassa.

And what is most compromising and most heinous of all is that the leader of the Conservative party in Canada has abandoned almost the entire Province of Quebec to these anti-British demagogues and traitors. To say that in only ten of the sixty-five constituencies in Quebec are there regular Conservative candidates in the field is to tell the ghastly story of weakness, cowardice, and betrayal which is the condemnation of Mr. Borden and his colleagues in the leadership of the Conservative party. A leader who submits to yielding in advance fifty-five seats in one Province to anti-British and anti-Canadian separatism is doomed to failure, no matter what his opportunities.

Were it possible that Mr. Borden should carry a majority of seats in the English-speaking provinces, he would be at the mercy of Mr. Bourassa.

The hope in the situation is that Sir Wilfrid Laurier and every one of his colleagues are loyal to the flag and throne and traditions of Britain. The Liberal leader denounced Bourassa and all his kind. He challenged them. He defied them. The Hon. Rodolphe Lemieux, like his chief, made no compromise with the Nationalists or their Conservative allies who conceal their disloyalty in the refugees of patriotism and religion. "I am as good a believer as any one of them," he declared, "but our only flag is the British flag, the emblem of justice and freedom, whose power is such that it can stand the Judas kisses without being stained."

When the smoke of this battle has cleared, the unswerving loyalty of true Britishers, French as well as English, will be the hope of Canada's national unity and the pledge of the larger Imperialism. But not in this generation shall loyal Canadians forget the traitor-alliance of Mr. Borden and the official Conservatives with the men who wave the Tricolor of France.

Westerners are interested in the Quebec situation. They will expect to hear from Mr. Haggart, Mr. Meighen, Mr. Aikins, and other representative anti-reciprocity candidates on the loyalty question. Their party has identified itself with the men who are opposed to Canada's Imperialistic position. Borden-Bourassa candidates in Quebec have been literally pouring the viols of wrath upon those who believe that Canada's destiny is to march shoulder to shoulder with the Mother Country in times of trouble as well as in the days of peace. If Canada's relations with the Motherland are only in name, the relations amount to little. Canada will not be slow to attend to those who, blinded by local surroundings to the real sentiment of the Dominion, imagine that a sectional victory means the end of Imperialism. Mr. Borden has indeed formed an unholy alliance. The fact that Mr. Borden's party has only ten regular Conservative candidates in Quebec, where there are sixty-five seats, is proof positive of the alliance. And several of his candidates indulge in even stronger anti-Imperialistic language than their allies, the Nationalists. What do our western anti-reciprocity candidates think of the alliance and the anti-British utterances?

Part VI

The Results and Post Mortems

When the votes had been counted on September 21, the government had suffered an overwhelming defeat. Eight cabinet ministers lost their seats, and a Liberal majority of forty-four had been turned into a Conservative majority of forty-nine. In almost every province, the Liberals lost ground. West of the Great Lakes, where party leaders hoped to make substantial gains, the parties broke even, the Liberals sweeping Saskatchewan and Alberta, the Conservatives Manitoba and British Columbia. In the Maritimes, Liberals dropped from 26 to 19 seats, winning a majority in New Brunswick and splitting even in Nova Scotia and Prince Edward Island. In Quebec Laurier was the clear cut winner with 37 seats, but 15 seats fell to the *nationalistes*. Ontario, however, held the key to the results. While the Liberals dropped to a mere 13 seats, the Conservatives ballooned to a record 72, a gain of 24 seats and the margin of victory in the election campaign.

Historians and contemporary observers alike have usually attributed the results to reciprocity. Although some, including Laurier and a number of Liberal leaders in Ontario, believed that race and religion had been decisive issues, the majority have concluded that the reciprocity proposals broke the government's back. O. D. Skelton, Professor of Political Economy at Queen's University, set the tone for much of the writing on 1911 in an article which he contributed to the *Journal of Political Economy*. An advocate of reciprocity, Skelton had prepared statistical surveys demonstrating the economic benefits of the proposed agreement for the Minister of Labour, William Lyon MacKenzie King. The agreement, he concluded, was economically advantageous to the Canadian people; it was rejected at the polls because it was successfully portrayed as disloyal and a threat to the preservation of Canadian nationality and the British connection.

A generation of historians played variations on a similar theme. Professor L. Ethan Ellis emphasized the role of the business and financial interests in a paper which he read to the Canadian Historical Association in 1939. The average Canadian, Ellis suggested, may have been seized by the fear of annexation. But it was the propaganda of the vested interests which implanted these fears and actively cultivated them as the controversy developed. Others have taken a wider look at the state of the Canadian economy and concluded that Canada had achieved a measure of economic integration by 1911 based upon lines running east and west linking the Prairies on the one hand to Great Britain on the other. Thus, as Clifford Sifton pointed out following the election campaign, the viability of Canadian nationality was closely linked to trade with the Empire and helps to explain the association of nationalist and imperialist cries throughout the debate.

The campaign in Quebec has not received the detailed analysis it deserves. The election, it seems clear from all accounts, did not revolve around reciprocity in spite of Liberal efforts to emphasize the issue. The naval controversy and the question of Canada's position in the British Empire were of greater concern to the Quebec electorate, mindful of the fate of French-Canadian nationality should Canada be drawn into closer alliances with Great Britain and her colonial possessions. In his doctoral dissertation for the University of Toronto in 1956, H. Blair Neatby suggested one line which further investigation might pursue. Of the constituencies which the Liberals lost, Neatby pointed out, thirteen were in northern and eastern Quebec where the *nationaliste* colonization campaign during the previous decade

had considerably weakened the influence of the Liberal party.

In more recent years another dimension has been added to the analysis of the reciprocity campaign. In a private memorandum to Laurier following the election debacle, Alexander Smith, the Liberal party's organizer in the province of Ontario, argued that the collapse of the party had been due to the lack of effective organization. Following this tack, two historians have looked at the campaign in the crucial province of Ontario and concluded that party organization was a decisive factor. In a paper which appeared in *Ontario History* in 1965, Robert Cuff maintained that the Conservative organization in the province was sufficiently strong the results would not have been substantially different whatever issue had emerged in the campaign. Looking at the Liberals Paul Stevens argued that the party was in consirerable difficulty even before reciprocity became the centre of political controversy. Lack of leadership and party division, he contended, seriously undermined the Liberal campaign to sell reciprocity and caused valuable ground to be yielded to the opposition as the debate unfolded.

John Dafoe, editor of the *Manitoba Free Press* came to a similar conclusion observing the campaign. The implications of the results, however, were of greater concern. In a letter which he wrote on the morrow of the campaign, Dafoe pointed out that the defeat would give the Liberals the opportunity to transform themselves into a party of the left with radical and progressive policies. Their failure to do so led Dafoe and others who shared his hopes to look to Progressivism as the true inheritor of the Liberal tradition.

James G. Foley, *Resumé of General Elections of 1896, 1900, 1904, 1908 and 1911 and of By-Elections Held Between July 11, 1896 and January 1st, 1916*, (Ottawa, 1916), p. 102.

Voting Pattern

SUMMARY, 1911

Province.	Voters on List.	Votes Polled.	Conservative Votes.	Liberal Votes.	Other Votes.
Ontario	693,485	480,572	269,930	207,078	3,564
Quebec	455,288	324,039	159,299	164,281	459
Nova Scotia	136,994	113,022	55,200	57,462	351
New Brunswick	101,112	79,072	38,880	40,192	
Manitoba	98,588	77,696	40,356	34,781	2,559
British Columbia	83,081	43,559	25,622	16,350	1,587
Prince Edward Island	*	28,636	14,638	13,998	
Saskatchewan	142,414	89,043	34,700	52,924	1,419
Alberta	107,228	69,775	29,675	37,208	2,892
Yukon Territory	2,552	2,114	1,285	829	
Totals	1,820,742	1,307,528	669,594	625,103	12,831

*No Voters' Lists in Prince Edward Island.

REPRESENTATION, 1911

Province.	Members.	Conservative.	Liberal.
Ontario	86	73	13
Quebec	65	27	38
Nova Scotia	18	9	9
New Brunswick	13	5	8
Manitoba	10	8	2
British Columbia	7	7	0
Prince Edward Island	4	2	2
Saskatchewan	10	1	9
Alberta	7	1	6
Yukon Territory	1	1	0
Totals	221	134	87

P.A.C., *Leighton McCarthy Papers*, Wilfrid Laurier to Leighton McCarthy, October 20, 1911.

Race and Religion

Ottawa, October 20, 1911

My dear McCarthy

I received in due time your kind note of the 27th of September. I was then and was kept ever since, so very busy that I could not dispose from day to day, of my ever accumulating correspondence; it is only this moment that I can convey you my gratitude first for having accepting at my request to be a candidate and still more for the plucky way in which you met defeat.

As to the courses; it seems now beyond doubt that an insidious and occult campaign was quietly going on for several months past. The argument used was an appeal to the protestant conscience, cleverly connecting together a roman catholic leader with the *Ne Temere* decree and other acts of the church. I often revolved in my mind your answer to an inquiry from me that but for my religion you would be elected by one thousand majority. We must take men as they are. In the province of Quebec, hundreds of men have cast their vote for me because of my race and religion. It is natural to expect that in the other provinces, men would be influenced by the same considerations to vote against me. This feeling was worked this year to a dangerous point, and has proved only too effective.

Of this I write not in sorrow, still less in anger. From the very moment that I took the leadership of the Party, I was prepared for ruin or catastrophe. I should no longer lead the party: we should have a Protestant at the head of it. For the moment I remain in the saddle and will show nothing but a serene face to the enemy, but the considerations which I have just placed before you, crowd heavily on me and seem to me unanswerable.

Once more let me tell you how grateful I am to you, and please tell Mrs. McCarthy that her also I thank most sincerely, for having, against her own inclination and judgment, given you such a free hand.

The present cabinet seems a queer combination and is not likely to long remain a happy family, if even it be now.

Yours most sincerely

O. D. Skelton, "Canada's Rejection of Reciprocity", *The Journal of Political Economy*, Vol. 19, No. 9, (November, 1911), pp. 726-731.

A Nationalist Viewpoint

The verdict of the people, it may first be noted, was given in a general election, not in a referendum. The fate of the government was involved, its general record was brought up for review, party ambitions and passions were stirred to the utmost. Fifteen years of office-holding had meant the accumulation of the regulation number of scandals, a slackening in administrative efficiency, and the cooling by official compromise of the ardent faith of Liberalism in its days of opposition. Yet the record of the government was not a main issue in the campaign, and the loss suffered on this ground was probably offset by the powerful pressure the Canadian party in power always exerts over constituencies, corporations, and individuals eager for favors. The opposition had gathered energy in fifteen years of fasting. Their newspapers were, on the whole, more aggressive and more effective than the government organs. It is significant also of the rôle played by party, that in the provinces where reciprocity was decisively rejected, Ontario, Manitoba, and British Columbia, strong Conservative governments are intrenched, which placed at the support of the Dominion party all their resources of electioneering skill and the prestige, in two of the three provinces, earned by progressive and honest administration.

Of the side issues introduced into the campaign by the party character of the struggle, the most important were the naval policy in Quebec and the race and religious issue in the English-speaking provinces. The government had to face what Sir Wilfrid termed "the unholy alliance" of ultra-Nationalists in Quebec under Henri Bourassa, and ultra-Protestants in Ontario. In the French-speaking districts the premier was attacked for truckling to the Imperialists, for establishing a Canadian navy which might involve sharing in Britain's wars, and for sacrificing the interests of the French-speaking Catholics in the West. In English-speaking districts a quieter but not less effective campaign was carried on against the continued dominance of Canadian politics by the French Catholic province and a French Catholic premier. It was in vain that the Liberals appealed to national unity or themselves started back-fires in Ontario by painting Bourassa black and declaring that a vote for Borden was a vote for Bourassa. The Conservative-Nationalist alliance lost the government fifteen seats in Quebec, and apparently did not frighten Ontario. Incidentally, the Nationalists overshot themselves; instead of holding the balance of power, they are faced by a Conservative majority sufficiently large at a pinch to do without their votes; for the first time since confederation the party in power might rule without Quebec.

Yet with all these cross-currents it was undoubtedly the reciprocity issue that decided the election. It is further beyond doubt that it was the political rather than the economic aspect of the case that carried most weight.

From the economic point of view there was little question that reciprocity would have meant gain for farmer, fisherman, and miner. Both on broad considerations of the mutual advantages of free intercourse between neighbouring peoples not unevenly matched in these fields, and on detailed study of market conditions in the two countries, the advocates of reciprocity had the better of the argument. Every agricultural paper in Canada and the most important farm organizations were heartily in its favor. There has, of course, been a levelling up of prices on the two sides of the border which makes the advantage less marked than in former years. There are agricultural products, especially fruit, in which it was plausibly claimed the Canadian producer could not compete with the United States. The free admission to Canada's markets of the products of Argentina, Denmark, Russia, the British colonies and other countries under existing favored-nation agreements or the fixed policy of giving no foreign country advantages over the other partners in the empire, threatened more severe competition; the government admitted the danger by taking steps at the Imperial Conference toward securing if possible exemption from the old favored-nation treaties negotiated by Great Britain and binding the whole empire. Yet had the economic issue alone been involved there is little question where the farmer's interest lay and how his vote would have been cast. In the prairie provinces of Alberta and Saskatchewan the economic issue was

most powerful, and here reciprocity swept the boards; had it been possible to pass a Redistribution Bill before the dissolution of Parliament, the additional seats due those provinces on the basis of the 1911 census would have cut down the anti-reciprocity majority—though redistribution would also have involved strengthening the cities of Ontario and Quebec as against the country. Elsewhere the rooted party prejudice of the farmer and the political arguments advanced prevented any government gain sufficient to counterbalance the loss in the industrial districts.

So far as the manufacturer was concerned, no serious inroad was made by the treaty on the protection he enjoys, though the milling, packing, canning, and brewing interests probably stood to lose by having to pay higher prices for their raw material. In spite of their comparative immunity, and of the private assurances that no further reductions were contemplated, the manufacturers and the allied banking and railway interests, afraid of the thin edge of the wedge, fought the pact in almost unbroken ranks. Prominent Liberal financiers broke from the party; manufacturers brought all possible pressure to bear on their employees and fellow-townsmen, especially when it became evident that there was a chance of beating the government and no further necessity for observing the neutrality declared since official Liberalism turned protectionist in 1896; the majority of the railway men attacked it, some openly, like the ex-American chairman of the Board of Directors of the Canadian Pacific, Sir William Van Horne, who made his first public entry into politics in order, in his own engagingly frank phrase, "to bust the damned thing," and some, more prudent because more actively in business, which in a railway-subsidizing country means in relations with the government, silently but not less effectively. The Liberal fifteen-year compromise with protection made it impossible to revive freer trade sentiment in a seven-weeks campaign. The endeavor made to catch the city consumer's vote by arguing that reciprocity meant both higher prices for the producer of the raw material and lower prices to the consumer of the finished and now protected product, while undoubtedly sound in some cases, was apparently too subtle for the wayfaring man to grasp. The prosperity of the country—heightened by big headline contrasts with the existing depression in the United States—lent force to the cry of "Let well enough alone." The fact that the United States had accepted the agreement was enough to convince many primitive reasoners that Canada must be getting the worst of the bargain. The city voter and the voter in the industrial towns scattered through the country flocked to the Conservative banners and turned the scale. Tacticians gifted with hindsight are declaring that the Liberal party would have gained if instead of attempting to placate the manufacturer it had boldly come to the relief of the consumer by increasing the preference on imports from Great Britain to 50 per cent; the opposition of the big interests could not have been greater, and the appeal to the British-born would have been effectively spiked.

From the outset the opponents of reciprocity concentrated on the political issue. The agreement was denounced as the forerunner of annexation, the deathblow to Canadian nationality and British connection. United States public men and newspapers played into their hands; indiscreet friend and astute foe of reciprocity alike fanned the flame by annexation utterances which were given the widest currency; every American crossroads politician who talked of the Stars and Stripes floating from Panama to the Pole was set down a statesman of national importance, voicing a universal sentiment; President Taft's parting-of-the-ways speech was unfairly twisted from its context and used with telling effect. The imprudent action of the Hearst papers in sending proreciprocity editions into the border cities of Canada made many votes —but not for reciprocity. The Canadian democracy proved it was unable to suffer fools gladly. It was in vain to argue that the men who counted in the United States had come to recognize and respect Canada's independent ambitions, that in any event it was not what the United States thought but what Canada thought that mattered, that the Canadian farmer who sold a bushel of good potatoes to an American customer no more sold his loyalty with it than did a blatant Kipling selling his tens of thousands of copies to the same American public, or that it was folly to assert that the political unity of Canada and the empire rested on the ban against Canadian exports which the United States could remove of its own volition at any moment. The flag was waved, and the Canadians, mindful of former American slights or indifference, and newly arrived Englishmen, admirably organized by the anti-reprocity forces, voted against any entangling alliance.

The success of the loyalty cry is viewed with mingled feelings by the Canadian advocate of reciprocity. He is proud of the sturdy feeling of self-reliance, the readiness to set ideals above pocket, which were the creditable factors in the decision; and he trusts that the demonstration of national spirit will not be lost on American prophets of manifest destiny. He regrets that in order to demonstrate a loyalty which might have been taken for granted it was considered necessary to sacrifice unquestioned economic advantage, and is not reassured for the future of democracy by the ease with which interests with unlimited funds for organization, advertising, and newspaper campaigning can pervert national sentiment to serve their own ends. However, this is a stage through which every young nation apparently must pass, and the gentle art of twisting the lion's tail has formed the model for the practice of plucking the eagle's feathers.

Clifford Sifton, "Reciprocity", *Annals of the American Academy of Political Science and Social Sciences*, (1912), pp. 22-28.

A Second Nationalist and Reciprocity

. . . the reciprocity agreement was suddenly and unexpectedly introduced. It is not too much to say that the whole proposition came as a complete surprise to both political parties in the country. No one was looking for or anticipating any such results from the negotiations. There had been a few public deliverances by men more or less prominent, nearly all of which, I think, were hostile to the idea of reciprocity, and a few business men had in a semi-jocular way expressed the hope that our negotiators would get back safely from Washington. I think, however, that I am quite within the mark when I say that there was no serious anticipation of anything important in the way of a treaty or agreement being arrived at. When, therefore, this far-reaching and revolutionary arrangement was announced it came as a complete surprise.

It was somewhat unfortunate in its introduction. In Canada all such matters are made the subject of a parliamentary statement by a member or members of the government of the day. In this case the business was in the hands of Mr. Fielding, Minister of Finance, and Mr. Patterson, Minister of Customs. No one doubts the ability of either of these experienced parliamentary debaters to bring to bear the necessary industry and capacity and to make the very most out of any case committed to their charge, but, strange as it may appear, neither Mr. Fielding nor Mr. Patterson nor the other members of the government ever seemed to realize that they were engaged in the fight of their lives, and that it was necessary for them to get to work and really argue the case. From the very first all of these gentlemen seemed to have been placed at a serious disadvantage by reason of the fact that they apparently thought a mere statement of the terms of the treaty to be sufficient to carry it without any backing of facts or arguments. This idea was due to what appeared to be a lack of realization of the changed conditions of commerce and industry as a result of what had taken place during the previous eighteen or twenty years. There was a time, for instance, when the cry of "free fish" would have swept the Maritime Provinces and when the cry of an enlarged market for hay, potatoes, barley, cattle and dairy products would have swept Ontario and Quebec, but conditions had changed in twenty years and the case had to be argued from new premises altogether. My observation led me to the conclusion that there was a very considerable lack of appreciation of this fact on the part of the government. As a result of this, while no doubt there was a fillip of favorable public sentiment on the first statement of the terms of the agreement, yet so soon as issue was joined in serious argument the impression went abroad that the government side was getting the worst of it. So far as the discussion in the press was concerned, the government side was not well served. The Liberal press, speaking generally, excels rather in attack than in defense. In this case, with one or two exceptions, there was a noticeable lack of thoroughness and vigor in the defense put forward in the Liberal organs. Naturally these papers took their cue from the government, and went in the early stages of the game too much upon the assumption that the mere statement of the terms would win approval. When in the middle of the campaign they found that this idea was fallacious, it was too late to retrieve the position, even if they had the weight of merit upon their side.

A considerable number of Liberals prominent in business openly and unequivocally attacked the reciprocity agreement. In the House of Commons, however, only three Liberal members broke away. The government was able to hold its following in the house and senate almost unbroken.

In the campaign which followed and terminated on the twenty-first of September, 1911, there was practically no serious discussion of any other subject than reciprocity. The government went into the campaign with a majority of about fifty. It came out in a minority of about fifty. There was no reason in the world to suppose that the opposition had any prospect of immediately defeating the government until this question came up. In fact, the opposition had in 1908 exhausted every possible effort and used every available weapon without success. At the beginning of the session of 1911 the opposition was to all appearances hopelessly out of the running and the government very strongly entrenched in office. The reciprocity issue arose. The government forced it forward in a general election. The opposition accepted the

issue and won the election upon it and upon it alone. There has been much talk about other influences affecting the election. It has been said that the *Ne Temere* decree affected the Protestant vote and that Protestants generally were disaffected toward Laurier. I think I know how far this idea prevailed. In my judgment, while no doubt a few hundreds of voters were affected by these arguments, as in every election there will be little eddies of sentiment which have nothing to do with the main issue, I am perfectly satisfied that these side issues were of comparatively little importance and that the victory of the Conservative party in the election was practically due to the reciprocity issue and to it alone. The reason that the Conservative party swept the Province of Ontario, where in fact the victory was won, was because the people of that Province were thoroughly and whole-heartedly opposed to the trade agreement.

What were the reasons?

The short recital given above affords the key to the most important arguments used in favor of the winning side.

Canada had time and again been refused any consideration by the United States and had finally, at great sacrifice and with tremendous efforts, made herself commercially independent. Her products went to widely scattered markets, but there was little or no chance that she would ever be put to serious inconvenience by the closing of these markets. A careful survey of her position showed a degree of commercial independence which under the circumstances was rather surprising and very gratifying to the national pride of Canadians. It was felt that if we consummated the proposed treaty with the United States our trade would follow the line of least resistance. As stated by a New York paper, the reciprocity agreement would check the east and west development of Canada and make that country a business portion of the United States with the lines of traffic running to the north and south rather than to the east and west. The immediate and inevitable result of this would be that Canada would become absolutely dependent upon the fiscal policy of the United States and at the mercy of American tariff changes. It might be said that the United States would be equally interested in our fiscal policy, but the conclusive answer to that argument was that what might be vital to Canada with its eight million people and its small production, would be of comparatively trifling importance to the United States with its ninety million people and its enormous volume of production. It would be, in fact, a case of partnership with one partner so undeniably predominant that the weaker partner would be in the position of the Roman philosopher who feared to press his argument with Augustus too far because it was not wise to press too hardly in argument upon "the master of thirty legions."

In a word, the judgment of the business men of Canada was that the reciprocity agreement, if carried into effect, would mean a commercial alliance which would of necessity have to be carried further, and that as a necessary result of such an alliance the United States, being the greater, wealthier, stronger and more populous country, would dominate Canada's commercial policy and development.

It was, and is, believed that reciprocity in natural products would lead to reciprocity in manufactures. It was, and is, believed that the predominance of the United States in commercial legislation would lead to loss of control on our part of our undeveloped natural resources and especially of our water powers. It was,

and is, believed that these results would not only affect us in the matters particularly mentioned, but would subordinate Canada to the United States in such a way as to interfere with her national independence.

Following this idea, it will be readily seen that Canadians who take seriously the idea of Canada's position in the British Empire had every cause to be alarmed. To place the most important unit of the British Empire, outside of the British Isles, under the domination of a foreign though friendly power would be a long step toward disintegration. Your publicists who said that this trade agreement would bind Canada to the United States and strike a blow at the consolidation of the British Empire were absolutely right and we who fought against it realized that fact and had a full appreciation of its importance.

Taking the Dominion by sections, the result was that Nova Scotia, Prince Edward Island and New Brunswick were on the whole slightly but still decidedly unfriendly to the agreement. In Quebec, strange as it may appear, I can find no evidence that reciprocity seriously affected the rural voters or influenced them in the exercise of their franchise. On the other hand, the manufacturers, financiers, railway men and commercial men of Montreal and vicinity were practically a unit against reciprocity and their influence undoubtedly accounted directly or indirectly for fifteen or eighteen of the Quebec constituencies which were carried by the opposition.

The Province of Ontario was almost solidly opposed to the agreement. My own belief is that even the election returns which gave seventy-three seats to the Conservatives and thirteen to the Liberals did not represent the real sentiment against the agreement. I knew fairly well the sentiment of Ontario as it was just previous to the election and I now believe that quite one-half of those who voted in favor of the Liberal government were at heart opposed to its policy. In fact, there was no heart in the contest on the part of the Liberal party in the Province of Ontario and there was apparently no mourning in its camp so far as the rank and file of the voters were concerned when it was defeated.

Winnipeg and the urban centers of the prairie provinces were generally opposed to reciprocity. The farmers were strongly in favor of it.

British Columbia was lost to the Liberals in any event on account of party disorganization and incompetent leadership, but it is fairly safe to say that the Province as a whole is against reciprocity.

Summarizing the case, we have the fact that a government strongly entrenched and well organized, led by a man who is perhaps the most striking and brilliant personality in the British Empire, with a record of statesmanlike achievement behind it, went into a fight on the question of reciprocity and was hopelessly routed. No single portion of the Dominion, except the farmers of the three prairie provinces, showed the slightest enthusiasm for the policy of the government, while in the other parts of the country thousands of ardent Liberals went over to the opposition.

The opposition remains unchanged and unchangeable to-day. It is a deliberate, calculated and determined opposition. I am perfectly satisfied that if the House of Commons were dissolved to-morrow and Sir Wilfrid Laurier proclaimed in unmistakable terms his intention of going to Washington to negotiate a new treaty or to consummate the old one, he would be disastrously defeated. In fact, his defeat would be more decisive than it was last fall.

But it is difficult to see how such a case can again arise. The proffer of reciprocity on what seemed very liberal terms by the government of the United States was undoubtedly a high political play on the part of that government. The play was made to meet a most unusual and embarrassing condition of affairs within the ranks of the Republican party. The measure was supported by the Democrats in congress, because to support it was at once the simple, straightforward and politic thing to do. But circumstances have changed and it may safely be said now that the conditions which brought the offer of reciprocity from the United States are not likely to recur.

Under all the circumstances, therefore, I conclude that reciprocity is not any longer in the least degree a practical political question. The question is not likely to return to the people of Canada in the form in which it was presented last year, but if it does so return it will undoubtedly be answered in precisely the same manner in which it was answered then.

Something should be said with regard to the ideas which in the main actuated the great body of those who were led to take an unusually active and determined part in the election. It should be stated in the most emphatic terms that there was no idea of hostility or unfriendliness to the United States at the root of their action. I think that most people thought that the treaty was a very liberal one from the standpoint of the United States. I never heard very much in the way of suggestion that the United States should have offered more or that our negotiators should have demanded more.

The underlying motive was of a different character altogether. The people believed that the development of the two countries under the reciprocity policy was bound to interfere with the commercial independence of Canada and that idea was fatal to the success of the policy proposed.

Our people thoroughly recognize the greatness of the United States and its phenomenal success along many lines of human endeavor. It is, however, the opinion of our most thoughtful people that your constitution is now approaching its supreme test. We look with some apprehension upon your labor difficulties. We think also that your attempt to regulate the great monopolies which have arisen will tax the energies of the nation to the utmost. We most sincerely wish you well in the efforts which you are so manfully making. Nowhere has the tree of Liberty borne more glorious fruit than in the United States, and it is the sincere hope of every true lover of freedom that you may go from triumph to triumph exhibiting to the world a shining and inspiring example.

Your present problems, however, are vastly more complicated and difficult of solution than our own. We shall have in one way or another all these problems to solve, but they will come in smaller volume and in a form much less difficult to handle. We anticipate no serious difficulty in curbing any trusts or combinations that may arise in Canada and in placing production upon a legitimate and proper basis. We feel also quite able to deal with questions affecting our great transportation systems. In fact, most of the machinery is already provided and working well. We, however, wish to deal with these questions and to regulate them in our own way without pressure from abroad and without feeling that great financial interests outside of our jurisdiction are being exerted to influence our decision.

L. Ethan Ellis, "Canada's Rejection of Reciprocity in 1911", *The Canadian Historical Association Annual Report*, 1939, pp. 101-110. Reprinted by permission of the Author.

The Historian and Reciprocity

. . . Why did an arrangement deliberately giving the products of an agricultural country a new outlet, representing the achievement of an end vainly sought for years by bipartisan efforts, and sponsored by a party long ensconced in power and led by the brilliant Laurier, go down to one of the most spectacular defeats in the history of the Dominion? The following pages attempt to trace the roles played by economic factors, by imperial relationships, by the United States, and by time itself in contributing to the mounting tide of loyalty to country and to Empire, and of accentuated fear of the neighbour to the south, under which reciprocity was buried.

It is obvious that Canadian beneficiaries of protection, Canadian railroaders managing lines built to defy natural trade routes by virtue of government subsidies, and bankers attuned to the interests of these powerful clients, would alike distrust any proposal which would lower tariff barriers or allow commerce to seek its natural level. These interests were geographically concentrated and numerically insignificant. Their influence, which it is here suggested was dominant in defeating the Taft-Fielding agreement, had therefore to be exerted so as to move popular majorities to hostility or to fear. Both time and circumstance aided these interests in the unfolding of a gradually-developing plan which used Conservative press and party as a vehicle of reciprocity's destruction. A number of factors forwarded this plan. The agreeement involved the United States, and pious platitudes about an undefended frontier had not yet sufficed to make all Canadians love their neighbours. Again, the alleged danger of a weakened imperial tie made a waving Union Jack an imposing weapon in the opponents' arsenal. A nearly parliamentary verdict (which contemporaries well-nigh unanimously agreed would have been a favourable one) was prevented by lack of closure and desire to move slowly lest the United States might act unfavourably. Congress failing to act in regular course, the necessity of a special session gave time for Canadian opposition to harden into obstruction, until Laurier had to leave to assist in the crowning of a King. When he returned the initiative had passed to his opponents, now in an excellent tactical position to force an election which could be fought on the positive side by appealing to national and imperial patriotism and on the negative side by saying "No" to the Government's programme without having to advance constructive measures of their own.

Parliamentary discussion opened February 9, two days before congressional oratory commenced. By this time Conservative spines, particularly from Ontario, had been stiffened by contact with their constituents. This enabled the party to unite upon a programme of opposition, after nearly a week of stormy caucuses which opened in an atmosphere of uncertainty and divided sentiment. Thus was launched a struggle covering twenty-five legislative days during February, March, April, and early May. This debate, carried on against a background of events in the United States, and of growing hostility in Canada, marked important developments in reciprocity's progress to oblivion. By the time Parliament adjourned to allow Laurier to attend the Coronation and the Imperial Conference, the Liberals had lost their advantage of surprise, had been forced on the defensive, and faced the likelihood of an appeal to the country.

At this point a brief recapitulation of events below the border may illuminate Canadian developments. President Taft's failure to secure passage of his agreement at the regular session of Congress has been noted. He was therefore forced to call a special session which assembled April 4. Here the House acted promptly (April 21), but Senate hearings lasted until early May and the bill was not passed until July 22. This delay, particularly failure to act at the short session, strengthened the position of the Canadian opposition—if the United States did not act, why should Canada hurry to bind herself? Again, the lengthy congressional debate furnished much ammunition for the Canadian discussion, particularly for the opposition, for every favourable argument below the border could be adapted into an unfavourable one above. Finally, American leaders themselves contributed a series of almost unbelievably inept statements which no Liberal glosses could free from damaging implications.

The parliamentary debates were significant along two lines: they served as a vehicle for the presentation of arguments on both sides, and they fore-shadowed opposition strategy. All the important arguments went into the record in February, when debate reached the high-water mark of parliamentary discussion. The national, imperial, and economic consequences of the agreement were canvassed thoroughly. Many followed Borden's lead and asked, in effect, "Why not let well enough alone?" Others argued that the ministry had no popular mandate for the proposed action. Others were alarmed at the uncertain duration of the agreement. On the national-imperial front concern was voiced lest reciprocity destroy Canada's fiscal freedom and endanger the tariff preference to Britain. The danger of annexation, prominent in the later discussion, was less noticed at this stage.

Among economic arguments, fear was expressed lest the most-favoured-nation clauses extend favours granted the United States to all of Britain's possessions and to many foreign countries. The imminent danger to Canada's far-flung east-west transportation lanes was noted. The whole Conservative argument echoed the refrain that the producer, in whose interest the Government had professedly made the arrangement, would be grievously injured by the competition which reciprocity would make possible. Thus reciprocity's opponents, in Canada as well as in the United States, made their chief plea to the producing interests; the farmer, rather than the manufacturer, was pushed to the fore as the principal sufferer. By the same token, Liberals emphasized the larger market which reciprocity would provide, while reciprocity's friends south of the border insisted that it would not harm the United States farmer. Liberal debaters spent most of their time refuting Conservative contentions, which exceeded their own both in number and variety. This first period of discussion launched the principal arguments on both sides, preserved a fairly high level of courtesy and urbanity, and stuck fairly closely to the point at issue.

This courtesy and urbanity may have had something to do with a revolt against Borden's leadership of the party in late March, seemingly led by Montreal and Quebec capitalist elements in disagreement with his too-gentlemanly conduct of the campaign. He survived the challenge to lead a further fight emerging in April as an evident effort to make Parliament a sounding-board to magnify the volume of hostility being stirred up in the country. Another note appeared in May—Why not wait until the United States acts by herself? This developed from the evident intention of the Democrats in the new Congress to attempt general tariff revision as well as adopt reciprocity. By late April the Liberals had passed definitely to the defensive and devoted most of their time to refuting the ever-louder Conservative assertions; furthermore, time was passing rapidly. The season for the Coronation and ensuing Imperial Conference approached, and presently a Conservative caucus decided to carry reciprocity to a bitter-end fight. With this Conservative strategy began to be apparent—they would postpone decision until after the Coronation, and would then try to force the issue to the country. The parliamentary recess could be used to good advantage in fanning the flames of hostility already burning.

Away from Ottawa the propaganda mills had been turning apace. The February memorial of the Manufacturers' Association to the Prime Minister exhibited a tenderness for the farmer's welfare, allegedly endangered by reciprocity, matched only by American manufactur-

ers' solicitude for the American farmer, also alleged to be facing ruin. This pushing forward of the farmer as the stalking horse of the protected interests was an outstanding as well as an adroit part of the campaign on both sides of the border. In neither case were manufacturers anxious to admit their own interest in preserving the tariff wall intact, though the files of *Industrial Canada* contain many articles openly deprecating any breach in the barrier. Boards of trade generally followed the lead of the manufacturers, though frequently adverse resolutions were adopted only after bitter internal struggles. Expressed sentiment of railroad leaders varied from Sir Donald Mann's belief that "no harm can come to our Canadian railways . . ." from reciprocity, to Sir William Van Horne's emergence from retirement in an effort "to bust the damned thing." The evidence indicates that strong adverse railroad influence was brought to bear behind the scenes.

February and March saw the press campaign gather headway, mirroring the parliamentary arguments. Hereafter the newspapers settled down for a time to reiteration, with Conservative organs occasionally discovering a new tack, which defenders veered to meet. As in Parliament, the Conservatives had the initiative, with Quebec and Ontario journals, particularly the Montreal *Star* and the Toronto *News* furnishing most of the ammunition; the stoutest pro-reciprocity fighter was the Toronto *Star*; the *Globe*, while active, was at first disinclined to a shirt-sleeves campaign. Declining during the Coronation season, the press drive revived rapidly during July to reach a crescendo in August and September. Opposition arguments first centred principally around the danger to national unity implicit in a reciprocity which would destroy the transportation bridge north of Lake Superior by turning western trade south to Chicago and the Twin Cities; stressed also were the threat to the imperial connection and the danger of annexation. In March the *Star* inaugurated a determined effort to prove reciprocity bad for the farmer; a widely-copied series of articles described, in words and pictures, the deserted farms of New England; Canadians were pointedly asked if these farmers, so close to a supposedly hungry market, could not meet the competition of the American West, how could Canadians overcome a still greater transportation obstacle? Again the *Star* launched (March 11) an argument designed to show how reciprocity would expose Canada to the hard times and unemployment said to be rampant in the United States. Two days later the *News* added a fear that the agreement would let the American trusts into Canada.

Liberal journals played up the argument that the agreement opened to Canadian producers a "Ninety Million Market." The next most important supporting claim was that reciprocity would benefit both producer and consumer, an unfortunate effort which subjected Liberals to no little ridicule in the controversy's later stages. Beyond these points, Liberal energies were mainly directed to refuting opposition sallies; this, in fact, became more and more the burden of the Liberal plea.

April saw a recurring appeal to annexation and the farm interest; Taft's unfortunate utterance of April 27 gave rise to a flurry of charge and countercharge on annexation and the Empire. About this time, too, Conservatives began to emphasize a series of alleged scandals in the Liberal administrative record. By the adjournment of Parliament the main outlines of the press campaign were evident—aside from the farmer's plight, matters of economic concern were to be soft-pedalled, it being the aim of opposition strategy to direct attention to more easily capitalized national, imperial, and political aspects. This strategy was possible because the opposition press seized and maintained the initiative, forcing reciprocity's defenders into a heart-breaking effort to overtake a strong front runner.

Laurier's decision to adjourn Parliament and go to London marked a turning point. Taken upon the advice of his Cabinet and against his own judgment that he should remain in Canada and fight reciprocity to a conclusion, whether before Parliament or country, the recess finally overcame the last vestiges of Liberal advantage so evident in January —surprise, prospective economic benefit, and entrenched power. The uncertain opposition, so hesitant in January, had been strengthened from powerful quarters, had profited by delay in the United States, and, after the recess took the offensive in Parliament and country to the point where it could enforce its demands for a popular verdict with the odds heavily in its favour.

His departure for London gave the Premier no respite from attack. The hostile press saw in adjournment evidence that the Prime Minister did not trust Fielding to manage debate on his own measure, and a quarrel between the two was intimated. Laurier's choice of an autonomist policy at the Imperial Conference allowed Conservative and Protestant to charge that he was trying to destroy the Empire at the behest of Quebec separatism. Meantime Borden, on a western tour, was facing the Grain Growers, who pressed him hard on reciprocity, and were satisfied neither with his stout refusal to co-operate in this direction nor his equally stout promises along other lines. The tour, however, gave him a chance to preach the national and imperial aspects of reciprocity and to de-emphasize its economic side. Though it made him little political capital, it showed the West and, more important, the East, what to expect from him, and gave him good experience in trying out his arguments before a hostile audience.

When Parliament reassembled on July 18, the Conservative strategy of obstruction was given full play until suddenly, on July 29, the Government stilled the repetition of old arguments by announcing an immediate dissolution with an election on September 21. The key to the bitter fight which followed is to be found in the Liberals' vain efforts to push reciprocity to the fore and in their opponents' more successful efforts (aided by left-handed allies in the French Nationalists), to drown it in a clamour of national and imperial interests allegedly more important. Both parties used the Eastern Provinces as sounding-boards for the leaders' oratory, leaving local campaigns in the hands of lieutenants. Laurier at first asserted valiantly that reciprocity was the sole issue, but ere long he abandoned this contention and introduced other matters into his addresses, particularly trying to lay the annexation spectre and to expose the "Unholy Alliance" between Borden and the French Nationalists. Toward the close of his tour he pointedly noted that the agreement treated the manufacturers kindly, and stressed again its great advantages to the farmer. Despite his stout front, he was obviously on the defensive, and privately began to

have his doubts about the result as early as three weeks before the election.

Borden spent over a third of his speaking time in the superlatively important Ontario. Like Laurier, he devoted considerable attention to the agreement's economic aspects, but generally connected these with its national consequences in an effort to show that reciprocity would endanger Canadian commercial, fiscal, or political independence. Using the unfortunate parting-of-the-ways remark in almost every speech, Borden made Taft his lay-figure, to be stood up and knocked down for the benefit of Canadian audiences. These, along with a plea to preserve the Empire, some attention to alleged Liberal extravagance and corruption, and the necessary promises of the out-of-office, comprised the burden of his argument. Next to the two leaders the most important speaker on either side was Clifford Sifton, whose trenchment criticisms of the agreement in many eastern industrial centres added to the influence he had already wielded as adviser to the opposition forces.

The position of the Quebec Nationalists, led by Henri Bourassa and the fiery *Le Devoir,* was a matter of moment to both sides. Bourassa at first favoured the Laurier reciprocity. The looming of a Dominion election complicated the Nationalist position. Quebec Conservatism, led by F. D. Monk, opposed Laurier and his reciprocity. Quebec Nationalism opposed Laurier's navy but not his reciprocity. To prevent this situation from creating three-cornered provincial contests which might result in the victory of Laurier men, a Monk-Bourassa arrangement produced Conservative candidates generally acceptable to the Nationalists.

This working agreement gave the Liberals an opportunity to assert that

Borden himself was allied with Bourassa, an accusation which he never formally denied. Solution of this problem lies beyond the scope of the present study; the possibility of the alliance alarmed much of the Liberal press to the point of hysteria and caused the Premier to spend over half of his campaigning time in Quebec; it injected the race and naval questions into the Quebec battle to such an extent that reciprocity became distinctly a minor issue there; it gave the Liberals a chance to assert that the Ontario Conservatives were financing the Quebec Nationalists and that while Borden was mouthing protestations of loyalty to the Empire in Ontario his Quebec allies were, in the Toronto *Globe's* words, "doing their treasonable utmost to inflame the minds of the French-Canadians against that very Imperial idea which Mr. Borden extols."

The reader of the Canadian press is struck by the bewildering reiteration of old arguments and the paucity of new approaches to what was now definitely a political problem. One is almost tempted to agree with *The Sentinel's* (Toronto) editorial writer who greeted election day with this effusion:

A careful reading of the party papers leads to the conclusion that Mr. Borden will be returned to power with a majority of thirty for Sir Wilfrid Laurier and the Nationalists holding the balance of power. This, of course, involves the defeat of the reciprocity pact, which will be put into effect as soon as Parliament meets, the United States already having adopted it.

This paradoxical situation will make Canada an ideal place to live, as the producer will get higher prices than before, while the consumer will get his goods for less money. Seeing that almost everybody in Canada is a producer of something, and seeing, too, that they are all consumers, it follows that everything a man has to sell will be higher and everything he has to buy will be cheaper.

The national song will be "Yankee Doodle's Maple Leaf," to be sung as a solo by your Uncle Samuel and Brittania [*sic*], who rules the waves.

Reiterated argument and phrase were dressed out in a tremendous variety of typographical pyrotechnics. Red ink, streamer headlines, cartoons, pictures of prominent deserters from each party on the reciprocity question, were all shaded by the Union Jack on front pages whence world news and the economic phases of reciprocity were pushed far into the background.

Liberal journals again had to devote much time to refutation; the principal positive arguments being their offer of the larger market to the producing classes, and the alleged Borden-Bourassa alliance. When, toward the end of the campaign, it became evident that the single appeal to the farmer would not win the day, attention was turned to reassuring industry and labour. At the last minute a prominent United States argument that reciprocity would lower food costs to labour was pressed into service. Finally, it was urged that the agreement should have a trial before it was condemned—an argument seized upon by the opposition as a counsel of despair. The last few days found the Liberal press striving valiantly to keep to the main issue, but being forced more and more into channels fashioned by the other side.

Conservative press strategy, as earlier, was to obscure the reciprocity issue by appeal to indirect and largely irrelevant matters, many imported from the United States for the occasion. Imperial loyalty, Liberal scandals, and annexation, the manna called down from Heaven by Champ Clark, the Missouri Moses, were much to the fore. The producer, as in the United States, was warned of dire disaster to follow in reciprocity's wake. The Canadian worker was proffered American hard times—duty free; at the same time charges were bandied that American money was pouring in to influence the Canadian issue. In the last days the worker was told that his job was not safe, as alleged by the Liberals, but in grave jeopardy unless reciprocity were defeated. Another American import was publicized: William Randolph Hearst, who in May and June had turned all the pressure of his powerful influence behind Taft in the United States, was charged with insinuating himself into the Canadian election. September 18, too late for successful contradiction, widely scattered journals announced a Taft-Hearst scheme to deliver Canada to the United States. Thus Conservative initiative led Liberals off the point of reciprocity despite valiant efforts, dissipated their energies, and forced them to reply in kind to Conservative appeals to race and to emotion. The result was a campaign which in intensity and picturesqueness has had few rivals in North America.

The end result of the forces surveyed above was recorded in the astonishing overturn of September 21. The first opportunity for this overturn came when the matter was opened to political discussion. This gave, on both sides of the border, a chance for protected interests to influence political events for private ends. In Canada, United States delay, Liberal unwillingness to force the issue to a vote, American indiscretions, and the passage of time conspired to raise opposition hopes and depress defenders' chances. The contest found one party on the way up and the other on the way down, and accelerated a change in the nature of things inevitable, but made more quickly possible when the 1911 campaign on the reciprocity issue alienated important interests which in 1908 had supported the Prime Minister. Having forced matters to an election, opposition chances improved rapidly, since the political arena was large enough to introduce extraneous issues more likely to appeal to patriotism or to fear; thus an economic programme of some intrinsic merit became the football of a political campaign in which the opposition won by an essentially simple tactic—of saying "No" to reciprocity and "Yes" to the British connection. Out of the whole episode Canada approached nationhood, under the British flag, and launched upon a period of high protection. This last result was the end sought by those whose agents filled the Dominion from ocean to ocean with propaganda.

Farmer, loyalty, imperialism, all meant one thing to the groups which used all these pleas to avert a danger which knows no national boundaries— the danger to a self-interest well-developed and long-entrenched. Any analysis of the reciprocity episode which stops with the explanation that the American farmer opposed reciprocity, and that it was defeated in Canada because of the annexation-loyalty cries, misses the fundamental factor involved; the farmer may have been opposed, and the average Canadian may have feared the United States, but this opposition and these fears were assiduously cultivated, if not implanted, by interests motivated by a common fear of the consequences of lower tariffs.

H. Blair Neatby. *Laurier and a Liberal Quebec: A Study in Political Management*, (Unpublished Doctoral Dissertation, University of Toronto, 1956), pp. 348-351. Reprinted by permission of the Author.

The Campaign in Quebec

In the campaign in the province of Quebec there could be no doubt that Bourassa was the most prominent opponent of the Liberals, despite the fact that he was not a candidate. His political assemblies drew enormous crowds and his continued emphasis on the issue of Imperialism put the Liberals in the province on the defensive. Liberal newspapers devoted a good deal of space to proving that Bourassa was mistaken in calling the navy an Imperial navy. *Le Canada* printed a series of political articles ridiculing the policy of *Le Maitre*, a name referring to Bourassa's apparent assumption of virtue and infallibility. *La Presse* repeated the theme that the battle was between Laurier and Borden, whatever Bourassa might claim. Towards the end of the campaign the Liberal press seems to have tried to shift the emphasis to the issue of reciprocity, with "Laurier et la Réciprocité" as the slogan, but Bourassa was not easily ignored. Nor was the policy of quoting Ontario Conservative newspapers embarrassing to an

opposition in Quebec which denounced Conservative as well as Liberal policies. If there were two protagonists in the province, they were not Laurier and Borden but Laurier and Bourassa.

Laurier won the election in Quebec. Of sixty-five seats the Liberals won thirty-seven. Laurier had expected even better results; more than a week before the election he told Fielding that the losses in the province would be "three or perhaps five" more than before the election, whereas actually fifteen additional seats were lost. It was a mathematical victory, but in comparison with previous election results it was a defeat. The "solid Quebec" had been split.

Nevertheless, the Liberal losses should not be exaggerated. With reference to the two national parties, Quebec was still predominantly Liberal. Most of the constituencies lost had been won by *Autonomiste* rather than Conservative candidates. It is not a coincidence that of the constituencies lost, thirteen were in northern and eastern Quebec—areas in which the *nationaliste* colonization campaign had played an important part in weakening the influence of the Liberal party. Even against a party, provincial in scope and *nationaliste* in policy, after fifteen years of office had dimmed the novelty of having a French-Canadian Prime Minister, the Liberals had won a majority of the seats. From a national point of view it was at least reassuring that so many electors had voted for a national party.

There was an indirect, but probably more significant result of the election of 1911 for the province of Quebec. The Liberal ranks had been decimated in the province of Ontario, and so the Conservative party could have formed a government even without an alliance with the *Autonomistes*. The scheme for a third party which would hold the balance of power at Ottawa had failed. The elected *Autonomistes* tamely accepted Borden's leadership, leaving themselves vulnerable to Liberal accusations that they were unprincipled office-seekers. Bourassa tried to console himself by a bold declaration after the election; "Nous avons aidé à jeter bas un gouvernement, nous n'hésiterons pas à mettre la sape au pied d'un autre, s'il forfait à son devoir." But this was cold comfort to the *nationalistes* who had just helped to establish in power the more imperialist of the two national parties, and who would wait many years for an opportunity to undermine it. The third party movement had failed in 1911. It never recovered from the failure.

P.A.C., *Laurier Papers*, Alexander Smith to Laurier, November 10, 1911.

The Organizer and the Election

Ottawa, November 10, 1911

My dear Sir Wilfrid,

In accordance with your suggestion, I am putting in Memorandum form, some of the cries which the Conservatives used against you and your Government in the recent election. These cries, each and all of them "cut deep" and largely because you had no organization.

The two main causes of your defeat were first fifteen years of power, and secondly no organization.

It is sad to think that our fellows in Ontario were just put up to be marked for slaughter. The Reciprocity Agreement was presented to the House in January, and it was six months after that (after your return from Great Britain) before any move was made to get the terms of the Agreement before the public, but during all this period, anyone who wished could go out and become a candidate for the sake of patronage. During the past six weeks, I have had the pleasant task of going over, assorting and

destroying a great mass of political (almost entirely organization) correspondence, for the Provincial Election of 1894, 1898 and 1902, and the Federal Election of 1896, 1900, 1904, and 1908, and the scores of by-elections contests from 1893-1904, inclusive, and it was evident to me that at no time during that campaign were we ever so poorly marshalled as in the recent campaign.

It behooved those in authority in organizational matters to be more on the alert than ever for in the campaign of 1908 some of those opposed to us in 1911 became thoroughly familiar with the personnel of the Liberal party in Ontario, its organization and its methods of education. The Conservatives in their methods of issuing their literary material followed the system which we adopted in 1895 and developed in succeeding years, whilst our people dropped back on antiquated methods. The other side were so equipped that they would feed mentally and otherwise any group of faddists and many groups sprung up when it was found they could get both pamphlets and support. Every man with a frenzy could get cash to go out and organize a group and many went out for the "interests" that supplied the cash.

We had nobody in charge. It was like playing marbles with marbles made out of ordinary roadside mud. Warnings, suggestions, directions and offers of assistance were all resented, and the result was that you had not the support of the lineal descendants of those who were proud to see you elected in 1896 and followed you until old age dimmed their ardour.

You were not defeated by these cries. The cries got the "start on you" because you had no organization—none whatever.

Some of the Conservative assertions throughout the Province of Ontario during the Federal Election Campaign which closed on September 21st, 1911, were as follows:—

(1) Borden will repeal the *ne temere* law, which the Pope got the Premier to pass.

(2) Borden will pass a law preventing the Pope from taking up his residence in Montreal.

(3) Borden will pass a law preventing another Eucharistic Procession.

(4) The Pope says that all Protestant fathers and mothers live in adultery and that all Protestant children are bastards.

(5) The Pope sent our Rev. Father Vaughan to declare this and he also sent out the Ne Temere decree—see how M. J. Heney, head of the Toronto Liberals, used his wife.

(6) The Catholics get what they want among themselves in Quebec, and they should not invade Ontario—see what Laurier has done for the Irish—all that is best he has given them—Even Justice is in their hands.

(7) Vote against Laurier and save the Flag.

Yours faithfully

Robert Cuff, "The Conservative Party Machine and the Election of 1911 in Ontario", *Ontario History*, Vol. LVII, No. 3, September 1965, pp. 149-156. Reprinted by permission of the Ontario Historical Society.

The Whitney Machine

In any election there are at least two levels of activity: the ostensible campaign of public issues, oratory and propaganda, and the less obvious one of party organization and electoral machinery. The relative importance that will be given to each as a factor in any election result will, of course, vary with the individual contest. Nevertheless, both features of the political campaign must be taken into account if the outcome is to be fully understood. Previous studies of the election of 1911 have been focused primarily upon the public issues involved: "Nationalism vs. Imperialism" in Quebec; reciprocity and the "loyalty" issue in the rest of Canada. A brief examination of the Liberal and Conservative party organizations in the Province of Ontario, however, suggests that the party machine has been previously underestimated as a factor in the Conservative victory of that year. . . .

. . . the Liberal campaign in Ontario [was] handicapped by haphazard organization, lack of decisive central control, intra-party squabbling, and inaccurate political reporting.

This was in striking contrast to the Conservative organization and the campaign it waged. Not only did Borden and the Federal Conservatives have a strong Provincial party with which to work, but they also had the personal co-operation of Sir James Whitney himself. The Premier and his organization were in constant contact with Borden and became, in fact, an extension of the Federal machine. Coupled with the vigor and efficiency of the Federal organizers, this close co-operation enabled the Conservatives to triumph over the Laurier Liberals on the battleground of constituency organization.

The reciprocity proposals were introduced in Parliament on January 26, 1911, and it was a dispirited Conservative Opposition that listened to what seemed to be a political coup of the first order. A groundswell of discontent, however, was not long in coming, and battered by a barrage of propaganda, the Government, in some bewilderment, suddenly found itself on the defensive. Nor could it count on solidarity among its own ranks. Sir Clifford Sifton soon made his objections public; a group of eighteen prominent Liberals from Toronto published its manifesto of revolt on February 20. The final blow came seven months later.

It was obvious to many Conservatives as early as April that an election might be called in the not too distant future, and action was initiated to whip Ontario into shape. Dr. J. D. Reid, M.P. for Grenville and the Conservative watchdog of Eastern Ontario, wrote Borden on April 15 with his evaluation of the situation. As far as the 22 seats under his aegis were concerned, all were in fairly good shape. Twelve of them did not require any attention at all. They were safe. But before an election was announced, active work had to be undertaken at once to ensure victory in the others.

Two days later the Conservative organizers for Ontario met in Toronto: A. E. Kemp, whom one observer later called, "the most useful adviser in the Federal Conservative party," without whom the party would have been "in wretched shape for the general election;" J. S. Carstairs, Secretary of the Liberal-Conservative Association and Dominion organizer; Frank Cochrane, member of the Whitney Cabinet and later put in charge of the entire Ontario campaign; and Dr. J. D. Reid. W. J. Hanna, Provincial Cabinet Minister, and E. D. Smith, former Conservative M.P. for Wentworth had been expected, but were unable to attend. The Conservative chiefs partitioned Ontario into areas over which they had personal supervision and responsibility to ensure that each district would have candidates who could carry the counties within it. The summation of Conservative prospects in Ontario that emerged from this meeting shows such prescience that it affords good ground for believing that a comparable Conservative landslide would have occurred in Ontario regardless of the reciprocity issue. There was no intimation that reciprocity was a controlling factor in their assessment of conditions or predictions of electoral success. It was rather a projection based upon careful consideration of existing Conservative constituency strength, and Liberal constituency weakness—a situation that was ripe for exploitation regardless of the issue that precipitated an election.

Of the 50 seats held at that time by Conservatives, 36, they believed, were "absolutely sure": Dundas, Grenville,

Leeds, Frontenac, East and West Hastings, East Peterborough, North Renfrew, South Lanark, Carleton, North Ontario, Durham, Victoria and Haliburton, South York, Centre Toronto, East Toronto, West Toronto, North Toronto, South Toronto, Peel, South Simcoe, Dufferin, East Hamilton, West Hamilton, Lincoln, Haldimand, Norfolk, East Elgin, West Elgin, East Middlesex, East Lambton, East Grey, South Waterloo, London, Parry Sound and Muskoka. The remaining 14, they estimated, would come under strong Liberal attack because of the small majorities by which they had been won in 1908. These were: South Bruce, East and West Huron, North Grey, North Essex, West and East Algoma, Nipissing, Centre York, Halton, Lennox and Addington, East Northumberland, North Lanark and North Simcoe. However, of this potential loss, only 4 were considered really very likely to fall. Of the 36 seats presently held by the Liberals, 14 were condeded: Ottawa (2), Russell, Prescott, Kingston, North York, East Kent, West Lambton, South Essex, Brantford, Welland, South Huron, North Waterloo and South Wellington. They believed, however, that the remaining 22 should be made the object of a "vicious attack," for nearfly all would be won: North Middlesex, North Bruce, South Grey, South Perth, North Perth, North Wellington, West Kent, West Middlesex, South Oxford, Prince Edward, Glengarry, Stormont, Brockville, West Northumberland, West Peterborough, South Renfrew, South Ontario, Thunder Bay-Rainy River, East Simcoe, Brant, Wentworth and North Oxford.

Besides the result of a general analysis of the political situation and a brief plan of attack, this same April meeting also provided a report on each one of the 22 Liberal constituencies likely to be won with suggestions as to who the best man would be for each. Comments on the candidates already nominated were also included. A comparison of these prognostications with the actual election results will show how well aware the Conservatives were of political realities and how effective their organization and candidates proved to be.

At the outset, much time was given to finding suitable Conservative standard-bearers. Eager to secure men who were certain of winning doubtful constituencies, the organizers often sought to induce members of the Provincial Legislature to give up their seats at Queen's Park and run for Federal office. This, of course, brought them into collision with Premier Whitney who was quite naturally concerned lest the position of his government be weakened by such raiding. He had already written to Borden stating his objection to Carstairs' efforts to move in this direction without consulting him first, despite the warnings the Premier had given him in that regard. In his reply to this note, Borden made it clear that upon all occasions Whitney should be consulted first, and he claimed that he had instructed Carstairs to do so. However, he went on to explain that there were several Provincial ridings which could be carried for the Conservatives by "any one of a score of good men" now in the Ontario Legislature. He had always understood that in such circumstances an arrangement could be made. He claimed to have spoken already with at least three of Whitney's colleagues on the matter and believed that the Premier had had no objection. Wanting very much to avoid any disruption of his invaluable relationship with Whitney, he concluded, "I am thoroughly anxious that no misunder-

standing or friction should occur with respect thereto."

But Whitney was not aggrieved so much at the actual arrangements contemplated as he was at the fact that Carstairs continued to make them without his official sanction. The Legislature and its members were, after all, his domain, and he had no intention of having his authority flouted or machinations effected behind his back. "There is not the slightest danger of any friction," he wrote. "I do not suppose there will be any real trouble in settling any such question as you refer to, whenever it may arise. . . ." In fact, he was willing to go "a long way" to comply, but only after such questions had been "discussed freely and openly by all." He was surprised, therefore, to hear that any one of his colleagues had given Borden to think otherwise. Furthermore, he knew of no case in which the knowledge of Federal intervention had come to him only long after it had been broached to the Member concerned. Borden, of course, took this brief exchange to heart. He later wrote to J. D. Reid, for instance, that before anyone pressured an M.P.P. he must talk to Whitney first, "as he becomes very angry if local members are asked to abandon the Legislature without consultation with him."

Save for such minor irritations, the relationship between the Federal and Provincial party organizations functioned smoothly. Borden not only had the personal friendship of the Premier, but also the full co-operation of the provincial machine. Such co-operation was crucial. On May 23, Kemp urged Borden to see Whitney and Hanna about four ridings. "Our success or failure in these constituencies rests with these gentlemen," he added. First of all, he had in mind Brant where J. H. Fisher, M.P.P. was willing to run, but awaited further instructions from Whitney. In North Bruce, Col. Hugh Clarke, M.P.P. of Kincardine was the man Kemp wanted, but nothing was yet definite; and since the Conservative Association there had decided to hold their Convention June 7 "without consulting anybody," quick action was needed. If the Conservatives of North Bruce were left to themselves, they would lose the constituency. It was Kemp's opinion too that only H. E. Eilber, M.P.P. could carry South Huron, and he also was waiting only for word from Whitney. In regard to West Lambton, Kemp felt that W. J. Hanna could get any Conservative elected there if he so desired. However, it was said, although Kemp did not know for what reason, that Hanna was not enthusiastic about defeating the Liberal incumbent, F. Pardee. Kemp warned Borden that there would be a Convention shortly and unless Hanna exerted himself the previous candidate would be nominated again. It was Kemp's judgement that if Hanna would only support either one of two other Conservative aspirants, West Lambton would be theirs.

Borden wrote Whitney immediately. He pointed out that at least three constituencies could be won if the present M.P.P.'s were induced to run. And since the election would no doubt come in the latter part of August or early September, the matter was urgent. He hoped that Whitney would use his influence to bring about the suggested conditions; it would strengthen the Federal Conservatives, he argued, without weakening Whitney's strong position in the Provincial Legislature.

Of the four seats that Kemp mentioned in his letter to Borden, it is significant that both Brant and North Bruce were on the list of Liberal seats calling for a "vicious attack," and South Huron and West Lambton were listed as Liberal strongholds. The Conservatives were following through with their strategy, even to the point of challenging seats which in theory, at least, they had conceded.

In subsequent correspondence with Borden, it was obvious that the indefatigable Kemp was making a concerted effort upon Liberal strongholds and doubtful Liberal seats. In the latter part of May, for instance, he wrote to ask Borden if he would clear up difficulties in several such constituencies. North Waterloo, where Mackenzie King held the fort, needed a candidate. South Wellington was admittedly a tough situation owing to Hugh Guthrie's popularity, but Henderson, the M.P. for Halton, should be consulted as to who the best candidate would be. The Conservatives had conceded both seats in April. A constant worry for Kemp was the problem encountered in North Oxford. Something had to be done swiftly before the Conservatives held their local Convention. Some kind of Farmer Candidate, he suggested, would be most suitable. He recommended further that T. W. Crothers, M.P. for West Elgin, be asked to visit West Kent to inform Borden as to whom the candidate should be. And in the same manner, J. E. Armstrong, M.P. for East Lambton, should survey the situation in North Middlesex. These last three seats were also held by Liberals, but could conceivably fall if the proper candidates were chosen. The Conservative organization made sure that they were.

Dr. Reid was enthusiastically engaged in Eastern Ontario, constantly radiating optimism and eagerly offering suggestions. Writing in May, he urged Borden to arrange a series of meetings in Ontario "without delay," securing the best available speakers and including "every county in which we have a fighting chance." He believed too that the Party should secure the assistance of prominent Liberals who were opposing reciprocity. He had his own county organized very quickly so he could assist any others that needed his personal attention. "You can depend on Eastern Ontario," he wrote, "it is being looked after perfectly. . . ."

By June, the Conservative electoral machinery was operating at an ever quickening pace despite the difficulties and enormous amount of time required to manage it. Nor were the Conservatives content, as Kemp's concern over local Conventions illustrates, to run merely a decentralized organization. On June 14, for example, they organized a meeting in Toronto of 50 Conservatives from constituencies where more work and cooperation were necessary. Moreover, Borden himself demanded a complete report on "Organization in Ontario" together with a list of candidates and prospective candidates before he left for the Northwest. Whether influenced by Reid's suggestion or not, he also told Kemp to hold a number of meetings during the summer throughout the Province. And not only were these anti-reciprocity public meetings arranged, but plans were also laid to obstruct anti-tariff speakers at farmers' rallies. Tried successfully at Woodstock, this tactic was also employed at meetings addressed by W. L. Smith, editor of the *Farmer's Sun*, E. C. Drury, and other Grangers. . . .

In early August, Cochrane was at Berlin arranging for a candidate against Mackenzie King. Reid wrote Borden, telling him Cochrane had suggested that Borden write Adam Beck to urge him to take "a personal interest" in getting out a good man to oppose King, as well as generally to look after the Middlesex ridings. "Cochrane says if you let him think he is a big man he will go right at it." Reid himself was becoming increasingly optimistic and he excitedly wrote Borden on August 3: "We have them on the run." By August 11, of the 25 seats in Eastern Ontario, he would not call one a sure loss. Every one was either safe or offered the Conservatives a fighting chance. Sure gains would accrue in Glengarry, Brockville, and Stormont, he predicted, and in at least one half of West Northumberland, Kingston, Peterborough West, Ottawa (2), Russell and Prescott. "Southern Ontario will be won. . . . We have the government beaten this time for sure."

In this particular correspondence between Reid, Kemp and Borden devoted to organizational activity, there was little mention of reciprocity or any other public issue. Success was apparently coming to the Conservatives by way of superior organization and superior candidates. Reciprocity, of course, did react positively for the Conservatives by virtue of the debilitating effect it had on an already weak Liberal organization. Yet the forecasts made by Conservative organizers in April strictly from the point of view of constituency organization were too accurate to be dismissed as merely dependent upon the accident of reciprocity for their realization.

The meeting of Conservative chiefs had predicted 36 seats "absolutely sure" of returning Conservatives; only one did not, Norfolk riding, but this was in fact the only new seat the Liberals gained in all of Ontario. They felt that the remaining 14 Tory seats would come under strong Liberal attack, but only 4 were likely to be lost. All remained Conservative. Of the 36 seats then held by Liberals 14 had been conceded, and although their prediction varied in regard to constituencies, it was exact in number. The Liberals did win 14 seats: 13 holds and 1 gain. But they lost the two Ottawas, Brantford, Huron South, Kingston, North Waterloo and York North, all former Liberal strongholds. The reciprocity issue did help to make some of these unexpected gains possible, but of the 22 doubtful Liberal seats the organizers had believed could be won, 16 did in fact come to the Conservatives.

It is interesting to note that in four of these latter constituencies an M.P.P. was persuaded to run: J. W. Fisher in Brant, H. Clark in North Bruce, G. Wilson in Wentworth, and Carrick in Thunder Bay-Rainy River. And in each case, it had been agreed at the Toronto meeting that if these men would stand, the Conservatives would win. Reid had written Borden that only Mr. Paul M.P.P. could carry Lennox and Addington; he did. The Conservatives also ran a member of the Provincial Legislature, A. E. Fripp, in one of the Ottawa City seats and this was one reason for the upset there.

In regard to the vignette in West Lambton, the Conservative organizers had agreed that Hanna, as Kemp had later written Borden, could win the riding for them if he wished to. However, Hanna apparently remained recalcitrant, for the Liberals won. In this light, such a Liberal victory was really victory by default and could have been altered with Hanna's co-operation.

Cochrane's work at Berlin against Mackenzie King was no doubt an important factor in the Conservative win there; and Adam Beck's interest in the Middlesex ridings may partially have accounted for a Conservative win in North Middlesex. Dr. Reid had been instrumental in getting Alquire to run in Stormont, and he won. Prince Edward had given the Doctor special concern and he had written Borden that if only he could get either one of the Hepburn brothers to run there, he would have a winner for sure. He "landed" one and Prince Edward went Conservative.

In summary, then, the Conservative Party swept the election of 1911 in Ontario by means of a superior political organization. Powerfully augmented by the many-sided co-operation of the Whitney government, the Conservative machine exercised a vigorous constituency control that took advantage of an increasingly weakening opposition. No matter what public issue emerged in 1911, given the existing state of party machinery, the electoral results in Ontario would have remained substantially the same.

Paul Stevens, "Laurier, Aylesworth, and the Decline of the Liberal Party in Ontario", *Historical Papers Canadian Historical Association*, 1968, pp. 94-113. Reprinted by permission of the Author.

Provincial Leaders and Party Organization

The Liberal party collapsed in Ontario in 1911. This was one of the most significant developments in Canadian political history for it resulted in the defeat of the Laurier government. Yet historians have failed to provide an adequate explanation. They have generally attributed the débâcle to reciprocity, although the proposal should have been popular in rural Ontario; or to charges of disloyalty to the British Empire, although Laurier and the Liberal party had survived a more blatant Anglophile and Francophobe campaign in 1900. For the most part they have overlooked the role which regional and provincial leaders play in the Canadian political system. Reciprocity might or might not have brought economic prosperity to Ontario and the Dominion. It might or might not have been destructive of a Canadian nationality. But in the face of growing skepticism about the nature of Laurier Liberalism and the social and political values of its chief spokesman in the province, the people of Ontario put the

American temptation behind them. At a time when leadership was essential, the Liberal party in Ontario was found lacking.

Ontario had been a predominantly Conservative province in national politics since Confederation. By the beginning of the 1890's, however, it was turning toward the Liberal banner. Laurier played a leading role in this transfer of political allegiance. In 1887 he had hesitated to accept the party leadership because he believed that a French-Canadian Roman Catholic leader would be a handicap in the English-speaking provinces, particularly in Ontario. But after assuming the leadership, he persistently pursued an Ontario policy to minimize the disabilities of his racial and religious background. He adopted a platform of unrestricted reciprocity to gain political support in the province. During the Manitoba school controversy, he maintained a position consistent with the principles of provincial rights and non-denominational schools, the twin pillars of Ontario Liberalism for over two generations. And in response to imperialist pressures from the province, his government introduced the preferential tariff and agreed to assist Great Britain against the Boers in South Africa. By the end of the decade Ontario had become a Liberal province.

But federal politics in Canada involves more than national policies and national leaders. The task of leadership in a national political party is particularly onerous because of the deeply-rooted regionalism which permeates Canadian life. The centrifugal forces of race and creed have been reinforced by geographical divisions, economic differentiation, and the beckoning smile of a wealthier neighbour. National parties have therefore been to a large extent merely the momentary reflections and temporary alliances of heterogeneous provincial organizations. The Liberal party remained essentially in this condition until 1896, anti-Catholic, anti-French Ontario Grits in an uneasy alliance with anti-clerical Quebec Liberals. Although Edward Blake and Laurier had begun to rid the party of its separate provincial outlooks and to formulate policies which would attract support from Ontario and Quebec, the ideology and traditions of the Grits and Rouges had not been obliterated, and it was of the utmost importance that the Liberals have effective leaders from both provinces to hold their followers in line. For Ontario the fact that Laurier was a French-Canadian Roman Catholic made this essential. John Willison reflected the views of many when he noted during the Autonomy Bill's debate: "I do not think it just, but it is nevertheless the fact, that a Protestant leader could do what Sir Wilfrid Laurier is doing much more safely, and that many Liberals will remember what they regard as the treason to their principles of a Roman Catholic, when they would not so remember if their leader were a Protestant."

One of the reasons for the success of the Liberal party in Ontario during the latter part of the 1890's was Sir Oliver Mowat's decision to become federal leader in the province. Liberal strategists portrayed Mowat as an English co-premier during the election campaign of 1896, while Laurier spoke rapturously of the days of Baldwin and Lafontaine. After Mowat's resignation in 1897, one of Laurier's weaknesses in Ontario was his inability to find a leader who could inspire a similar confidence. The stalwart old warhorses of Ontario Liberalism, Sir Richard Cartwright, David Mills, John Charlton, Richard Scott and William

Paterson were all in the twilight of their political careers; and William Mulock, though an effective administrator, lacked the oratorical force and eloquence necessary to a man who sought political power. The loss of 16 constituencies in Ontario in the election of 1900 was in part a reflection of the belief that the Liberal party was dominated by Quebec and under the influence of individuals whose Liberalism was incompatible with the province's social and political values. "Our province is hopelessly overborne in the councils of the Liberal party by the strong delegations from Quebec and the East," observed one member of the Ontario caucus, "and the resultant effect upon Ontario is that of apathy and indifference throughout our ranks."

The man whom Laurier selected as "political boss" in Ontario was Allan Aylesworth. The son of an eastern Ontario farmer of United Empire Loyalist stock, Aylesworth was imbued with the contempt and scorn of the Upper Canadian reformer for the despotism of the Family Compact and the aggressive tendencies of a centralized authority. He was a brilliant student at the University of Toronto and rose quickly to a prominent position at the Ontario Bar. In 1903 he was one of Canada's nominees on the Alaska Boundary Tribunal, and his refusal to sign the tribunal award won him popular acclaim. Since 1900 Laurier and his Ontario strategists had been attempting to induce Aylesworth to enter federal politics. Optimism was widespread that Aylesworth could provide "the vitalizing influence necessary to raise the party in public esteem and restore its former prestige." Aylesworth, however, was reluctant to relinquish his briefs until he had provided for the future of his sons; and, when in the general election of 1904, he agreed to take the plunge, he was defeated in the eastern Ontario constituency of Durham. In October 1905 he finally entered the House when Mulock resigned after a by-election in York North. He immediately became Postmaster General and eight months later succeeded Charles Fitzpatrick as Minister of Justice.

Aylesworth was well suited for the position of chief lieutenant in Ontario in many ways. Laurier and Aylesworth were intellectually and temperamentally congenial; and in Aylesworth, Laurier had discovered a colleague to whom he could give his complete trust. On most of the important issues of the day, and particularly on the subject of imperialism, the two had common principles and common opinions. Like Mowat, Aylesworth's Reform credentials were impressive. He was a staunch defender of provincial rights and economy and efficiency in government. Although his political support came primarily from the farming population, he had roots in the business and financial community through his legal practice. He was a strong orator on the political platform, accurate, lucid and disarmingly frank, and his speeches were continuously dignified and convincing. "I have never listened to any Ontario minister who enthused Liberals as he did" applauded one Ontario Liberal. "He simply electrified the electors here, both Grits and Tories." ...

It was becoming apparent [following the election of 1908] that Aylesworth's leadership in the province was far from secure. In the midst of the campaign, he had begun to grow deaf, and he told his constituents that he would be forced to retire from politics unless his hearing improved. At the beginning of 1910, his troubles continued when he became embroiled in bitter controversy with the leaders of moral reform in Canada, undermining his authority with a wide section of the Liberal party in the province. In December 1909, H. H. Miller, the Liberal member for South Grey, proposed an amendment to the criminal code which would have prevented professional gambling on Canadian race tracks. The measure was supported by the Moral and Social Reform Council of Canada which represented all the major Protestant denominations, the Canadian Purity Educational Association, the Trades and Labour Congress, the Dominion Grange, and the Farmers' Association. Laurier voted for the proposal himself, but he refused to adopt it as a government measure, and in committee the chief clause was defeated by one vote. For the promoters of the bill, the villain of the piece was the Minister of Justice. Aylesworth had little use for the puritan conscience of Protestant Ontario, and he possessed neither the inclination nor the political dexterity to conceal his impatience. He maintained that the legislation would make a crime of something "which the ordinary sense of the average man does not consider a crime." Rubbing salt into the wound, Aylesworth derided those who supported the bill. "Very possibly before the end of this parliament, we shall have a proposition to make it a crime to play cards, or to dance, or to indulge in any of the other amusements which there are some in the community think constitute, very nearly, if not quite a sin."

Aylesworth's attitude angered many Liberals in the rural and Protestant sections of the province. N. W. Rowell, a young Toronto lawyer and a leading spokesman for Canadian Methodism, informed Graham that he now regarded him rather than Aylesworth "as the real leader of the Ontario Liberals in Dominion politics."

There appears to be on all sides the deepest regret, and on many sides the deepest resentment at the spirit and character of the speech of the Minister of Justice in opposing the bill, not that he should not agree with the principle of the bill, but that in voicing his opposition he should have treated with contempt the conscientious convictions and the sentiments of the church-going people at least of the province, and, I believe, largely of all the provinces. As a man said to me last evening in the car, whatever Conservatives may do, Liberals will not follow that leadership. They may not say much about it, but they will not vote or work for its support. . . . There is the belief that had one of the influential members of the Government who are believed to be in sympathy with the bill spoken at all as strong in favour as Mr. Aylesworth did against it, the bill would have been carried, and however correct the theory may be that the government is in no way responsible for the bill, it will be difficult to remove from the minds of many that had the members of the Government who are nominally in favour of the bill, really desired that it should pass the vote would have been different. The strength of the Liberal party throughout this country will be found in those classes who believe in the church and in religious institutions and who have strong views on moral issues, and who do not believe in legalized professional gambling, and while up to the present time the agitation has not been strong in my judgment it is because the issue has not been raised, and unless during this session something is done to retrieve what appears to me to be the serious blunder which has already been made, you will inevitably find an agitation during this coming year which necessarily will, by reason of the speech delivered by the Minister of Justice, more or less reflect on the Government however

little those concerned in it may desire to do so.

The editor of the Toronto *Globe*, Rev. J. A. Macdonald, also rebuked the Minister of Justice. "It would be to Canada's discredit if, with a new start in a new country, free from the incubus of age long social custom, we were not able to lead the way into a cleaner democracy." On April 15 the House reached a compromise that allowed legalized bookmaking but limited race meetings at any track to two weeks a year. Although the *Globe* and the Moral Reform Council were far from satisfied, they accepted the legislation as a step in the right direction.

But the conflict between Aylesworth and the "church-going" section of Ontario Liberalism continued over another issue which lasted for several months. On March 4 Aylesworth announced the release of two men, King and Skill, who had been convicted of selling obscene literature, after they had served only two months of a one year sentence. Aylesworth explained that in his opinion the two men were not guilty of the offence with which they had been charged. He admitted that certain passages in the books in question, as well as in "that best of books that we all revere", might properly be described as indecent. But he declared that the books themselves, which included the English translations of Balzac, Petronius, and Brantôme, were classics "which are to be found on the shelves of our own library." New evidence later revealed that salacious advertising had been used to sell the books, but Aylesworth remained adamant. He admitted that though his judgment might have been at fault, his opinion had been a purely legal one, which he still thought to be right.

The decision outraged the "Ontario puritans." The protests were led by Macdonald in the editorial columns of the *Globe*. For Macdonald, the affair was another example of a dangerous tendency in Canadian society "to regard lightly offences against purity in life and morals." "Canada," he explained, "can do without the 'science' of depraved perverts or the 'classics' of the modern French lust-sewer." Politically, the question was charged with explosive potential. "There is more political gunpowder in this than in almost anything else that has come up of late," Macdonald warned Laurier. "Following hard upon Mr. Aylesworth's speech on the Gambling Bills, it makes things well nigh intolerable." The Minister of Justice, he contended, had lost his hold on the Ontario Liberals.

Men who care nothing at all about the ethical interests involved, but who are interested only in the popularity of the Government, do not hesitate to say that Aylesworth can never be anything but a weight. If this is true, it is largely the result of his own persistent blundering in dealing with questions in which public opinion is involved. I say this with the utmost frankness . . . I do not propose to say anything against him, but I shall never have the least enthusiasm for him so long as he follows the lines he has pursued in the past. . . . And more than that, the great body of the Liberal Party is with me and not with him.

Macdonald was not the only Liberal to express alarm. As one leading Protestant clergyman explained, "the people of Canada are a moral people. They love purity in their homes. They will not tolerate a Minister of Justice whose sentiment and opinion would allow the circulation of literature so loathsome as to affront and shock the moral sense of all decent people.

Throughout the dispute, Laurier stood firmly behind the Minister of Justice. He explained that Aylesworth had not condoned the sale of immoral literature but had merely expressed on opinion that the sale of books which were acknowledged as classics could not be held to be a violation of the criminal code. "I am quite familiar with Brantôme," he added. "It is one of the classics of the French language of the sixteenth century. It is coarse, as were the manners of that day but it is not lascivious. It deals with matters of rather risky character but he does not write with the view of exciting passion but rather of provoking mirth. I do not consider it half so dangerous for youth as some other books of almost daily circulation such for instance, as Shakespeare's sonnets or Shakespeare's Adonis." He agreed that King and Skill were not respectable book-sellers and admitted privately that Aylesworth's opinion had been "too drastic." But he was content to point out that "this is one of many questions as to which lawyers can disagree."

In the midst of the controversy, the divisions within the ranks of Ontario Liberalism were publicly and dramatically exposed. For some time a young and ambitious group of Toronto Liberals had been disenchanted with the lack of active and aggressive leadership in Ontario. At the end of April, Hartley H. Dewart, a prominent member of the Ontario Bar, and the son of a former editor of the *Christian Guardian*, charged in an open letter to the *Globe* that the Liberal party in Ontario was lamentably weak in its organization. For Dewart, the responsibility for the apathetic condition of the party's electoral machine lay with the Ontario ministers. "A commander-in-chief, even if he be as brilliant and skilful as Sir Wilfrid Laurier undoubtedly is, cannot be expected to achieve the success that he should without able tacticians between himself and the men in the ranks." But it was upon Aylesworth as leader of the Ontario Liberals and central Ontario's representative in the cabinet that Dewart fixed his sights.

In the City of Toronto and the surrounding ridings we have suffered and are suffering as a party because the Minister who is supposed to represent this district is not a political force or even a factor in organization. A district or even a constituency may be lost if featherweight advisors are the main sources from which knowledge of the political situation is derived. The local Minister should at least be the mouthpiece through which the political views or needs of the district are expressed. . . . The consideration locally that these matters have received and to which they are entitled is due in nearly every instance to the direct representations made by active Liberal workers to the Minister in charge of the department interested. Surely the public at large are justified in expecting the directing force of the Minister of Justice in these matters of local policy, just as much as Liberals are in matters of political organization. If our policy is sound and our views are right, as we believe them to be, the party leader who sees to it that organized effort and wise direction are brought to bear to achieve success performs a public as well as party service.

Dewart concluded that the country was entitled to the "best service of the best men" and that political prescience as well as sound executive ability was needed.

The charges were not without secure foundation. Although one political observer had described the Liberal electoral machinery in Ontario during the 1908 federal election as "the most effective organization that had ever been known in a Dominion election," it had fallen into disrepair particularly in Toronto and central Ontario. "With the present organization" admitted one party stalwart, "it would be impossible to elect St. Peter to any one of our seats." So exhausted was the provincial organization that party officials were forced to cancel a proposed policy convention for September 1910 because none of the local constituency associations had prepared policy measures for the organizing committee. That conservative strategists could predict with such accuracy the results of the election in Ontario in 1911 was indicative not so much of the strength of the conservative organization, for the Tory machine had been unable to deliver significant results in 1908, but of the moribund state of the Liberal organization.

Moreover, Aylesworth had done little to enhance his position with the political activists in the party. A master intellect, of high character, and with rare executive ability, the Minister of Justice had many deficiencies as a practical politician. It is one of the remarkable aspects of Laurier's career that, though an astute and calculating politician himself, he was more concerned with the administrative capacity of his political advisors than with their ability to master the details of political organization and to keep the party in line. Aylesworth had little interest in the intricacies of party organization, while frequent forays to Europe and the United States took him out of the political arena for months at a time. In cabinet, he seldom spoke on political matters, admitting to Laurier on one occasion that "in all such respects I am content to trust you blindly." One of the reasons was his deafness which limited further his effectiveness as the spokesman for Ontario

Liberalism. As he pointed out to Laurier some years later:

My last four years in the House at Ottawa were purgatory to me. To sit there like a dummy when perhaps something I knew all about was being discussed—to know absolutely nothing of what was being said and then to read next day in Hansard speeches that I could have torn to tatters if I could have heard a word of them—kept me raging in impotent anger. And it was even more dreadful in council when there was something under consideration that I knew about or was perhaps specially interested in. I might talk a little while and then somebody across the table might say something—or even if you spoke, sitting by my side—I had no idea whether it was in agreement with me or in criticism. . . .

On the eve of his departure for the Hague Tribunal at the beginning of May, Aylesworth informed Laurier that his continued presence in the cabinet would be "a weakness and an injury" to the government and offered his resignation.

Laurier, however, stood by his beleagured colleague and refused to agree to his leaving the cabinet. "I am only too well aware," he explained, "that there are in the ranks of the party, some, who, I regret to say, are your personal enemies, but they must learn that, outside their very limited number, the whole party is behind you." There were a number of reasons for Laurier's loyalty. The Liberals could not afford to have Aylesworth resign under a political cloud and thereby give credence to his critics' charges. Another factor undoubtedly was the failure of the younger Liberals in the province to emerge as potential successors to the Minister of Justice. Moreover, Laurier had personal motives as well. The aging Liberal leader had become increasingly withdrawn from his political colleagues in Ottawa. The retirement of most of his friends from public life had contributed to a growing sense of isolation. Aylesworth was one of the few men with whom Laurier still enjoyed intimate companionship, and he was determined that this not become the victim of the political wars. But in spite of Laurier's determination, it was clear that Aylesworth had little control over the Ontario Liberals. At a time when new issues demanded party cohesion and unity, the Liberal party in Ontario was divided and leaderless as it had seldom been in the past.

In time Laurier might have been able to put the pieces together, particularly as Graham and the new Minister of Labour, W. L. M. King, began to emerge as political forces in the province. But the debate over reciprocity threw the party into complete disarray. . . . The revolt of the Toronto Eighteen and the widely-held fear that the lowering of duties on farm products would be followed by similar reductions on manufactures were the expressions of a business and financial community which no longer felt it had adequate representation at Ottawa; while the strength and resilience of the loyalty cry was in part the result of long-standing doubts and suspicions about the nature of Laurier Liberalism. Aylesworth did his utmost to ease these apprehensions. "There is not a thought, nay, not a breath drawn by Sir Wilfrid Laurier that is not single to the good of Canada and her people. He is a loyal subject, a true believer in that form of Imperialism which he thinks and I think is the true form; that Imperialism which gives to every component part the fullest freedom and seeks equally the well-being and closer binding together of the whole. But Aylesworth's influence in the province had been greatly weakened; and the Minister of Justice had already advised Laurier that he would not seek re-election in the next election. Indeed effective leadership in Ontario had passed into the hands of the Young Turks of the party, Graham and King who had few ties with the old guard of Ontario Liberalism. King summed up the situation: "With the exception of one colleague, Mr. Graham, who is much over-worked, I have no other who is in shape to do much work through the province, in the way of speaking. There are six of us from Ontario, two are too old and infirm to get about, one is deaf, the other is there mostly because he is an Irish-Catholic— and that leaves Graham and myself."

The weakness of leadership in Ontario also hampered efforts to place the case for reciprocity before the province. Liberal leaders in Ontario were unable to provide the direction necessary to galvanize party spokesmen into action and launch a concerted and effective campaign in the constituencies. Plans for a public meeting in Toronto to answer the charges of the hastily-formed Canadian National League did not get off the ground. Graham complained that "the discouraging part of it is the apathy of the members in the House, whom we have been after for weeks, begging them to hold meetings, but they seem to be standing it off until the roads will be so bad that there will be little use in calling a meeting." Early in March, the Ontario Reform Association set up a committee to provide speakers for political meetings throughout the province, and constituency associations were urged to arrange meetings to pass pro-reciprocity resolutions. Conservative obstructive tactics in the House, however, demanded that Liberal members be in Ottawa and the brunt of the campaign

thus fell upon the lacklustre provincial leader, J. F. Mackay. In April, the death of Graham's son forced Laurier's chief strategist in Ontario to withdraw from the campaign for over three weeks, further decimating the Ontario contingent. Moreover, as the summer began and the pamphlet propaganda of the Canadian National League flooded into the province, the Liberal counter-attack had yet to begin. Graham was dismayed that "not a blow has been struck. It is discouraging here—not a single envelope. . . . There is literature waiting to be sent out, but it will take a long time to address the envelopes after they come." The sluggishness of the Liberal machines in Ontario was serious. As one Liberal organizer warned, "Unless a very vigorous educative campaign is undertaken, taking township by township and polling subdivision by polling subdivision, I would not like to do any prophesying as to the result. Our fellows simply MUST realize that it is their business to dig in and earn their indemnity."

But little time remained as the Ontario Liberals suddenly found themselves in the midst of an election campaign. Their task was immense. Liberal stategy was designed to enlighten a misinformed and befuddled electorate. "I must confess," wrote King, "I find everywhere the need of the people in different ridings being more fully informed as to just what the nature of the proposal is. The press and the speakers are taking it for granted that the people know the agreement and that it is only its effect that needs consideration. The truth is our strongest side of the case is the agreement itself." Liberal strategists believed that once the province was fully aware of the true character and extent of the proposed pact, it would readily see that there was nothing disloyal in it. But as the campaign began, the Liberals had clearly lost the initiative. The argument that the agreement would open a vast third market to the Canadian farmer was no longer useful, particularly in the cities and towns where the consumer was convinced that greater farm prosperity would result in an increased cost of living. One Liberal candidate advised Graham "to say very little about the farmer, which I find has the same effect on my constituents as a red flag is supposed to have on a bull." Efforts to present candidates from the business and financial community to counter the impression that the agreement would imperil their interests were largely unsuccessful. Charles Hyman turned down Aylesworth's overtures to return to public life: "I could not hope to carry the city of London at the present time, the party organization is gone, the party itself only a skeleton of its former self, and enthusiam over reciprocity in a city constituency could hardly be expected." In the end, Laurier and the Ontario Liberals were forced to concentrate on the British and Imperial question; and by focusing attention upon the dangers of a Borden-Bourassa alliance, they brought into play still further the racial and religious question upon which they were already so vulnerable.

Laurier lost the election of 1911 be-cause he lost Ontario. Of eighty-six seats in the province, the Liberals won only thirteen, a loss of twenty-three seats from dissolution. In spite of his efforts, Laurier failed to win in Ontario the support he felt his policies deserved. He had persistently tried to keep in personal contact with the province. His failure to find a lieutenant in whom the province had implicit confidence might be attributed to his instinctive preference for advisers with intellectual and executive talent over political astuteness, to his own withdrawal from his political colleagues, or to the vagaries of fate which took from him some of his brightest supporters. Perhaps no one man could effectively represent and speak for Ontario like Fielding in Nova Scotia, Blair in New Brunswick, or Sifton in the west. For its geographical extent, religious and racial diversity and economic disparities makes Ontario a province not like the others. But Laurier never lost sight of the importance of regional and provincial leaders in the Canadian political system. In the final analysis, they provide one of the keys to the collapse of the Liberal party in Ontario. Laurier's inability to secure a strong leader acceptable to his Ontario supporters left the party deeply divided and swung the electoral pendulum in the province toward Borden and the Conservative party.

Public Archives of Canada, *J. W. Dafoe Papers*, Dafoe to George Iles, September 27, 1911.

A Final Word

Dear Iles:

I am not going to say anything about the election beyond that, while I think the decision of the people of Canada on the issue submitted to them was idiotic and will be so adjudged by history, I am not, on other grounds, disposed to complain about the fate that has destroyed the Laurier Government. Regarded simply as an administration it has been growing weaker for some years, and, failing the reciprocity matter, it would probably have gone out of office at the next election. It is better that it should fall on a big issue, which covers its defeat with a tragic dignity, than that it should have died of old age and incapacity.

The fact is, as I have long known, Canada is now and has been for a generation, an essentially Tory country. That is to say, the right of corporations, moneyed interests, etc., to determine the policy of the country is recognized by the majority of the electors. Laurier achieved office in 1896 mainly through a series of blunders by his opponents, supplemented

by their loss, in rapid succession, of able men; and upon obtaining office he held it for a long period of time by placating various powerful interests at the expense of the general public. The moment he showed signs of putting real Liberal doctrine into effect, the interests combined and crushed him. I should be very well content to see the Liberal party remain in opposition for the next fifteen or twenty years, if it will devote itself to advocating real Liberal views and building up a party which, when it again takes office, will be able to carry out a programme without regard to the desires and feelings of the privileged classes. It is quite possible, however, that the real advocacy of an advanced policy might bring results much sooner than most people think. I believe we are on the eve of big changes in all the Anglo-Saxon countries. I should not be surprised if, before many years, a rise of democratic sentiment in Canada should make possible a reforming and radical government at Ottawa.

2 3 4 5 6 — 76 75 74 73 72